The Red New Deal
When Everything is Free, You are the Price

Dmitri I. Dubograev

The Red New Deal

When Everything is Free, You are The Price

Copyright © 2023 Dmitri Dubograev

All Rights Reserved. No part of this book may be reproduced or transmitted in any form or by any means, electronic or mechanical, including photocopying and recording, or by any information storage and retrieval system, without permission in writing from the publisher.

ISBN:978-1-967887-09-5

Dedication

Dedicated to my dear mother, the strongest and kindest person I know. Like other strong-willed women of her generation, she rose above the ravages of socialism and the modern red/brown plague, and left a legacy of enduring love and courage for her family.

Acknowledgements

I am eternally grateful to my wife, Svetlana. You are my love, my best friend, my guiding light, and my inspiration. Your unwavering support, undivided faith, loyalty, dedication, resilience, intuition (you did marry me, right?) and unmatched cooking bring out the best in me. You take me to new heights in life and my legal career. I couldn't imagine this journey without you, my true soul mate for life.

I am thankful to all of my family: Sergei, Leigh, Luka, Nikolai, Kira, Ru, Masha, Steve, Alaina, and Obi who give my life purpose, integrity, and eternal joy. Our strong family and your undivided love are all I need to succeed and make sense of my life.

Special thanks to my publishing and editing team, especially Barbara Markland, whose guidance and editing kept me on course, helped me clarify my thoughts, provided valuable feedback, and relentlessly cut my long sentences. You have made this book immeasurably better.

I also want to thank the kind people of Gander, Canada, who provided us with shelter and comfort (and bear cutlets and warm clothes!) on September 11th when our airplane was diverted there. You helped us cope with very difficult times, making sure we made it home to our families (despite the airline's determination to fly us back to Europe, which took some effort to overcome!). I still view showering in the town's hockey locker rooms equivalent to being invited into your most sacred chapel. But, knowing your love for hockey ... still, ...go Caps!

Special thanks and eternal gratitude to my Slavic brethren who selflessly face the fight against tyranny--Zelensky and the entire Ukrainian people, Navalny and his brave team, Babariko, Tikhanovsky family, Kolesnikova, Tsepkalo, Belarusian partisans, Kastus Kalinovsky regiment, HelpPeopleOfUkraine, Athletes for Freedom, and each and every citizen of Russia and Belarus who find the courage to sacrifice their livelihood, and even their lives for the bright future and freedom of their children. A portion of the proceeds from this book will be redirected to your cause.

About the Author

Dmitri Dubograev is an American information technology and corporate attorney of Belarusian descent. Prior to graduating from The Washington and Lee University School of Law in 1994, he graduated with honors (~cum laude) from the Belarusian State University, Law Department in Belarus, in 1991. He was the winner of the military pentathlon (GTO) in Belarus in 1985 (18 and under) and the winner of the Law Student Olympiad in Belarus in 1988.

He published numerous articles on corporate law and human rights in the former Soviet Union. As various cooperation agreements were developed by Ronald Reagan and Mikhail Gorbachev by the end of the Cold War, Dmitri Dubograev was chosen by his faculty to represent Belarus in one of the first USA-USSR student exchanges in 1988.

Dmitri Dubograev has acted as an advisor to several Eastern European governments, under the auspices of USAID and the World Bank, in legal reform projects. He represents numerous clients in connection with the protection of IP and corporate transactions.

Mr. Dubograev is a member of various corporate boards, including Nonprofit organizations HelpPeopleofUkraine.org and AthletesForFreedom.org

Preface

When I first came to the United States in 1989, people would ask me what surprised me the most about their country. Obviously, upon arrival to study at Washington and Lee in 1989, I eagerly embraced everything that I faced for the first time. That included the style of American education with its focus on the humanities, the Socratic method of learning, and the practical aspects of education. It also included the American social system and legal system which I was familiar with only through books, particularly property rights, and the way that an individual and their freedoms became the cornerstone of society in the United States. This was so different from utopian and power-centered government goals. Having lived my childhood and youth in the socialist environment--though I still feel young!--that was all I knew.

Based on my almost immediate observations, one of my responses to their question was that I was shocked to see how much 'socialism' permeated the fiber of society in the United States. Sadly, I now wish America could return to that kinder, gentler level of 'socialism' of 1989. It's amazing that 30 years ago, I was yelled at for opening a door for a lady as a sheer courtesy. These days I'm listening to the likes of Bill De Blasio, the New York Mayor, declaring *"There is enough money in the state, it's just in the wrong hands,"* which mirrors the war cries of Lenin and Castro with their 'red terror' and devastation. It was like a bad dream, like déjà vu, for me to hear an American politician make such a statement.

'Wisdom' such as that sends a chill up my spine, because I recognize that mindset all too well. I lived it. My ancestors were persecuted and died because of it. I fear that if the spines of Americans do not begin responding, they may soon be living it too.

In light of statements such as that, I am writing this book in hopes of giving Americans of all ages a glimpse of the ordinary life of a Soviet person during Soviet socialist times. I remember and will share the perceptions, ways of life, and ideologies that were prevalent in my youth in the Soviet Union. If history does indeed repeat itself, at least the ugly and unpleasant eras, then we must educate ourselves and our children. Allow me to enlighten you with my first-hand perceptions of life under the 'red dream.' Actually, 'nightmare' is a much more accurate word here.

I grew up during the '70s and '80s in the Belarusian Soviet Socialist Republic (one of the 15 'states' comprising the former USSR). It should be noted that the Belarusian Republic was probably one of the most advanced societies in the former Soviet Union. If anything, it would represent the so-called 'Developed Socialism.' The communists developed this term to describe the advanced forms of socialism in a society before the entire civilization actually reaches communism--the dubious ultimate goal of human progress. I am sad to say, but we are beginning to see signs of 'Developed Socialism' in our beloved America.

Belarus did not have many of the economic problems that other republics suffered, such as long lines for essential foods or staples, or rampant nationalism. So one could perhaps view Belarus as the 'maximum' standard of prosperity that one could reach when a nation is driven by socialistic principles in building its economy and society in general.

My paternal ancestors were Cossacks. The Cossacks were viewed as a spunky lot of freedom seekers and defenders, as Putin's army is discovering now. Historically, they were formed by essentially runaway serfs, outlaws, and other 'adventure seekers' who got their freedom and recognition in the 17th and 18th centuries. The Cossack society's composition, purpose, and way of life was similar to those who came to America escaping persecution for a better, independent life with a determination to defend it by all means. They were eventually granted freedom in exchange for military service and grants of lands, similar to squatters or frontier population in American history.

These tough 'adventure and freedom seekers' made up one of the most fierce and able parts of the Ukrainian army--and later the Imperial Russian army- -which eventually helped to defeat Napoleon and later occupied Paris. The term 'Ukraine' described what was originally Kyev's Russia (or Kyevan Rus'). It originated from the word 'Krai' meaning 'border' or 'frontier.' Cossacks served as a virtual wall shielding Russia from a southern invasion, while also providing the 'elite' troops for various military conflicts, including numerous wars with Turkey, the Crimean War, and World War I. Even communist ideologue Karl Marx noted that, "Russia, having nothing to do with Russia and stealing its current name, however, arrogantly claims the historical legacy of Russia, created 800 years earlier." That ill-fated imperial claim for cultural and social leadership of Slavic nations was certainly one of the reasons for Putin's warring attempts--which are doomed to fail miserably-- at erasing Ukrainian and Cossacks legacy in favor of his despotic and autocratic way of life.

The moral strength, work ethic, tenacity, and determination of the Cossacks made them relatively wealthy through hard work and service to their country. While hard work and service to country should be lauded and rewarded, the Bolsheviks, however, feared Cossacks' free spirit and wealth. They eventually expropriated all family lands and heirlooms--the plight of most Cossacks. A few family members bearing our last name and my grandmother's maiden name were found on the historical 'repressed' lists. People on that list were usually executed or exiled to Siberia. Socialism has its own cruel way of issuing rewards for success and even the slightest hint of freedom.

My family's Cossacks history matches the misfortunes of numerous other peoples who got caught in the evil whirlwind of socialism. Those were painful and dangerous times, highlighted by government's unfettered abuse against those it deemed 'privileged'--despite the fact that 'privilege' was earned through hard work and service to country.

Similarly, the "woke" crowd in America today has a very skewed and artificial view of 'privilege,' largely based on skin color. In that light, can someone from the current "woke" crowd dare explain the 'privilege' unabashedly ascribed to my family simply because of our lighter 'skin color' or 'European descent'?

Perhaps you are one who ascribes to the popular notion today of "white" privilege. Maybe you include my family in that notion. Allow me to tell you what "white privilege" brought to my wife's family. You might change your mind. My wife's "white" grandparents, though of noble Polish descent, were executed by Germans for participating in the resistance. Their "white" children--my wife's dad and his sister--were forced to serve as blood donors for Nazi soldiers. By sheer miracle, they survived when their aunt bribed the Nazi guard to write them off as dead and let them go.

Along with most Belarusians, my mom also suffered under "white" privilege as a child. She lived through three long years of Nazi occupation, hunger, and bombings. Maybe you would also consider my mom's "white" cousin privileged. He was sent to one of Germany's labor camps. Later, he boldly pretended he was Polish rather than Belarusian. Ironically, the word Belarusian means "White Russian," so his "white privilege" could have gotten him killed. That courage, plus the fact that he ended up at the American zone of German occupation, saved his life. It allowed him to emigrate to America and escape being sent to Stalin's gulags. In Stalin's world, "white" POWs were viewed as traitors who should have, of course, all died fighting. My family's hardships, along with the hardships of other families, are proof that being "white" brings no privilege.

Many Americans have endured legitimate grievances and hardships, whether one generation ago or five. But the degree of grievances of people of other socialist and communist nations, races, religions, or origins was on par with the hardships of people in the New World. Frequently far worse.

I admit, it is unbearable to me to listen when historically uninformed and logically inconsistent people argue that another country has surpassed the United States. No country has ever surpassed the USA in its key and long-standing achievements, or in being the economic and social engine of the world. Every nation has its flaws, but the USA continues to offer more opportunities for equality and justice to all people. Despite its relatively short history, only 240+ years, America stands alone as the beacon in the dark night, the social and economic engine, and the moral compass of the world.

It has been a great surprise to me that Americans are fascinated with fine points, such as how much light is reflected off one's skin or the hyphenation of the 'type' of an American. I do hate the hyphenated references-- 'Jewish-,' 'Belarussian-,' and 'African-' before 'American.' Such pre-designation divides Americans instead of uniting us. We are all Americans here. Our heritage, religion, or body propensities should precede such facts purely in timing rather than their significance. This kind of attitude and 'class' division is one of the reasons why so much of America's 'racism' is artificially inflated. Anything and everything has become 'racist,' a reference to everything bad. It's another marker of socialism inching closer to our shores and into our society.

One of the greatest American actors, Morgan Freeman, responded to the question of how to stop racism. *"Stop talking about it,"* he spoke. *"I'm going to stop calling you a white man, and I'm going to ask you to stop calling me a black man."*

Great words from a great actor. A great action item for ending the artificial division between various artificial "classes" of Americans with allegedly irreconcilable conflicts. This peculiar gain-of-power tool and theory has been employed by socialists since

Karl Marx. I am concerned that few today recognize that, so they are fascinated by an evil system they do not understand.

No matter how you describe all these far-fetched leftist fringe theories, regardless of the "color," they all continue to revitalize the virtually dead 'RED' or communist ideology. In this book, the color 'red' will be attributed to the intrinsic color of Communist movements, not the familiar GOP red on election maps. A large part of the communist ideology is based on the victimization of certain classes. Consequently, the stratification and separation of society, largely on an arbitrary basis, is done into classes of 'victim' and 'oppressor.' We see the roots of that phenomenon infiltrating our American culture today.

As socialism's main foundation, Marxism embraces 'proletarians'--or the chosen ones--as the only class that can rule fairly in the futuristic society. Intelligentsia and peasants, on the other hand, are not fully 'ideologically fit,' regardless of the traits of one's character, actual skills, efforts, achievements, actions, or ambitions. In socialism, your class dooms your plight and you are powerless to change that. No matter how productive or loyal the "whites"-- primarily the intelligentsia, military, scientists, and peasants--were to the Soviet regime, they should endlessly carry the guilt of the oppression held by their parents and ancestors. America, does this mindset remind you of anything? It should.

A lot of people from the former Soviet Union who lived through those dark years, when asked to describe leftist/socialist trends in politics and society, they used just one word to describe it-- 'sovok.' For those of you who do not have a feel for the Russian language, it's somewhat of a derogatory term combining 'scoop' and 'Soviet.' By 'sovok,' we primarily mean the society's fascination with socialism, socialist principles, political correctness, and 'woke-ness' which brings its inevitable double-speak and hypocrisy. America, did you know that socialism also contains its own "woke-ness" and political double-speak?

At the end of the 1980s, when the Soviet Union 'woke up' from the coma of socialism, the U.S. was far removed from what we're experiencing today. America today features Leftist and utopian movements along with continuous propaganda from the media and politicians, open propaganda of mass media and politicians perpetuating the need for socialist revisionism. For example, various programs, theories, and aspirations such as 'the Green New Deal' and 'Critical Race Theory.' Despite the different 'colors' assigned to these 'deals' and 'theories'--namely green or black--they are nothing more than America's frightening fascination for socialism with its ideological dogma and underhanded agenda. Hence, America's "Green New Deal" and other "progressive" utopian ideas today actually reek of yesterday's Soviet "Red."

While American Leftist Reds have essentially adopted the ideology of the communists, thankfully, they lack the strength and raw audacity of hard-core communists. Similarly, the reason for the inevitable defeat of Putin's regime and his embarrassing war in Ukraine could be ascribed to his desire to live like Rockefeller but govern like Stalin.

In America, the Left pundits, while still being drawn by the same far-fetched utopian goals, could only softly operate in the free and humane society they are trying to destroy. They want to live like capitalists but govern like Stalinists. But it just doesn't work-- economically, socially, or politically.

Therefore, when they faced the force of today's dictatorial "Reds," whether it was the Chinese Communist Party or Putin, the Left failed. They were unable to stand up to them or negotiate on an equal footing. Only former President Trump, in stark contrast to the Left, had the force of character and strength to hold the dictators at bay. I offer this example. Putin annexed territories of its neighbors under Obama (Georgia in 2008 and Crimea in 2014) and under Biden (the territory-grabbing war in 2022). But Putin did not dare to attempt such things while Trump was President. This cannot be just a coincidence. We must all recognize and admit this fact, regardless of political affinity or level of personal sympathy to his persona.

Some think that Biden's timid warning to Putin--namely that 16 critical areas of the American economy were off-limits for hacking--was an effective way of dealing with the "Red" culprit. If you are one of this group, I suggest you make 16 post-it notes which read, "Don't hit me here!," stick them on your chest and other body parts, and walk into a late-night bar scene. You will soon discover those timid notes will not protect you, but rather, will encourage less-than-scrupulous bar attendees to jump you. This is exactly how Putin felt about, "Don't you dare hit our 16 critical areas." (By the way, why 16 and not 17? If law firms are in the 17th category, am I not protected?) Or Biden continuously proclaiming that no matter how far Putin's atrocities go, he will not face a US or NATO response.

Such "soft speak" actions by the U.S. administration, mismanagement of the Afghan troop withdrawal, and sheer lack of common sense are primary reasons for lowlife like Putin to mistakenly equate American indecisiveness with weakness of the entire Western world. Such soft speak simply emboldened Putin to wage an unprovoked war against the people of Ukraine. That war is nothing more than yet another communist hare-brained messiah-like project by Putin--though the 'World Revolution' is conveniently replaced by a nebulous 'Supremacy of the Russian World.'

The West has made a series of grave errors regarding Putin, and the world is now suffering the consequences. Such underestimation of the clear and present danger posed to the world and the United States by Putin, and even a slight chance of his success in Ukraine, comes from both the Left and the Right. The West willingly closed its eyes on Putin's annexation of parts of Georgia, followed by then Ukraine's Crimea in 2014. These were the first annexations since WWII. But we did not learn our lesson from expansionist policies and war crimes committed by Putin's murderous and looting army.

I want to show you examples of policy statements and official propaganda by Putin and Lukashenko's socialist dictatorships showing that the war in Ukraine is not "Europe's problem" and that "we should stay out of it."

- This is the Russian explanation for the war in Ukraine. --The USA and Western Europe designed special bio labs in Ukraine to create DNA-engineered geese and mosquitoes as biological weapons capable of killing only Slavic people. Russia is now freeing its "territories" from the West's bloody experiments directed toward extermination of the Ukrainian and Russian people through this "special military operation";

- This is Russia's explanation for its military goals. -- Russia's military operations will stop only when its troops reach Stonehenge or, at a minimum, Reichstag in Berlin, proving that Putin does not intend to stop if he takes over Ukraine;

- This is the Russian explanation for its hatred of the West and the goals of the war. --Western democracies are "puppets" of transnational corporations. Russia is the only barrier against the invasion of capitalists, whose sole purpose is to exploit other nations and their vast resources. These words come right from 1970s Marxist propaganda;

- Russia, by attacking Ukraine with assistance of Belarus, pre-empted an attack ("here, to these four places on the map!") that was "prepared" and ready to go by Ukraine and NATO, Great Britain, and the United States against Belarus and Russia. (Yes, these people really think that some would believe their nonsense.);

- This is Russia's explanation for its perceived role in the world. -- Western ideology is rotten, i.e., Parent Number One/Parent Number Two families, mandated sex change surgeries, gay marriages as a tool to limit Western population growth and enslave the rest of the world as servants for its privileged few. Hence, Russia is here to stand in the way and revert the world back to its "traditional values."

As you can see, Putin is paranoid about the so-called Western threat. Here is the great paradox--Putin considers it his messiah-like mission to do the same thing and turn the world into Russia's slave! As proven by the 2014 annexations, Putin does not intend to stop at the Western border of Ukraine.

As shown by Russia and Belarus, socialist leaders cannot be trusted by either their own people or the nations of the world. Here is a vivid example. Ukraine voluntarily gave up its nuclear weapons, dismantling its last Tu-22 bombers and X-22 missiles over 15 years ago. These same types of weapons are now being used in 2023 by Russia *against Ukraine*, bombing her peaceful cities. Ukraine's voluntary surrender of nuclear capabilities was done under the Budapest Memorandum on Security Assurances, in which both the U.S. and Russia agreed to respect Ukraine's "sovereignty in the existing borders" and provide other security assurances.

Clearly, that promise was not kept. Certainly, our moral compass should show that our assistance to victims of war atrocities is crucial and inescapable. In addition, if we do not help Ukraine to defend herself, it will send a clear signal to any country that by demilitarizing and ceding nuclear weapons, they also become vulnerable to outside aggression without them. Putin has proven once again that no international agreement signed by Russia or any socialist leader is worth the paper it's written on.

We cannot allow socialism to invade the hearts and lives of our people, nor any other NATO lands, nor any other countries valuing freedom. Consider what will happen if Putin should be successful in crushing Ukraine. The U.S. will inevitably be called upon to send our young people to fight and die defending the rest of Europe under Article 5 of the NATO Charter.

The heart of America is, first and foremost, about personal and economic freedom, opportunity, and equality for each of us under the law. These Leftist attempts to attach guilt to one's heritage or skin color are disgusting, divisive, and frankly, extremely counterproductive. Concepts like redistribution of wealth--which is a thinly-veiled cry for retribution--and widespread utopia-like socialist programs are the greatest threats to the United States and our free capitalist society today.

I've spent 30 years living in this nation, being grateful for its freedoms, its unmatched opportunities, and the decency and ingenuity of its people in pursuit of a fair society. Before that, I lived in the Soviet Union under communism as a youngster. Because I see the signs of socialism and recognize its insidious threat, I decided to write this book.

I am driven to point out to all who will listen the parallels between what was going on in the Soviet Union at the various stages of its socialist development, and the current state of American social tendencies. Throughout the book, you will see the sign *||* *followed by text in italics.* This is designed to bring your attention to clear parallels of the abysmal failures of socialism elsewhere compared to events and social phenomena spreading like wildfire in the Western world, and the United States in particular. In my humble view, having lived through it, I want to fire a warning shot to all Americans.

One may argue that "socialism" in the Western World takes a "soft form" and there are no mass murders and purges in the U.S. as of yet, although the deceptive "letter" concocted by 50 security officers exonerating Hunter Biden comes really close to the practice of "KGB/people's letters" in the Soviet Union. Without denigrating the lives lost under socialism, it should be noted that destroying one's life, at least in principle, comes fairly close to destroying another's livelihood or career due to 'ideological purity.'

In other words, today's rhetoric and policies regarding misplaced priorities, virtue signaling, and suppression of freedoms only differ in the degree of "Redness." They give us no comfort as to the future of this country. We can only hope that people will wake up and get re-educated quickly. We hold fast to the expectation that our founders' visions and social architecture were strong enough to withstand the assault on freedom, equality, and quite frankly, common sense which is definitely coming our way.

Table of Contents

Dedication i

Acknowledgements iii

About the Author v

Preface vii

Chapter 1 The Great Red Socialist Revolution 1

Chapter 2 This Free Speech, That Free Speech 45

Chapter 3   Perception of History 103

Chapter 4 Fundamentals of Society 160

Chapter 5 Political Correctness and Canceled Culture 233

Conclusion How to Spot and Say "No" to Socialism 267

Epilogue 299

Chapter 1
The Great Red Socialist Revolution

Today's current events in America are troubling. Though some say history teaches us that history teaches us nothing, nevertheless, history has a way of repeating itself. When a nation does not learn from past history, its own or the history of others, that nation is vulnerable. Allow me to share some very pertinent Russian history beginning a century ago, which may shed some troubling light onto current events in America today. Watch for decisions and comments by today's newsmakers that bear an uncomfortable resemblance to the historical details I am about to share with you.

In 1921, Russia emerged from civil war as the world's first Marxist-Communist state, the newly created Soviet Union. This was brought about by the Great October Socialist Revolution of 1917, which overthrew the centuries-old Romanov monarchy. The 1917 Revolution was aptly called the Red Plague. At its zenith, the United Soviet Socialist Republic--otherwise known as USSR--comprised approximately one-sixth of Earth's land surface, including Armenia, Azerbaijan, Belarus, Estonia, Georgia, Kazakhstan, Kyrgyzstan, Latvia, Lithuania, Moldova, Russia, Tajikistan, Turkmenistan, Ukraine, and Uzbekistan.

The USSR was one of the world's largest and most powerful nations until its eventual fall and ultimate breakup on December 25, 1991.

The Russian Revolution

First, let's witness the birth of the Soviet Union, the first socialist state. By 1917, the Russian Empire undertook significant reforms and sported a formidable army. Its grain production and exports were bigger than that of England, France, and Germany combined. By then, as manufacturing and trade developed, the nobility and monarchy gradually ceded their dominant grasp, allowing self-governance of localities, territories, and certain elections. The ruble was one of the strongest currencies in the world. In World War I, the tide turned in favor of Russia and its "Antanta" allies, as it was locally known in Russia (aka Triple Entente--Russia, France, and Great Britain). This brought the German and Austro-Hungarian empires to the brink of defeat.

During WWI, change came through revolution. The Russian Bourgeoisie February Revolution occurred when Czar Nicholas II abdicated the Russian Imperial throne. However, the Provisional Government led by Kerensky was weak, unable to effectively resist the society's anti-war sentiment, and called for immediate and more sweeping reforms. The Bolsheviks were led by Lenin, who was unable to attain any significant number of votes in the actual elections to the representative body known as the Constituent Assembly. Yet the Bolsheviks could not "let a crisis go to waste" and effectively seized the moment. They overthrew the Provisional Government and brutally executed a Czar and his family. This brutal event gave birth to the "new" state--the Soviet Union. It comes as no surprise to many of us that this clustering of various nationalities, born in brutality, continued its brutal ways through revisionism brought by Putin, Lukashenko, and other loyal followers of the "Red" ways.

This new state refuted and dismantled its predecessor's social system and religion, demolished churches and statues, and even replaced its "oppressive" flag and anthem. It is not clear to historians how a fringe but active and loud political minority of Lenin followers, associated with murders and terror, first gained so much influence on the populace and then quickly obtained so much power.

|| *Much like the "Squad."*

Next, let's witness the power tug-of-war which followed. It should be noted that one of Lenin's strategies was to cause the defeat of Russia in the war. This then helped ignite the "World's Revolution." When the Germans realized that Lenin and his policies were their best "allies" in the act of unprecedented sabotage of the Russian state, they secured a safe passage for Lenin from Europe straight-through front lines in a heavily guarded train to St. Petersburg--a feat that was not possible without Germany's blessing. Germany's intent was clear: they would assist the Bolsheviks in the Revolution to weaken Russia as its war adversary.

In other words, the goals of the Germans and Bolsheviks coincided for the same narrow political purpose: to achieve their goal by inflicting maximum damage on others, in this case the economic and social system of Russia.

|| *Bill Maher: "I hope for a recession to get rid of Trump. Sorry if that hurts people." Mr. Maher felt perfectly justified wishing financial hardship, in this case on his entire nation, for his narrow political purpose of replacing a president he disliked. His wishes appear to have materialized in 2022.*

As Churchill noted, the Germans "[t]urned upon Russia the grisliest of all weapons. They transported Lenin in a sealed truck like a plague bacillus from Switzerland to Russia."

Once Lenin's coup was achieved, Russia signed an embarrassing surrender treaty in Brest-Litovsk, ceding a large portion of its territory to Germany in the war. Let me repeat it again--Lenin made Russia lose in the war that *its allies* had won in just a few months (albeit without Russia). He inflicted defeat on Russia to serve his purposes of gaining power. In a desperate but unsuccessful attempt to turn the tide in WWI, Germans effectively aided the Bolsheviks in succeeding to bring an end to centuries of Romanov monarchy. The result proved devastating-- the founding of the first socialist state. This event would indeed change the face of world history all the way to 21st century America.

The defeated Russian government was taken over by the Communist Party (earlier formed in 1898 as the Russian Socialist

Democratic Labour Party, "RSDRP" in Russian). Ironically, this occurred in Minsk, the city where I was born. The first Congress of RSDRP occurred only a few hundred meters away from the place where JFK's killer, Lee Harvey Oswald, lived in Minsk.

Shortly after the Bolsheviks' coup, significant repressive and regressive changes occurred under the misleading banner of 'Progress and Reforms.' Take note of these similarities:

As a mechanism of "imperial oppression," the entire police force was effectively canceled (*||*: *defunded?*). Property rights were abolished. Factories were nationalized (*||*: *redistributed?*). As a natural result, crime was rampant and unpunished (*||*: *Think of NY and Chicago*). Corpses, typically stripped and robbed, filled the Russian cities and were observed by the rare contemporary foreign travelers. The Bolsheviks continued in their plan of total domination by enticing the Russian populace through redistribution of wealth.

||: *Free stuff! Minorities with phones in their hands crying out, "Vote for Obama and he will give you a free phone!"*

Empty promises were offered, including "Lands to Peasants!" and "Factories to Workers!" Furthermore, Lenin declared Dictatorship of the Proletarians the key governing principle. He intended to "counterbalance the prior oppression" of the working people with the "Red Terror" (i.e., mass murders, expropriation, taking hostages from families of those fighting against the "red"). Lenin termed such terrifying acts as the "language of persuasion."

---

* A shout out to self-proclaimed 'social democrats' caucus in the U.S. Congress.

As a response to Bolshevik atrocities, a long and terrible Russian civil war ensued. The White Army, which was made up of monarchists, anarchists, capitalists, Cossacks, and advocates of different versions of socialism, was eventually defeated by the Bolshevik's more powerful Red Army. This was accomplished by conscripting large masses of peasants and proletarians through fear, terror, and more empty promises of an "equitable society." Once again, this included "free" land and other "free" property.

All the norms of the "prior oppressive traditional society," regardless of their positive achievements, were effectively abandoned in favor of one ephemeral goal: building Communism. This would be accomplished by sacrificing anything and everything (people, law, freedoms, prior social and economic achievements, etc.) that stood in the way of "masses" marching in lockstep under the new bloody flags of political, economic, and social correctness. As I said, these events would change the course of the country, and even the entire civilization, in devastating ways.

In those early years of the Soviet Union, there were attempts to radically change the family unit. This included abandoning the institute of marriage, or sexual consent, and destroying the traditional family and marriage. Per communists, "A true revolutionary does not have time to court a mate."

Perhaps the most terrifying piece of social "reforms" was their plan to unite all the children into a single "community family" with the "new" society's specific focus on "newspeak" (*||*: *"Cancel culture and revolutionary political correctness".*) and blue-collar language purity (*||* *"Woke speak"*).

|| *It is the American Left's position that parents should not interfere with their children's education, but instead relegate that function entirely to the state. Such government attitude to "community children" has deep roots in the Soviet approach to family and education. At least we can rejoice that such an approach brought a crushing defeat to Democrats in Virginia's gubernatorial elections*

which will reverberate for decades. That defeat gives Americans hope and a hint of cure against the Red Plague.

In that "new" society of the Soviet Union, government-- not the family-- would now play the dominant role in raising the children and making choices for their education.

|| *President Biden told America's teachers that when students are in the classroom, those children belong to them. Republicans replied they are not co-parenting their children with the government. The response of parents, judging by sheer numbers of both Republicans and centrist Democrats in Virginia contributed to that parental "revolt" and GOP landslide victory in the 2021 election. The fight against the woke ideology permeating our schools with sexually explicit materials and openly racist CRT studies continues today in towns all across America.*

While the "communal families" concept was abandoned fairly quickly by the rulers, the trend toward total domination of education in the Soviet Union remained until its demise in 1991. I must impress upon you how restricting those new educational components were, and how different from what you are used to in American schools. Soviet education provided no elective courses. None. All school programs were completely pre-determined and implemented by the state. There were no opportunities for input offered or allowed by parents or students.

While such uniformity raised the average level of knowledge in concrete areas such as biology, geography, and math, any free thought, critical thinking, or even debate about social issues, market economy, or history were completed "canceled." Such expressions of individual thought were viewed as dangerous for both kids and parents.

|| *This very same issue and argument over parents' rights in their children's education, and focus on problem solving, enabled Governor Glenn Youngkin and Lt. Gov. Winsome Sears to claim*

victory in the 2021 Virginia Gubernatorial elections. *It will be interesting to see how many states will seek to do the same in subsequent elections.*

In the Soviet Union, this went so far as to often abandon the traditional Christian names for children in favor of the atrociousness of Electraficatsia (electrification), LEM (Lenin, Engels, Marx), Dazdraperma (Long Live the First of May--the 'Labor Day'), and later, Pofistal. No, that was not the name of a potent drug, but an acronym that stood for 'the victor over fascism, Iosif Stalin'. We were all baptized by our grandparents in secrecy. By the 1960s and '70s this practice with "weird" names subsided (thank God!). That trivial example of Soviet "cancel culture"--canceling the "outdated" world--only shows how ridiculous and senseless change is when it's made solely for the sake of change itself.

American women have many more benefits than Soviet women. Equality between women and men was declared, but this was in lip service only. Even during the later Soviet times, there was a list of more than 400 vacancies which women simply *were not allowed* to fill. In an unprecedented and "enlightened" move in 2020, Russia reduced the list by about 25%. This inequality between men and women flies in the face of America's current cultural struggles.

During the entire existence of the USSR, not even one woman served in the Politbureau, the effective highest ruling body of the Communist Party. For all practical purposes, no women served in the top ranks of the state's governing body, which was declared the sole Ruling Party in all four Soviet constitutions. The state structure and the golden ruling principles were simple, if not primitive. Marxist ideology is flawless, so it must be the party representing such an ideology. Any dissent or even casting doubts about Communist theory or the Party was not allowed. Such actions were heavily prosecuted as a state crime.

|| *In America today, it's "Are you against the environment? Are you against equity and progress?" This is painfully similar to: "Are you against communism?"*

Speech was neutered entirely. Any meaningful political discourse was wholly eliminated by one single party line in every field of the "sovietikus"-- the term coined for the new type of human being. Despite freedom of speech being declared as a right granted to the people,*† in actuality, only speech that fell squarely within the "Course of the

Party" was allowed. Political 'elections' were a farce. There was neither an alternative party nor any alternative candidates. Any mention of God was strictly forbidden. Raising any questions or discussion about election results was highly toxic.

|| *It's almost akin to discussing possible irregularities or media bias in the 2020 American presidential elections on Twitter, particularly media suppression of the Hunter Biden laptop story.*

Even an attempt at placing a candidate on the ballot was not approved by the Party. Seeking an audit of election results was considered treason. Alexander Lukashenko, a learned student of his communist predecessors, puppeteered kangaroo courts in Belarus. One such infamous trial sentenced Sergei Tikhanovsky to 18 years in jail just for trying to get *onto* the voting ballot.

In a similar fashion, Putin keeps piling criminal convictions on Alexey Navalny for contrived and ridiculous charges, including essentially a charge of "hurting the feelings of war veterans," after an unsuccessful attempt to assassinate Navalny which was clearly orchestrated by Putin and his FSB. We are sure Navalny's courageous reporting about corruption and Putin's opulent palaces with golden

---

*Compare to the opposite approach by the U.S. founders – human rights are God-given.

toilet paper holders worthy of a small city budget had nothing to do with those prison sentences, or the attempts by FSB operatives to kill Navalny by rubbing poison into his underwear.

|| *Socialists everywhere are disturbingly deeply concerned with words and "feelings," raising them to the level of social or even criminal offenses, particularly when dealing with the feelings of despots.*

A large credit for the success of the Bolsheviks' keeping power is given to the secret police, known as ChKa (Extraordinary Commission--later transformed into NKVD, KGB, and now FSB in Russia, still KGB in Belarus). Most Americans equate KGB to men in dark suits featured in James Bond movies. However, rather than fighting MI-6 or CIA, the true danger with this oppressive state's tool came from spying on its own citizens for "thought" crimes. These secret police and their broad network of informers were very real. They carried out a campaign of mass murders and random arrests during the Red Terror. Perhaps you are familiar with the Olympic opening ceremonies in Sochi, Russia, in 2014. Portraits of famous Russian or Soviet writers/poets were shown. What you may not know is that the vast majority of those faces shown as a 'pride of the nation' were, in fact, executed or died in what were deemed suspicious 'suicides.' I was not able to identify even one exception.

|| *Any cues about a suspicious set of circumstances of people committing suicide when being deemed a liability for the 'Swamp'?*

Here are just a few examples out of millions of others. Osip Mandelstam drowned in the toilet as he served his five-year sentence, convicted essentially for being a poet. Nikolai Gumilev and Isaac Babel, along with thousands and thousands of other prominent artists and scientists, were charged with espionage and executed. Some "credible" charges, in a Steel dossier style, included a plot to dig a tunnel to Western Europe. On the bloody October 30,

1938, more than 100 prominent Belarusian politicians, artists, writers, and the very elite of Belarus society were rounded, executed, and buried at Kuropaty.

Imagine what it was like to live in those days under this oppression when poets, artists, and scientists were executed for treason simply for being too daring, speaking too freely, undertaking any initiative, or showing even a hint of desire for the same freedoms Americans enjoyed then--and are perhaps taking for granted today. A sad postscript to that horrible event in Belarusian history: the memorial of this atrocity is now being meticulously dismantled by the neo-communist Lukashenko.

The socialist regime often used the death of a Bolshevik as a pretext for further repressions. For instance, Sergei Kirov, a prominent Soviet politician, was killed by an NKVD officer. Many, including Nikita Khrushchev, believed this was a hit job organized by Stalin himself against a popular political opponent.

The murder, however, was used as a huge pretext for even more repressions against the Soviet population to instill fear. Fear was always an effective means of intimidation in the Soviet world, "encouraging people to keep their heads down and their mouths shut." Retribution, even for the smallest deviation from the Party line, was another effective intimidator. As a true devotee of the retribution theories, one of Lukashenko's generals declared they would kill 100 people for each member of the KGB killed. Much like NKVD and Nazis in the '30s and '40s. Much like crime bosses in 1930s Chicago who ran the violent world of organized crime through fear and retribution, yet at the government level. This disturbing threat by an active general was annunciated in the aftermath of the incident when Andrey Zeltser, a member of the Belarus underground resistance, was killed along with a non-uniformed KGB agent in an apparent shootout.*‡ Imagine a general essentially labeling the people of his own country as "enemies." Why would he do that? Misguided loyalty to an unscrupulous tyrant not willing to part with power, privilege, and palaces.

|| *Should we then say that those U.S. politicians who declared the half of the country that voted with and for the "wrong party" were "a basket of deplorables" or "most extreme political group" were half as shameful?*

History and economic laws follow their own path. It's so important that Americans know and understand history. Consider this: Russia in 1919, despite its recent prosperity and abundance of goods and food, had suffered terrible famines and essentially turned into a failed state. This was due to incompetent and brutal Bolsheviks' policies, including the deliberate destruction of their own economy through nationalization and turning all private property into communal ownership for the universal welfare.

Did you notice the same words are being bantered about today? America would be wise to listen closely when the Left uses phrases such as *"communal"* and *"universal,"* or makes excuses for their abysmal policies by claiming they are *"temporary"* or *"transitory."* Even more so, when they blame Putin for their own messes. Why not blame Martians or UFOs? Soviet Russia always sought internal and external, usually imperialistic, "enemies" and their "saboteurs," never considering that the Communist government itself was indeed the "root cause."

|| *Ironically, as much as Biden blames Putin for high inflation, Putin blames Biden and the West for Russia's economic misfortunes, even for provoking the war. But Putin would never put blame on his own decision to wage a brutal war against a neighbor.*

Take note of the irony in a "cry for help" letter of 1920 from Maxim Gorky, a famous Russian writer, displayed at Stanford University. Gorky begged President Herbert Hoover for help to feed starving Russian children, the result of those failed Bolsheviks' policies. Eventually, the ARA (American Relief Administration) was formed, which is believed to have saved the lives of tens of millions of Russians. Help from the ARA was given even before the formal diplomatic relationship was established between the new Soviet State and the USA, in spite of the negative propaganda about Western and American Imperialism fed daily to the Russian people by their government.

These propaganda exercises have amplified to levels not even seen during the Cold War for the USA's recent assistance to Ukraine in defending its independence.

In other words, the humanitarian help Russians needed so desperately came from the same "greedy and ruthless" capitalists who were the very target of the Bolsheviks' sweeping revolution. This is yet another historical example of the generosity and integrity of the American people. They offered timely aid to others in need without regard to political differences or even adverse consequences to their own economy, which were partially due to sanctions imposed on Russia for war crimes.

|| *I guess all those angry proponents of the 1619 curriculum who shout that America has never been a good nation have never bothered to study any history, nor do they understand how lucky they are to live in the USA and enjoy its freedoms and fortunes. There are grateful people in nations all over the world who would vehemently disagree with their accusations.*

By the end of his life, Lenin realized how inefficient the Soviet system was so he initiated the New Economic Policy. This initiative included a return to some private property, a return to a money-based economy with taxes rather than the forced requisition of harvest and even seedlings, and small-scale entrepreneurship. At this time American businessmen were allowed to enter Russia and contract with the Russian

*An uncanny parallel can be drawn using January 6th's riots in the U.S. as a pretext for the Left to go after those who speak against the Swamp.

government again. You might recognize the name Armand Hammer. Along with Albert Kahn later, American entrepreneur Hammer built Soviet factories, including the famous Stalingrad tractor factory, at an unprecedented rate.

Nevertheless, Stalin eventually canceled the "counter-revolutionary" measures of Lenin's New Economic Policy. Foreigners were expelled, killed, or exiled. What followed was the policy of "collectivization"--forced unions of the farmers, called "kolhoz," and forced industrialization--essentially expropriating everything from the peasants for the sake of "industrial development." Citizens must beware when their government introduces programs with lofty names. They frequently come with devious intentions.

// *The U.S. Inflation Reduction Act immediately comes to mind as an epitome of cover-up and hypocrisy, inevitably bringing the opposite result of its shamelessly titled declaration.*

Again, several waves of famine rolled through Kazakhstan, Russia, and Ukraine, starving innocent millions. The repressive economic and labor laws caused the workers to have little incentive to help their government or country, and even less passion toward slogans and ideology. One example of this repression was the law of "three spikelets"--any individual stealing three spikelets from a field already harvested could be executed and all his property confiscated.

|| *Obviously a different direction than taken by the State of California, which decided not to prosecute unless at least $950 worth of goods was stolen. Thieves are having a field day in California, but they would not dare to be so arrogant in the Soviet Union.*

As kulaks (relatively wealthy farmers) were executed, the remaining peasants had no incentive to produce anything because they knew the government would confiscate it. Instead, they were coerced to rely on the government as the supplier of all necessities, while the government could rely only on forced labor.

Of course, forced labor could not survive without its martyrs. It also required approaching economic production with the same brutal force and ferociousness as fighting in Stalingrad. All of us who grew up as kids in the Soviet Union were fed the stories and images of Pavlik Morozov as a "role model." This boy *reported his own father* to the authorities for having hidden some of the grain so he could feed his family and save them from starvation. Fear and retribution were always at the forefront of Soviet life, but even they paled in comparison to the cult of showing Party loyalty. After his own relatives later killed the boy, his image was made into a martyr by the Soviet propaganda. However, among us kids, his name had a negative connotation. We viewed him as a snitch who cared more for his own hide and state crumbs than the lives of his family. Take it from me, you do not want to be called Pavlik Morozov by a Russian speaker! This would be worse than an American calling someone a Benedict Arnold.* §

Lenin and Stalin are the two forefathers of socialism, which seems to hold fascination for some Americans. However, even a brief glimpse at history will make you understand the dangers of socialism as it was designed and developed by those evil geniuses. Following Lenin's death in 1924, Joseph Stalin rose to power. Through Gulags, mass oppression, and terror costing tens of millions of lives, Stalin converted the Soviet Union from an agricultural civilization to an industrial and military superpower. His iron-fisted reign lasted until he died in 1953.

During Stalin's rule, you could get arrested for even a slight sign of disloyalty. Through fear, Stalin developed the culture of "reporting" on your neighbor to help the government seek out "enemies of the people." Today we call that a snitch. Did you notice that "snitching" was very prevalent in Soviet culture? An enemy of the people was not an evil mass shooter dressed in black. To the contrary, an enemy could be anyone who dared to think independently or show disbelief in the value of the communist cause.

The anecdotes that we learned in childhood reflected the "culture" of those times. One of them went like this: "Stalin lost his smoking pipe." The head of the KGB reported to Stalin that they arrested 25 people, and 24 of them had confessed to stealing the missing pipe. Stalin's infamous response: "Just 24? Please continue the investigation."

Numerous "collusions" with the West were invented. (*||*: *Similar to the bogus Russian collusion in America today based on a made-up dossier.* Most people confessed to the alleged crimes following torture, were then charged with treason, and summarily executed. Genetics and Cybernetics, among other sciences, were rejected by the Soviet regime because science, natural selection, and proximate causation interfered with the harvesting and other development plans of the Communist Party. Proponents of such things were arrested as saboteurs and then executed, including Nikolai Vavilov. Such an "applied" attitude toward science is essential and, thus, true if it falls within the accepted political concept. And if not, and if reality shows it to be a fact contradicting the Party line, then it is not science.*"*The socialistic approach to science cost the Soviet people dearly, i.e. "It's science *if* we like the results and *if* they are politically proper."

In addition to the very fact of prosecution of innocent prominent people, the Soviet society hampered true progress and development in all spheres of life, including the military (which, with the German invasion, contributed to the heavy losses suffered during WWII).

* One could conclude that the Washington bureaucracy is filled with Pavlik Morozovs, who answer their "higher calling" to "save" the country from the "Orange plague" by leaking critical information and instructing the FBI agents investigating General Flynn – "just make him lie" – and even walking on the edge of treason, warning Chinese counterparts by members of U.S. upper-echelon military who essentially sided with the potential enemy over the Unites States – all due to their pitiful grudge against Trump and his intolerance of the Swamp culture.

Notably, Sergei Korolev, the father of the Soviet space program, was arrested on contrived charges, beaten, and tortured. He even had his thumb and jaw broken in jail during interrogations designed to get confessions for non-existent crimes. Eventually, the broken jaw injury killed him by preventing the attending doctor from resuscitating him. Korolyov, one of only a few lucky ones, was moved to a "special prison," enabling him to work on the Soviet airplane and rocket program.

Thousands and thousands were executed under the same false premises. These included the creators of the famous Katyusha, the first mobile multiple rocket launcher and predecessor of the famous HIMARS, which played a huge role in the World War II victory. Sadly, a modified version of this same rocket launcher is being used today in 2022 to turn Ukrainian cities to dust as Putin, yet another communist, comparing himself to Peter the Great, declares himself a "messiah" and "gatherer of the Russian lands." The vast difference in physical height (at least a foot--hence the "Napoleon complex") and historical stature notwithstanding, it is ironic. You see, Peter the Great was a devotee of Western culture and is credited with "opening the window to the West."

Putin, on the other hand, has succeeded in slamming that window closed. He also succeeded in making the height difference with Peter the Great smaller by ordering special heel inserts for his shoes, effectively causing him to walk on tippy-toes. Even more comedic, while standing and speaking in public (at his usual 30-foot distance), when fidgeting, he starts bringing his toes up. The result causes it to appear that his shins bend back, akin to the back legs of a horse. Putin's inferiority complex

> * One could wonder if an ever-changing stance on masks, lockdowns, inexplicable partiality to vaccinations over natural immunity, unreasonable measures such as wearing masks outside, and the dystopian Big-Tech and Mass Media censorship on truly scientific, empirical studies and discussions regarding the origin of the virus, efficacy of the vaccines, and therapeutics as imposed Left-wing agenda had more to do with control and the unflawed "Party line" than the actual science.

and the need to recompense with his "greatness" manifests itself in his each and every action, whether it be an overuse of Botox or feeble attempts at resurrecting the Soviet Empire.

The socialist regimes were readily joined by the mass hysteria on the Left in the U.S. regarding the intrinsic flaws of capitalism. However, as they were unable to win in a fact-based argument or a meaningful competition, they resorted to other means--brute force, Soviet Union prisons, censorship, cover-ups, and personal "cancel-culture" attacks against opponents in Western society.

Most recently, Putin is waging war against Ukraine on false premises of "Nazism." Note the irony: In a country led by a democratically-elected actor of Jewish descent, Volodymir Zelensky's courageous stature and stoic character propelled him to Churchill-like heights of admiration among the people in his country. At the same time, Putin's regime, through his pawn Foreign Minister Lavrov with his wicked logic and lies, insulted Jews around the world, implying that Jews were to blame for the Holocaust. Why? Because Hitler was Jewish!

|| *Such nonsensical and insulting comparisons and conjectures have certainly taken deep root in contemporary American politics when a black conservative politician is called a "black face of white supremacy and racism" just because he or she decided to break out from the "party line" of the Left. I could not even try to repeat all the insulting epithets the Left reserved for Nikki Haley when she chose to run for president on a conservative platform.*

In even more sinister rhetoric, many war-hungry Russian ultra-patriots who supported Putin's war on Ukraine called their Ukrainian war mission a "Hohlocaust"--a disturbing term concocted as the derogatory label for Ukrainians and Holocaust. What a great way to make friends with a "brotherly" nation and people around the world!

Gabriel Garcia Márquez, a Columbian writer and Nobel Prize laureate, while visiting Moscow in 1957, was asked what he found to be essential in the Soviet Union. He had an insightful response. He said the Soviet rulers and Soviet people were "really lucky" that the people simply do not know how miserable their lives are. His books were banned in the Soviet Union. This simple example bears a logical conclusion: the key to covering up the incompetence, corruption, and hypocrisy of socialism was to keep people away from facts. In other words, simply twist reality. The Kremlin's assault on independent journalism added war crimes and the state of affairs of their crumbling army to that list of things that must be zealously concealed by this modern-time self-declared Hun.

Eventually, the Red Terror turned against the revolutionaries in a few sequential waves. Again, note the irony: killers were killing the killers of the prior killers. The dangers of Red Terror are demonstrated by this simple fact: of about 70 people in the Congress who declared "Red Terror" as a necessary means of the new political will, 75% were eventually executed. Stalin, in his typical socialist grasp for unlimited power, was afraid the "true revolutionaries" taking part in the Civil War or Revolution might turn against him. He responded by merging those "true revolutionaries" with other "enemies of the state."

He even left evidence of his evil, several of which were somewhat humorous. There is a chain of several historical pictures with Stalin and five or six of his comrades. The photos were contemporaneously "modified" by erasing people as they were executed. This was long before Photoshop so it took some creativity! The eerie sequential photographs showed awkward repositioning of hands and legs of the persons remaining--for the time being anyway. As is the case with dictators who see enemies at every turn, by 1940 virtually everyone had become Stalin's enemy. Eventually, Stalin ended up in that picture alone. The last one standing. The last of the Mohi... "true" Bolsheviks.

Those who were lucky enough to be "only" jailed, typically without the right to "exchange correspondence," were turned into an effective slave force responsible for the quick Soviet industrialization. Four out of five Marshalls were "purged." Tens of thousands of high-ranked officers were summarily sentenced to death. At one point, the highest-ranking officer remaining in the Southern Caucasian District was a captain! Stalin's cruelty to his own army was so massive and severe, he literally left the Soviet Army helpless against Germany's invasion in 1941 with a few million PoWs and massive loss of lives and armaments.

One of the shortages and, hence, most coveted possessions of my boyhood in the Soviet Union were books. I recall that my aunt had a version of the 1953 Large Soviet Encyclopedia with certain duplicate pages in the "B" chapter referring to Beria and Bering Strait. Lavrentiy Beria was one of the brutal and murderous leaders of the KGB/NKVD. Along with his usual prosecution of "enemies of the state," he routinely tortured and executed the husbands of the women he raped. Beria himself was ultimately declared an "enemy of the state." Owners of Soviet Encyclopedia books were sent an insert with instructions to remove the page about Beria and replace it with a new page about the Bering Strait. My aunt, certainly in a daring move, kept both pages! Yes, in the Soviet world you could just "cancel history" as if nothing actually happened.

|| *It seems that in America in 2022, some are trying to do the same thing--simply ban someone from social media, omit his or her opinion or view, and pretend that they or it never happened.*

To drive economic growth and transformation in the Soviet Union, Stalin established a series of Five-Year Plans. The first Five-Year Plan prioritized agricultural redistribution and rapid industrialization. Manufacturing of arms and military build-up became the emphasis of subsequent Five-Year Plans.

Between 1928 and 1940, Stalin forced the agricultural sector to be collectivized. Peasants in rural areas were compelled to join collective farms. Citizens who possessed land or livestock simply had their holdings taken away. Imagine the government simply taking your land from you and evicting you for no other reason than you, as a result of your hard work, are relatively wealthy-- or at least not dying of hunger--in the name of universal equity. Even worse, hundreds of thousands of kulaks--higher-income farmers -- were gathered up and killed, and the lucky ones were exiled to Siberia. Their land and property were seized for the "common good." Intelligentsia and clergy were subject to the same type repressions. Over 90% of priests were executed because the Soviet Union could have only one religion-- namely, Communism and the World Revolution.

Individually-owned farms were seized and consolidated into enormous state-run collective farms. The Communists claimed their plan would increase agricultural productivity. Nothing could have been further from the truth. Agricultural productivity fell because farmers in the countryside resisted having their farms seized, so they sabotaged expropriation of harvest and operations of collective farms. A severe food shortage followed--the natural result of abysmal mismanaged government policies.

|| *Much like record-setting high gas prices in the U.S. or sporadic shortages of various staples due to Biden's "monkey wrench" policies.*

During the Great Famine of 1932-1933, millions of people died. For years after, the Soviet Union denied the Great Famine. The government tried to conceal the findings of the 1937 census which would have revealed to the public the true scale of the disaster. In typical Soviet fashion, everyone responsible for conducting the 1937 census was executed. The census was redone shortly afterward by people who had quickly learned the lesson from their deceased predecessors. The new census produced results that satisfied Stalin, enabling him to victoriously claim a falsified "growth" of the country's population.

That same "wishful-thinking reporting" in 2022 caused Putin to grossly underestimate the resistance and will of the Ukrainian people fighting for their motherland and freedom. Putin failed to take into account Russia's corruption, failing economy, or the abysmal state of affairs of the Russian army. Putin's commanders eagerly reported about the "unmatched capabilities" of the Russian army. North Korea's commanders practice the same type boasting.

The facts tell a very different story. Reportedly, some Russian troops which suffered significant losses from the Ukrainian resistance were equipped with 1943 Mosin rifles. My grandfather fought with that same rifle in Stalingrad! Putin's 2022 army is wearing WWII helmets. The expiration dates on their food supplies are older than some of the Russian soldiers!

It seems the "second" best army in the world turned out to be second best in Ukraine. If the promised munitions and supplies arrive in Ukraine in timely fashion, the Russian army is destined to suffer a crushing defeat in the near future. As you may recall, President Zelensky responded to Biden's offer of evacuation by saying: *"I don't need a ride. I need weapons."*

At the time of this writing, the Ukrainians and their brave president still need weapons to defend their country, and perhaps the entire civilized world. For our part, we can help and pray. Hopefully, leaders of the world will listen. More than that, they will have enough intestinal fortitude and self-preservation instincts to bring about a quick victory. Hopefully, such a historical military defeat of "red/brown" evil will drag the misguided communism-inspired tyrants, headed this time by Putin, down into the abyss once and for all.

Otherwise, the occupation of Ukraine will be only the beginning for Putin's insatiable appetite. History repeats itself. As Hitler started his march for world domination in Poland, Putin will do the same unless he is stopped in Ukraine. In his own terms, Putin said, "Russian borders do not end anywhere." While he perhaps sounded half joking, history proves that "many a true word is said in jest."

Putin's actions, which began with soft occupations of its neighbors in 2008 and culminated in all-out war in Ukraine in 2022, carry serious consequences for the future of our children. We can't afford to laugh this off. We can't afford to be afraid to "provoke" Putin because, as with any bully, he will not stop unless he is stopped. He is obsessed by his insatiable messiah fight against the "evil and corrupt West." How many more children in Bucha and Izium need to be tortured to death before people around the world realize that Putin's army has already reached its peak of atrocities and war crimes? Blackmailing the world with nuclear weapons and high gas prices can only be stopped by calling Putin's bluff. Calls for negotiations with Putin while he occupies and loots a large part of Ukraine, and calls seeking an "off-ramp" by various people-- including Elon Musk and even Donald Trump--are missing the critical point. It was well put by Golda Meir, former prime minister of Israel who was actually born in Ukraine: "*We intend to remain alive. Our neighbors want to see us dead. This is not a question that leaves much room for compromise.*"

In the Soviet mindset, if socialist goals could not be achieved, whether by ignoring economic laws and any sense of causation, you just played with numbers and switched the propaganda machine into high gear. The game plan is simple: Continuously instill your "truth" in people's minds. Anyone who dares to doubt or question the veracity of your successful "matchless" results is punished for "disinformation." Give the people a steady diet of your version of the "truth" and they eventually believe it.

|| *Compare this with the Left's perception of "misinformation" and effective cancellation of non-liberal views by the Leftist media. The steady diet of "talking points" comes down from the White House and is repeated again and again and again by multiple 24-hour newscasts and print media.*

In my boyhood in the Soviet Union and now in Russia today, the fact-checkers were the KGB (aka ChKa or FSB). Belarus's leader, being true to his Soviet past and present, even kept the name KGB. It was their job to police the Soviet version of "truth" and eliminate any dissent at its root, be it school, university, or social interaction of any kind.

|| *Much like today's Facebook and Twitter fact-checkers--the American version of 'thought' police as they ban Nobel laureates for "misinformation"---report the activity of conservative groups to law enforcement and suppress conservative opinions. By and large, many of the so-called "conspiracy" theories, as labeled by the Leftist media, such as the source of the virus, Biden's family ties to foreign agents in China and Russia, and FBI interference with social media, etc., ended up being true or at least subject to a legitimate debate and discovery.*

An alarming trend in the United States government is to "re-invent" today's reality to meet their agenda. We've seen this trend with the border crisis, the energy crisis, and the uncontrollable inflation. You declare "sanctuary cities," but refuse to take in refugees and paint the moving of migrants to the cities as a "political stunt." You beg Saudi mullahs to produce more oil, but ignore U.S. oil producers. You "fight" inflation by pursuing more spending on social programs and student loan forgiveness. The world and logic of the Left are just upside down.

Our government declares: *"We spent $3 trillion, and it's not going to cost you anything."* Really?? This sort of statement is squarely in line with the impractical socialist ideology and methods I witnessed in the Soviet Union. Pursuits of utopia pet projects cannot rely on facts or science because there are none. Instead, they give projects a trendy name and new "spin"--all designed to convince the public of their new make-believe "reality." Then tell them again and again, and eventually they believe you. But when reality hits you with inflation (surprise, surprise!), you can blame "the other guy" (or Russia) for it.

Putin has always been a master of this as well. When facing obliteration of his ground forces in Ukraine, Putin claimed, "Everything goes according to plan." He also rebranded the embarrassing Russian loss at the Battle for Kyiv as a "sign of goodwill." Then he rewarded Russian troops who were charged with credible reports of war crimes and atrocities against the civilian population. To save face, he reported that new goals were now set calling for "regrouping" of the armed forces. A move by a bully who unexpectedly met his match!

According to one estimate, the Ukrainian famine of 1932-1933—known as the Holodomor, a combination of the Ukrainian words for "*starvation*" and "*to inflict death*"—killed 3.9 million people, roughly 13% of the population. Stalin used his secret police to terrorize Communist Party officials, the military, and the general population. He killed or imprisoned millions to effectively eliminate any potential challenge to his power. That, my friends, is the true face of socialism.

Notice that when Bernie Sanders is called a "socialist," he immediately corrects people by adding the word "democratic." Bernie is making a gross error. He has the same distorted and glorified image about socialism that most Americans have. Bernie spent his honeymoon in the Soviet Union so he's likely confusing his romantic memories with reality.

Those of us who are truly aware and actually lived under socialism and its bloody history know the same "positive" connotation could be achieved by adding Bernie's adjective "democratic" in front of many other words too. "Democratic "murderer." "Democratic slave owner." "Democratic arsonist." I wonder if Bernie intended that? Or was he simply using typical socialist word games for his own power trip? A dangerous game to play as he deceived the unwary youth who followed him.

Between 1936 and 1938, at the height of Stalin's terror campaign known as the Great Purge, an official count put the number of people executed at around 600,000. Even more astounding, many believe that number was greatly underestimated by at least 20 times. It did not take into account the people who were tortured to death, committed so-called "suicides," or had "heart attacks" in Gulags. Consider this example of the brutality of Stalin's regime and the arrogance of his domination. Some prisoners as punishment for not reaching a plan, for instance, would be tied to a tree to have Siberian ruthless mosquitoes suck the blood out of them until they died. Of course, the official cause of death would be "heart attack." To prevent even a chance of an escape from a desolate Siberian location, the dead in the prison would have their skulls crushed with a hammer before their bodies were buried or dumped in the river.

Dear fellow Americans, are you sure you want Communists to run your prisons ... or your government, for that matter?

The Cold War

Following Nazi Germany's surrender at the end of World War II, the already uneasy wartime alliance between the Soviet Union, the United States, and the United Kingdom began to fall apart. By 1948, the Soviet Union had installed communist-leaning administrations in Eastern European countries liberated from Nazi rule after WWII. The United States and the United Kingdom were concerned, with good reason, about Communism spreading over Western Europe and the world.

The North Atlantic Treaty Organization (NATO) was founded in 1949 by the United States, Canada, and its European allies. This

Western bloc alliance was a political show of force against the Soviet Union and its allies.

In reaction to NATO, the Soviet Union formed the Warsaw Pact in 1955 to consolidate power among Eastern Bloc countries. This ignited what was known as the Cold War. The Cold War power struggle between the Eastern and Western blocs was waged on political, economic, and propaganda fronts, and continued in various forms until the Soviet Union fell apart in 1991. There were no free movements of people inside the country. The passport system and various "domicile" registrations ("propiska") made a move to even a different region inside the country difficult, and a foreign move virtually impossible.

Even travel inside the country was hampered by restrictions and formalities requiring a state-approved "reason" for virtually every trip. Soviet peasants or collective farm workers, for instance, were issued passports in the late 1960s even to enable them to travel or move within the country. Passports were seen as a privilege, as "revered papers" signifying and entitling them to their rights rather than rights given by laws or God. Notably, the collective farmers were not even allowed to leave their work at the collective farm until the later years of the Soviet Union, thus being effectively enslaved to the state.

Attempting to escape the Soviet Union was a high crime. To Americans, it sounds ridiculous that people would be forbidden to leave their own country. People by the thousands try every day to force their way illegally *into* America! But I remember that in my school days, we were told a story about a famous heroic border guard who stopped over 150 "breaches" of the Soviet border. It turned out that all but one (!) were breaches where people were *trying to escape from the Soviet Union*. As for traveling abroad--since 1935, free travel outside of the Soviet Union has been banned, effectively making the country a prison for its citizens.*†

As I said, the idea of being banned from leaving your own country is a foreign concept to Americans. But to a communist regime, any travel abroad by its citizens would be dangerous to the system because viewing life in other nations would prove the advanced decline, rather than "progress," of the Communist society. Particularly in the abysmal economic sphere. Consumer needs and well-being of its citizens were largely ignored in the Soviet Union in favor of military might. Remember, the Soviet goal was not happy citizens. The Soviet goal was the spread of communism around the world. Each and every tenet of Soviet social life was made to serve only that high purpose. Each and every personal goal or desire was publicly ostracized and labeled as "greedy" or "selfish."

|| *Much like all those "greedy" capitalists "driving up" the prices in the U.S. under Biden's dreadful abysmal economic policies.*

Permission to leave, known as an "exit visa," was not easily granted, not even to go to other socialist countries. The humiliating process required a lot of "red tape" and haunted Soviet citizens until the dissolution of the Soviet Union. As Russia and Belarus suffer consequences today for the current war against Ukraine, both governments have restricted travel abroad for IT people and state workers, at least for now.

Khrushchev and De-Stalinization

After Stalin's death in 1953, Nikita Khrushchev rose to power. Khrushchev was appointed Secretary of the Communist Party and he served during probably the most stressful years of the Cold War. In 1962, he sparked the Cuban Missile Crisis by placing nuclear weapons in Cuba, just 90 miles from Florida's coast. This frightening conflict was eventually resolved, and mutual tensions reduced through negotiations with the Kennedy administration.

Khrushchev instituted a series of political reforms during a period known as "Warming Up" which reduced the repressive nature of Soviet society. During this time, known as de-Stalinization, Khrushchev chastised Stalin for detaining and deporting political opponents, took steps to improve living conditions, freed many political prisoners, relaxed artistic censorship, and closed the Gulag work camps.

---

* If you vie for socialism, imagine you live in a society that has such a grasp on your life, you are not only prohibited to travel outside the country without government permission, you cannot even freely move within your own country. Constant control by Big Brother is apparent on the streets with no "probable cause" limitations on police power. Police can demand your passport and other papers for your proper justification for simply being where you are.

However, he never blamed the system or socialism. Instead, he pinned the blame solely on the "Cult of Personality of Stalin" and "overbending" [of the repressive mechanism].

In the Communist Party leadership's view, Khrushchev's legitimacy was damaged by deteriorating relations between the Soviet Union and neighboring China and food shortages across the USSR. In 1964, Khrushchev was seen as "too progressive" and viewed by many as betraying the communists' true calling. He was deposed by members of his own political party.

The Collapse of the Soviet Union

During the 1960s and 1970s, the Communist Party leadership and its bureaucratic machine amassed riches, power, and access to all needed resources. At the same time, millions of ordinary Soviet residents struggled with their daily lives. The Soviet Union's rush to industrialize at any cost led to routine shortages of food and consumer goods. Throughout the 1970s and 1980s, although hunger or famine were no longer an issue, routine queues for essential goods or food were widespread. The Soviet Union sent Gagarin to space in 1961, but didn't start producing toilet paper until 1968. Thus, "Pravda" and other lead-ink printed newspapers had dual-use!

Soviet life meant a constant search for necessities. When people saw a queue, one never asked, *"What's on sale?"* or *"What are they selling?"* Instead, they asked, *"What do they 'dayut'?"* which translated, *"What do they 'give' or 'let us have'?"* In Soviet daily life, money was not essential in satisfying your needs. Access to privilege or resources was far more valuable. Essentially everything the state was willing (and able) to produce and then sell was viewed as both rarity and charity. In addition, a tight leash through distribution meant that people could be easily manipulated. Hence, the main principle of Soviet management was for the government 'apparatchiks' to distribute or "give" *("dayut!")* the people something they did not have before *and* which could be easily taken away-- goods, travel, career advances, etc. As there was no private enterprise in this culture, citizens were at the mercy of the state and its planners. The state was omnipotent, "giving a generous hand" when it so desired and removing that hand just as easily.

I remember very well feelings of helplessness and constant dependence on the "parental" and omnipotent Soviet state. I also vividly remember my family's constant focus on trying to "get" things we needed. Particularly when those things we needed, such as a quarter pound of butter, required standing in line for two hours. No kid in any nation anywhere enjoys standing in line for hours, especially for butter ... but maybe for a new iPhone!

|| *Current shortages of baby food, cars, women's hygiene products, and energy in the U.S. caused by overregulation and "progressive" woke policies are only an apprehensive glimpse at what socialism is all about. In addition, under ineffective economic policies, woke or socialist alike, high inflation acts as a tax depriving you of the fruits of your labor.*

That power of the Soviet government over the people extended to education, career, promotions, salaries, apartments, bonuses, cars, any daily privileges, as well as obtaining better food, goods, or staples. You must understand. There was one and only one employer--the State. If you were fired, you would essentially be re-hired by the same "employer." Firing was not easily or routinely done, however, because the State killed all initiatives. To get your salary, you simply had to "be there." Simply show up. No extraordinary performance was required, except in areas relating to military production where extreme pressure, large benefits, and coercion were applied. Military strength was the focus of the regime. Not much was expected of workers or peasants, other than loyalty to the regime. The focus of the workers was on avoiding hard work and "cooking" the books. There was a familiar saying: *"They pretend that they pay us, and we pretend that we work."*

We witness similar results in Ukraine today as we observe the "mighty" Russian army, whose main weapons are "cannon fodder" and "scorched earth tactics."

For the worker, bargaining powers were, to put it mildly, limited. You were fully and completely at the mercy of the government as your single paycheck provider. At the same time, there was no competition for your skills. Everyone was "equitably" paid, as determined by the State. All advances were pre-determined and exactly the same throughout the society. There was no incentive to advance and virtually no route to do so anyway.

That is why participation in sports was such a coveted privilege in the Soviet Union. Only in sports could you experience competition. Only in sports would your actual individual result matter. I cannot stress this enough. Competition was non-existent in all other areas of Soviet life. Sports provided privileges that citizens could not achieve otherwise. Sports also offered an opportunity to travel outside the Soviet Union. This was huge to citizens living in a nation that refused to allow them to leave. My parents were both prominent athletes. Participating in sports provided them the coveted opportunity to travel, while also securing for their family a relatively comfortable living in the early years.

Allow me to share with you a personal example of the Soviet approach. The Soviet Union sought to secure higher country participation in the 1980 Olympics held in Moscow, which were boycotted due to the Soviet invasion of Afghanistan. My dad was assigned and assumed the role of the Olympic coach in Seychelles. To ensure that my parents returned from their overseas trip, the Soviet government forced them to leave one of their children behind. That dubious honor fell to yours truly. While my younger brother explored the beaches at Seychelles, I had the "privilege" of being raised by my grandparents for two years without seeing or visiting my parents. In this Facetime culture of immediately seeing the faces of anyone anytime, I'm not sure you can imagine what it was like to be 12-years old and go two full years *without seeing the faces of my parents.* I didn't even talk to them more than once every few months. But then, who needs the beaches of Seychelles when you can have the pleasure of standing in line for hours for butter!

Sports also entitled athletes to certain privileges within the Soviet system. Much like Hitler's Germany and today's China, sports continues to be used as an important propaganda tool. Parading winning athletes before the world's cameras is an apparent outward evidence to the world of the successes and achievements of the communist society as a whole.

America is in stark contrast with this Soviet mindset. In America, people are individuals. Hard work is rewarded. In all walks of life, not just sports, anyone can roll up their sleeves, apply their ingenuity and resourcefulness, and know it is possible to achieve the "American dream." Did you ever wonder why you do not see any immigrants from Africa, Asia, or countries of the Soviet Union among the homeless? From their perspective, the hard work and effort required to reach for the American dream are far easier than fighting government abuse and enduring dominance.

To illustrate this better, imagine a situation where your only choice of being hired in the U.S. would be the DMV or Post Office. I am sure there are a lot of decent, hard-working people in these organizations. But DMV workers are not usually as pleasant and excited to see you as waiters in a restaurant. Why? Because even though waiters are not the restaurant owner/capitalist, waiters know their paycheck *depends on you,* the consumer. In contrast, no consumer has any influence on the paycheck of a DMV worker. There is no incentive to be either friendly or efficient. Economic incentives eventually take over upbringing or habits. And there you have the difference in overall attitude and, I would dare to say, the eye contact.

The Politburos and other upper echelons of power in the party and their children, known as "boys Majeure," lived vastly different lives from the ordinary people. Children of the powerful carried on luxurious lifestyles. They acted with impunity, taking significant advantage of their parents' influence and power, much like spoiled American children of movie stars, wealthy professional athletes, and successful music artists. These "privileged" rulers accumulated great wealth. Vested with virtual impunity, wealth, and other related powers, they exerted a heavy influence over the "commoners" who were continually deprived of basic freedoms and choices. Lack of freedom and the dismal existence of the Soviet people resulted in backlash and complete nihilism, especially among young people who saw through the hypocrisy and refused to follow in their parents' footsteps in the '70s and '80s.

The new generation of Soviet people grew more and more disenchanted with the regime. This was made worse when news and stories about Western freedoms and wealth leaked into their society, overturning the Communist Party beliefs which had been universally and persistently indoctrinated in school and media. Any stories about the United States were of great interest to young people, including me. In fact, continuous Soviet propaganda against the U.S. had an opposite effect. Even when state-run media correctly identified some of the true problems of Western society, we refused to believe any of the negative information. Instead, we mistrusted the Soviet state all the more.

Studies of the natural sciences required for military production--math, chemistry, physics, biology--were the government's primary focus for students. Soviet leaders had learned their lessons from WWII and Stalin's purges. Military power was foremost. Subjects such as economics, law, history, or any social studies for that matter were permeated and polluted by mind-numbing

Communist ideology. Strict censorship implicitly encouraged and provided incentive for inquisitive students--such as me--to learn from books, Western short wave radio stations such as Voice of America or BBC (whose signal was suppressed by the KGB) or "read between the lines" to discern the truth or at least an alternative point of view. And we did. Soviet social studies courses taught you virtually nothing practical or universally useful. Their sole purpose seemed to be filling the minds of students with excuses and contrived arguments for the very existence of socialism. Dare I say, defending socialism?

When socialism--as both a concept and a desirable achievement--has to be defended continually to its youngest citizens mostly through hypotheticals, despite ample horrendous historical evidence, perhaps something is wrong with socialism.

Most school exams could be passed simply by praising the Communist Party and its sacred role in building the future. Assignments were typically to create essays or "cliff notes" of the works of Lenin and Marx. These escapades had no educational, practical, or intellectual value. In fact, they were universally despised by students. However, since this rotten "ideology" was the alleged foundation of the society, approximately half of the Soviet Union Ph.D.'s were issued in the field of the subject titled, "The History of the Communist Party of the Soviet Union." This was all despite the fact that archives on the real history of the Soviet Union were classified. Lukashenko and Putin both shared an ardent desire and practical intention to hide the real history of Communism from the public eye.

With the current war being waged against Ukraine, is Putin now repeating that "secret red sauce" without enabling the public to preempt it?

Such Marxist studies diminished the value of societal education, provided no universal value outside the socialist society, and reduced these professions to the obedient servants of the Communist regimes.

|| *Every immigrant from the Soviet Union or Cuba recognizes an immediate, virtually exact match in the uselessness, indoctrination nature, and artificially inflated academic value between the former Communist studies to which they were exposed and the current "woke" materials with their various gender studies and CRT studies being presented in U.S. schools and universities today. The focus of such materials, Communist and "woke" alike, in their destructive and illogical nature, is incitement of hatred of one class of people toward another, intolerance of a competing view, noticeable lack of any scientific basis, and complete lack of any practical application.*

If it pays to learn from history, here is a vital lesson the Americans have clearly not yet learned. However, there is hope. The level of sheer disdain and anger exhibited by parents, prompting an FBI task force, shows that the parents in America vying for true education for their children are waking up to the call of the "woke."

The Soviet economy was also subjected to outside pressure. President Ronald Reagan separated the Soviet economy from the rest of the world in the 1980s, helping to bring oil prices to their lowest levels in decades. When the Soviet Union's oil and gas revenues plummeted, the USSR's hold on Eastern Europe began to erode. Similarly, during Trump's presidency America secured U.S. energy independence and low energy prices. One of the many benefits of energy independence was that American consumers no longer financed Putin's insatiable appetite for land and egomaniacal plans for supremacy expansions. As a result, the Soviet-style tyrant's power deteriorated, and no land annexations were even attempted by Putin during the formidable Trump administration.

If you remember, under the previous feckless Obama/Biden administration, Crimea and parts of Georgia were virtually annexed by Russia. Under this subsequent, even weaker Biden administration, Putin wages war again and this time attempts to annex the entire Ukraine, the second largest European country? Is there something to be noted here?

Meanwhile, Gorbachev's reforms were slow to yield fruit and contributed more to the Soviet Union's demise than to its preservation. Despite the wrong perception by most people in the West, Gorbachev did not want to destroy socialism. He wanted to do something even more innovative. The previous plans to improve the reputation of the decaying corpse of socialism had not included embellishments for the people's sake. On the contrary, all ideological efforts were laser-sharp focused strictly on achieving one sole valuable goal: build Communism at all costs.

Gorbachev wanted to build "socialism with a human face." Much like Bernie Sanders with his "democratic socialism" escapades, trying to put a softer adjective in front of the horrendous pile of garbage known as socialism. In his view, hypocrisy, corruption, and pretense should have been eliminated in the socialist society. Truth, freedom, and practicality should have become the prevailing model for socialism. However, that is simply "pretend-reality." Truth and freedom are incompatible with socialism, much like CNN is incompatible with fair reporting, Skid Row with hygiene, or the "Green New Deal" with reality.

Pursuing utopian projects, most of which are cruel and contradict every law of nature, economics, and humanity's strive for freedom, is not a firm foundation for a naturally evolving society. Especially when such projects denigrate the daily needs and concerns of individuals, which cause inflation, low supply, and high prices for daily essential goods. Whether under Brezhnev, Gorbachev, or Biden, the results are the same for the citizens, though they may vary in degree

As a result of the turn to reformation, the Gorbachev era indeed became a time of openness and truth. People started speaking up and opening up the historical material about the atrocities of the Communist Party. Truly independent media evolved, some economic freedoms were introduced, and even rock 'n roll was legitimized. By the way, rock 'n roll was again made largely illegal in 2022 in Russia and Belarus due to rock musicians taking a strong stance against Russian aggression and atrocities. Furthermore, Putin's propagandists (of which are many such as Sheinin, Popov, Simonian, Skobeeva, Solovyev, and Kiselev threatening to turn Europe and the US into nuclear ash and calling to drown Ukrainian children) are now part of the Rock history earning a song by Boris Grebenschikov, one of the leaders of Russian underground rock movement since the 1980-s, called "Vecherny Mudozvon" (loosely translated as "Evening Bulls**tter").

All these natural social elements of human liberty spearheaded an unbelievable transformation of the Soviet society that left no chance for the Soviet Union's survival. The relaxation of Soviet authority over its people boosted independence movements in Soviet satellites in Eastern Europe as well. But as the Soviet perspective changed and its people yearned for the freedoms Americans enjoy, ironically the American perspective also began changing. The current generation of Americans seems to take freedom and much of their first-world amenities, wealth, and liberties for granted. In the past decade patriotism has waned. Fascination with socialism has risen. America's freedom may soon be in danger of being greatly weakened or even lost entirely.

The fall of the Berlin Wall was largely initiated by a political revolution in Poland in 1989. This event spawned additional, usually peaceful, upheavals across Eastern Europe. By the end of 1989, the Soviet Union had disintegrated. In August 1991, a failed coup by Communist Party hardliners sealed the Soviet Union's destiny by weakening Gorbachev's grip on power. Democratic forces led by Boris Yeltsin were thrust to the forefront of Russian politics.

Gorbachev resigned as Soviet leader on December 25. On December 31, 1991, the Soviet Union ceased to exist. It should be noted that Gorbachev was a communist believer. He, along with many others at the time, truly believed in the principles of Communism and that, if they were to be applied appropriately, one could build a fair state. However, the truth about the corruption, repressions, and actual causes of the dreadful state of the economy surfaced. Once the Soviet people caught a glimpse of the achievements of the rest of the world, they no longer trusted that socialism was the way to go.

Nevertheless, as Putin came to power, he claimed that the disintegration of the Soviet Union--rather than Holodomor, Holocaust, World War II, or Stalin Purges--was the "greatest tragedy" of the 20th century. Putin is a former KGB agent (though once a KGB, always a KGB), a card-carrying communist, and a thinly-veiled loyalist of the socialist (even Stalinist) system. Naturally over the course of 20 years, Putin gradually turned Russia with its unstable and evolving democratic institutions into a new version of the Soviet Union, a red/brown mix with Nazi-like supremacy claims culminating in a war. However, in his governing of the Soviet state, Putin cunningly replaced the term "Ideology of Communism" with the more palatable "Russian Orthodoxy" and its derivatives, such as "Russian World," "Historical Lands," or "Traditional Beliefs." Many viewed this as phony and insincere, especially since Putin and his lackey clergy continued to glorify Stalin and Soviet achievements.

It has become even more insincere with his current horrendous war against Ukraine, continued adherence to socialist tenets and ways of governance, and unequivocal hatred toward all Western values and liberties. Putin's new values are simply reinvented, re-packaged "traditional largely socialist values."

Putin also built in Russia what he terms "capitalism." However, this version of capitalism is not what you would recognize or what exists in the Western society. American capitalism is rooted in entrepreneurship, free trade, competition, and innovation. Putin's capitalism is derived from the pages of Pravda--greedy, crony capitalism where a few "close friends and loyalists" have everything, and their riches are closely related to their proximity and level of loyalty to the throne. Not surprisingly, the vast majority of the population has very little material wealth. A quarter of the "Great Russia" population--yes, 25% --live without modern running-water toilets. Most houses in Siberia--you know, the place where most of the natural gas comes from--have not been gasified (though the leftist New York appear to have the urge to follow that trend). Yet, for the large part, they still hate "capitalism" and "Western liberties" and still blame the West for their misfortunes.

Furthermore, as the pretext for that hate, even as justification for the aggression against Ukraine, a large portion of predominantly poor Russian population sees it as a pre-emptive war against NATO, who would otherwise come to take their "wealth."

How can this be? Putin's relentless propaganda to hate "capitalism" and "Western liberties" as concepts has blinded the Russian people. While they live miserable lives, they do not associate their misfortunes with Putin's socialist and totalitarian agenda. Rather, they gullibly believe that it is the main goal of the West to humiliate Russia. Hatred-based revisionism has been used by Putin and Lukashenko--much like it was used by Hitler in the 1930s--as an effective ideological weapon. Meanwhile, it has been reported that the savings and wealth of the 24 richest Russians equal the savings of the rest of the population.

Another example of the trend of modern-day falling "Back to the USSR" is demonstrated by the current regime of Lukashenko in Belarus. The regime is replete with killing and terrorizing opponents, arresting bystanders for wearing the wrong color sock or playing the "wrong songs," and drumming up criminal charges against anyone daring to challenge Lukashenko in the elections. Lukashenko's "stolen" victory confirmed this. His opponent, Svetlana Tikhanovskaya, picked up the baton after her husband was arrested just for trying to participate in the elections. Lukashenko still lost as he refused to believe that a woman could beat him.

In Belarus, even the lawyers were thrown in jail and disbarred just for representing the opposition leaders or raising their public voice regarding the outcome of the elections. These events sound chillingly similar to anyone even remotely familiar with Red Terror or Stalin's Purges.

We could be witnessing something similar here in the United States as well. When some questionable statements were made by lawyers taking it upon themselves to verify the outcome and validity of the unprecedented 2020 U.S. elections, immediate censorship and persecution resulted. Although those attorneys and activists only intended to go through a proper legal process, excessive political discourse erupted, causing further division to the society. This is ironic since Democrats challenged Trump's 2016 victory for the entire four years he was in office, under the false premise of "Russian collusion." Their persecution was based on totally bogus materials created by the opposition with the Russian FSB's help. The Durham investigation finally unveiled the deceptive chain. But American society suffered irreparable damage to the civility fiber of our political system.

There was other damage as well. In 2022, while the falsehood of the Trump dossier had been proven by the Durham investigation, Michael Sussman was acquitted by a District of Columbia jury. The charge was lying to FBI investigators relating to his connection to the Hillary Clinton campaign after reporting about the dossier in September 2016 to derail Trump's election chances. Hence, although the evidence for falsehood was clear, the legal system has yet to lower its sword of justice on those liars who made Americans live on the edge of their seats worrying about potential corruption and vulnerability of their elected President. There is great danger in spreading false information and breaking the law. Even greater danger in repeatedly getting away with it. For the sake of the integrity of our future elections, we can only hope that truth will prevail. May the scales of Lady Justice, or 'Femida' in Greek, be weighed in favor of truth and righteousness.

During the 2020 election, there was a clear thumb on the scale by the media propaganda. Their activities included suppressing damaging materials relating to Hunter Biden, banning of conservative groups (including Russian-speaking Republicans), and reporting so-called "suppression" polls which portrayed Biden's lead over Trump to be in double digits. (Interestingly, people tend not to vote if the media repeatedly reports their candidate seems destined to lose.)

Various states had a host of apparent problems in 2020 with mail-in ballots, missed deadlines, improper interference by state executives, issues with identities of voters, "dead voter" counts, double counting, and more. Facebook spent hundreds of millions of dollars for questionable "improvements" of the electoral system, etc. As we now *know*, Twitter was pressured by the FBI, clearly in collusion with Democratic operatives, to suppress information unfavorable to the Democratic candidates, and Biden in particular. If there were no violations, and there was nothing to hide, then inspection would only serve to solidify and reaffirm that the American system works. Pundits should have found nothing to worry about, right? Unless, of course, there were things to worry about. Why would one need a Russian collusion if we have our own--even more ominous and clearly more influential than the made-up overseas "remote control" by Putin?

In that case, claims and wholesale labeling of "conspiracy" and "racism" against the conservative movement were being unveiled. Again, this is not about propagating "lies" or "conspiracy," but rather, the ability of citizens to ask honest questions about the integrity of their political and voting process. My prediction is that when the proverbial shoe eventually ends up on the other foot, many such irregularities and manipulations will be uncovered, and the documentary "200 Mules" will have only scratched the surface.

In a socialist state, criticism is never welcomed. Any criticism of a despotic ruler or even his extensive bureaucratic apparatus is deemed as traitorous. This mindset was evident when Belarusian sprinter Kristina Timanovskaya, an Olympic athlete, was not even allowed to criticize the members of the National Olympic Committee for its recent failure to submit timely doping tests. Andrei Kravchenko, a silver Olympic medalist in decathlon, was detained simply for signing the letter against violence and torture. The co-founders of the Athletes For Freedom Foundation, Alexander Apeikin and Alexandra Herasimenia--also a silver-medalist in Olympic swimming--were recently convicted *in absentia* with an ominous 12-year prison sentence for their active social stance and support for freedom and non-discrimination of athletes.

Regrettably, socialism did not die in 1991 along with the Soviet Union. It is being resurrected now by neo-communists and their Western followers (or "useful idiots") who have been duped into believing in socialist dogma. Sadly, socialism is still alive, but not at all well. Alive not only in the minds of a few deceived Westerners, but also in countries such as Russia and Belarus, which have become victims of dogmatic dictators who overstayed their terms. Now those dictators are applying, yet again, the same thinking, methods, strategy, and repressive tactics used by their communist predecessors. While publicly distancing himself from Communists, Putin's actions prove otherwise. Russian occupational forces recently renamed Liberty Square in the occupied city of Mariupol in Ukraine as Lenin Plaza. Lenin's bloody way of governing with total disregard for human lives is not simply an influence upon Putin. Regrettably, Lenin's principles continue to be Putin's--and, by and large, Russia's--feed and foundation.

Now the Red Bolshevism of Belarus and Russia has naturally blended into Nazi-brown, producing a dangerous red/brown replica of the Third Reich. The same terrifying tactics are seen again--widespread hatred, nationalistic supremacy at the expense of other nations and countries, claims regarding new world order and spheres of influence as a coverup for aggressive international policies, disdain for personal liberties, subversion of private business, disinformation, the cult of personality, persecution of journalists and critics, jailing of opposition, and militarization of internal and external policies. Even today the Russian army commits horrendous atrocities and war crimes worthy of their Nazi predecessors, yet receives only praise and awards from their irreplaceable imperial kingpin.

Anti-Semitism also remained alive and well in 2022, demonstrated in repugnant claims by Putin's government that Hitler was a Jew and Ukraine's President Zelensky is a Nazi. Putin displays similar disdain for Ukrainians and Belarusians as he refuses to recognize them as nations, nationalities, or even truly independent countries. This led to his abhorrent attempts at elimination of the culture, language, traditions, and sovereignty of both Ukraine and Belarus. In the case of Ukraine, Putin waged a bloody unprovoked war on a peaceful neighboring nation. In the case of Belarus, Putin provided security to a power-grabbing dictator who lost his election in a landslide and is loathed by his own people.

A ridiculous *casus belli* was developed by Putin and his eastern lapdog vassal under three equally preposterous false premises. First, the "denazification" of Ukraine, whose President Zelensky is a Russian-speaking Jew with relatives who were persecuted during WWII. Second, the preemption and prevention of an omnipotent "Western threat," despite Russia's enjoyment of Starbucks, iPhones, and other popular achievements of the Western civilization. Third, the need for an ever-expanding and morally superior (?) Russian World.

Let me mention it again. This is what happens when Bolshevism and Naziism blend together. Power-hungry dictators apply the same thinking, methods, strategy, and repressive tactics used by their Communist predecessors––adding a dangerous

Nazi-like hatred toward Western civilization with the new insignia in stylized V and Z, which repackages and repurposes the Nazi Swastika.

The bright red of Nazi and Socialist flags, symbolizing the color of blood, eventually blends into the brown societal wounds and puddles of dried blood. If we do not stop the neo-Reds at work today, as in the case of Russia and Belarus, the government will indeed blend into the dangerous red/brown.

There is nothing new under the sun. These are nothing more than poor, ill-contrived excuses for yet another grand socialistic "project." Its purpose? To satisfy the Nero-like ambitions of one psycho--this current case, Putin-- and his willing followers who are being pumped up with "patriotic" propaganda. How will this current "project" end? Thankfully, the Russian Army is as corrupt, incompetent, and inept as everything else built by communists and cronies of Putin.

To the great embarrassment of Russia, Ukraine has become the spiritual and military pinnacle, shining light on the determination of people all around the world fighting for freedom and liberty. That light cannot be extinguished, not by inept Biden and his weak administration, nor corrupt liberal European rulers, nor even the horrendous actions of Putin's murdering and marauding hordes. The world's unity and fiery determination is assisting Ukraine in its righteous fight for freedom and independence while shielding the rest of us from this warring plague. Ultimately, this battle is for the freedom and independence of *all* civilized people in the world.

DMITRI I. DUBOGRAEV

Chapter 2
This Free Speech, That Free Speech

What is capitalism and why do communist leaders like Putin hate it so? With its incentives and protection of the private property system, capitalism has always been the most potent force for economic and social advancement. Capitalism is the antithesis of socialism. Let's consider just three of its many accomplishments. Capitalism has lifted billions of people out of poverty and elevated living standards to previously unfathomable heights. Its influence has permeated technological advances throughout the world. Perhaps this third point most profoundly highlights its radical difference from communism. Capitalism is responsible for an extraordinary blooming of productive creativity throughout the last century.

America should be singing the praises of capitalism. However, it is being put to the test among young Americans in light of their "woke-ness" culture and dangerous misperception of other social forms--socialism in particular.

Similarly, a large portion of the population of the former Soviet Union has become disillusioned with the crony capitalism built by Putin. In fact, the only similarity between Putin's capitalism and America's capitalism is the use of the name itself. Putin's discontented population, now pumped up with Nazi-like propaganda of the superiority of their "Russian World" and their alleged affinity with it, is entertaining the idea of reverting back to the full-blown socialism. With a "New Stalin"--Putin--at the helm. In their nostalgic and misguided utopian view, they dream of a more fair and equitable society. And sincerely believe it can be ushered in through socialism.

The rulers of both Russia and Belarus tune their ears to such sentiments. Reintroduction of socialistic principles with overwhelming control over the economy, speech, and social institutions of society, especially media and courts, will enable those rulers to accumulate even more power.

Both contemporary Russia and Belarus, by the spirit of their rule and the belligerence of their deeds, are true ideological successors of the Soviet Union. The Soviet Union declared "freedom of speech" in all four versions of its constitutions, then ignored it entirely. Soviet "freedom" was interpreted as the right to say only the right things that were strictly within government-approved content. Certainly that did not include anything that hinted at questioning a left-wing utopian ideology or inept government actions.

Let me share a few examples of the Soviet version of "freedom" of speech. A little boy pees the word 'Stalin' on the snow. His father is sentenced to ten years in a Gulag (forced labor camp with an incredibly high level of mortality). A person writes "comedy" on the voting bulletin referring to a no-choice predetermined charade. His "freedom" to vote got him eight years.

|| *Trying to cancel someone, though not yet literally, for a joke or an unpopular opinion appears to have gained speed within the Western Left in the past decade.*

In this dismal society, the essence of such arrests was reduced to kitchen talk anecdotes. Gulags became the butt of jokes in the most masochistic way. Here's an example that would be funny if it weren't so frighteningly close to the reality of Soviet life.

A guy asks an inmate, *"What are you in for?"*

The other replies, *"I did nothing."*

The guy quips, *"You are lying. They give five for nothing, but you got ten years!"*

Here's another eye-opening example. A publisher makes a simple mistake in a poster. Rather than, "The life got better, Stalin," the poster instead read, "The life got better for Stalin." For one wrong word (which in Russian was a one-letter mistake: instead of "Stalin" it read "Stalinu," which means "for Stalin"), the publisher was arrested and ended up in Gulag.

At this juncture in Russia and Belarus, people get actual jail sentences just for re-tweeting or posting "likes" to comments questioning the legitimacy of prosecuting people who file anti-corruption reports. Other offenses include questioning a "hardline" interpretation of history. "Hardline" mostly means "Russia = good, West = bad." Questioning election results, criticizing government policies, or daring to question an unfair outcome of a criminal case are all viewed as "incitement of hate toward social institutions" such as state courts. Any social media or public display of protest or even dissent against the Russian aggression in Ukraine is deemed "dissemination of disparaging information about Russian troops." Such an action carries a real prison sentence.

We see another example of such tensions in flags and historical symbols or coats of arms. The Belarus white/red/white historical flag (known as B.Ch.B.) symbolizes the people's protest against fraudulent 2020 elections in Belarus, tortures, and political violence. The Canadian flag, by unfortunate historical coincidence, sports the same colors. If people in Belarus even display the Canadian flag with its similar color scheme, Lukashenko's 'karateli' (a reference to Nazi SS troops now attributable in Belarus to the regime's violent defenders) will throw them in jail.

Imagine that today in Russia, you will be thrown in jail just for saying or liking "World Peace," or for appearing at a public square with a poster that reads "*** ******" –the number of asterisks equal to the letters in the phrase "Net Voine" ("No to War!"). Even asterisks on a poster will land you in jail. On a humorous side, a resourceful lady was able to prove that by "Net V***e!" *she could have meant* "net voble" *or* "No to 'vobla'" (a type of dry fish). Fortunately for her, she was released! In a more creative way of approaching protest, one Russian recently walked the street with a poster – "Arrest me if you are against the war!" Not succumbing to irony, Putin's orcs did arrest him, of course.

Putin claims he is fighting against fascism in Ukraine and the West. Yet, right there in Moscow you will be immediately arrested if you appear on the street with a slogan reading, "No to Fascism!" It appears that the Kremlin apparently knows more than the rest of the world about Naziism and its actual location. Russia seems to be aligning itself to a prediction made at the end of WWII --namely, the next wave of fascism will take the shape of anti-fascism.

|| *Much like Antifa, an organization with all the attributes of the Sturmabteilung (or, in German, SA, "Storm Units,") the Nazi Party's militia founded by Ernst Rohm, (the only person that Hitler regretted killing during the internal power struggle among Nazis) sweeping over the U.S. today.*

State spying on citizens on social media became a routine in Russia, with jail sentences handed out for "liking" posts that the people in power viewed as anti-government or "extremist." There were over 100 arrests for social media posts praising the heroic death of Andrei Zeltser for his resistance while he defended himself and his family during a secret police raid of his apartment. His wife, who survived the attack, was reportedly subjected to torture.

Sending someone to jail or torturing them for verbal expression in Russia is obviously not the same as destroying a person's career in America. But when we routinely "delete" people from Western social media, ostracizing them both professionally and socially over their drastic "crime" of apparent lack of "woke-ness" or expressing an "unpopular" opinion or even a "wrong" pronoun, are we then really that far apart? What would happen if our Western society actually empowered our social media "Nazis" with the same unchecked government enforcement powers wielded in Russia? Do you really think possessing such power by the "progressives" would cause them to suddenly exhibit "mercy"?

According to the GenForward Survey of Americans aged 18 to 34 conducted by the University of Chicago, 62% of America's future believe, "We need a strong government to address today's complex economic problems." While only 35% believe, "The free market can handle these problems without government involvement."

Consider this--sixty-one (61%) percent of Democrats and twenty-five (25%) percent of Republicans actually think socialism is a good idea. Overall, this group has a favorable view of capitalism, with 49% favoring capitalism and 45% favoring socialism. Asian-Americans, African-Americans, and Hispanics actually rate socialism higher than capitalism. This is both scary and abhorrent.

I wonder which of the "practical benefits" of socialism they find most appealing--the mass murders, starvation, or perpetual (but mostly equal and equitable!) lack of toilet paper? You are "enjoying" a glimpse into socialism under the microscope of Biden's socialistic policies, which have already caused unprecedented disruption of supply-chain in the U.S. with shortages of some basic staples.

If you think the current occasional empty shelves and intermittent supply problems are an issue in the United States, stay tuned. If this current trend of reckless government policies continues, you may soon enjoy the pleasure of standing in line for hours for baby food. Maybe even one day for butter!

Let's compare and contrast the views of millennials with their parents of a generation ago. You may find the results disturbing. According to a survey conducted last year, only 26% of baby boomers desire to live in a communist country. The figure was nearly doubled to 44% among younger individuals. These figures are still way too high for both generations. They demonstrate how brainwashed today's contemporary society is by the media and liberal academia, whether through naiveté or a sheer lack of historical and social perspective. Liberal academia is responsible for our historical illiteracy.

Once the true facts and knowledge about life under socialism surface, any attempts at creating a rosy perception of life in a "fair" communist society hit a brick wall. Statistics point at more than 100+ million innocent people dead due to attempts to implement socialism, mostly by force and misery. That alone should open the eyes of even the most clueless young individuals.

Still, there is a clear generational divide, not to mention a very scary trend toward infatuation with socialism. What's the cause for such a divide or trend? The first aspect is that young individuals may take the benefits of capitalism for granted. Today's young people in the West take many practical benefits for granted--free movement and travel within and especially outside their country, daily conveniences such as a cell phone continually in their hands, an unending supply of fresh food, clothing, and other goods, running water, hot water, and modern toilets! In Russian everyday "fair" life under socialism, more than 20% of the population does not even have sewage or running water. They are forced to use a crude wooden hut with a hole in the ground. There have been recent reports of people falling through rotten boards and drowning in human waste. I'm wondering how long pampered Americans would put up with that?

The younger generation in the West has no recollection of a time when things such as microwaves, cable television, or 24-hour access to food, beverages, gasoline, and banking did not exist. Sadly, they do not realize the reason why they live with such an abundance of resources to meet their daily needs and whims--namely, capitalism. Thus, they are clueless to give credit. All this abundance is solely due to the development of a capitalist society. Not a socialist society. Even the recent "economic miracle" in China is largely credited to their adopting Western-designed principles of economy, use of Western technology, and trade with the industrialized free world. However, much like German leadership in the 1930s controlling a country's private enterprise, the Chinese private industry is largely under the thumb of the Chinese Communist Party. As an indicative observation, consider the fact that Chinese nationals do not consider themselves rich--regardless of how much money they have--until they, their family, and their money are moved outside of China.

Perhaps our youth do not realize this, but their baby boomer parents have not forgotten the anguish and uncertainty brought about by the devastating recession of 2007-09, from which it took years to recover. Disenchantment with the economic order is the usual response following a financial disaster. While it was "devastating" in both emotional and relative capitalist terms, the "suffering" endured in capitalist America was relatively mild compared to the daily distress that accompanies socialism. People who live or have lived under socialism develop a much higher tolerance to pain and suffering. For us, "devastating" involves words like mass deaths or famine, or at least inflation with multiple zeros.

When capitalism "corrections" cause painful dips in the stock market and inflation hits the 20-50% range, Americans will feel devastation.

Now imagine the truly devastating situation when your money is devalued 20 *million* times! This happened to the people of Belarus between 1991 and 2021. The blame fell squarely on the government of Belarus which failed to implement market reforms, clinging instead to the remnants of socialist principles which ruined a post-Soviet economy. Imagine you had 20 million dollars--and now your savings are worth a single dollar. One dollar.

Maybe you are among those who think, *"But that would never happen here."* Think again. No one would have believed 18 months ago that gasoline prices would approach $10 per gallon in 2022. All it took was a few small strokes of Biden's presidential pen to cause a chilling effect on the entire energy industry.

51

The sloppy economic policies of the Biden administration, sending prices and inflation to unprecedented levels (at least for the past 50 years), and insane politicians pontificating that spending $3.5 trillion "*will cost us nothing*" seem uncomfortably similar to the 'efficient' socialist tools. While claiming to promote universal wealth and prosperity, instead they were actually used to promote equity, resulting in misery and poverty.

Higher gas, car, energy, and foodstuff prices, "transitory" inflation, Grinch-like problems in the supply chain, and the inability of small businesses to fill almost 9 million vacant employment positions is a clear demonstration of what happens when you start throwing socialist monkey-wrenches into the carefully designed, well-oiled engine of a sensitive capitalist market economy.

By the way, I learned a long time ago that "transitory" is a socialist double-speak cover-up word for "*It's here to stay.*"

If these changes do not scare you yet, imagine a scale of 10-fold economic devastation. If the Left's full-blown "Green (well, Red...) New Deal" or other similar planned reckless expenditures and regulations were to be implemented, that is exactly what awaits you.

The Great Depression of the 1930s left two scars--a considerably more powerful, intrusive federal government, and acceptance of communism by some Americans. This was amplified during the Great Recession when a large number of young people reached adulthood in a depressed job market. Their incomes and advancement suffered as a result. The consequences are still felt even today. Unfortunately, many of them now connect capitalism with failure and eternal struggle, rather than advancement. As the economy continues to grow, this could alter. However, some of capitalism's more fundamentalist proponents have harmed it in the long run.

Many Republicans have portrayed President Barack Obama as a socialist bent on destroying the free market during his eight years in office, even as the economy improved. Many argue that the economy grew despite Obama's reforms, rather than due to them. Yes, he was the president when that growth occurred, although it was the slowest recovery from recession in U.S. history. As a result, Obama had a 77% approval rating among millennials when he left office. How could this be? Since many millennials are relatively uninformed regarding the workings of the economy, they probably concluded that if Obama was a socialist, then socialism must not be all that bad.

Similarly, Bernie Sanders would not have been so close to winning the Democratic primary in 2016 if the new generation hadn't had that experience. Socialism has lost much of its painful stigma, partially as a result of the Right's wholesale misuse of the socialist label. Bernie presented a seemingly appealing socialism without the stigma. At the same time, virtually all of Trump's speeches were labeled as "worse than Watergate."

The fall of Marxism in so many nations has really benefited the Left. Once upon a time, socialism was thought to be a stop on the way to communism, as the ultimate utopian society being the final goal of happy and equitable mankind. Those anxieties have diminished now that the Soviet Union is no longer in existence and China is merely pretending to be socialist, at least from the economic standpoint.

On the other hand, many who are adamantly opposed to government overreaching intervention and redistribution are perceived by millennials to be "boring" and at odds with them, especially on social issues such as LGBTQ rights, racial inequity, immigration, gun control, and abortion rights. None of these issues improve the perceived values of capitalism or the image of its vehement proponents to the younger generation. Conservatives need to do a better job of demonstrating tolerance and open-mindedness on social issues, particularly to millennials, as well as receptiveness to reasonable reforms where reforms are due. Otherwise, when the Left makes reform a winning political token or, as in the case of the Green New Deal, takes their rhetoric so far as to threaten the republic's existence, the Right often finds itself playing catch up.

In the crucial upcoming 2024 elections, the Right must recognize the need of reforms when reforms are truly due, especially in the eyes of millennials.

The failure of most conservatives to acknowledge humanity's higher responsibility regarding environmental protection alienates its supporters, who fervently believe they will live with the environmental devastation caused by their forefathers. Thus, due to certain stereotypes, left media indoctrination, and tactical failures of the Right, supporters of the free market are disrespected by millennials. They are viewed by the next generation as rejecting science, disrespecting the poor, and being intolerant.

Needless to say, Republicans need to be armed with specific disadvantages of socialism along with demonstrable advantages of a free society. This may reach millennials more effectively than slogan-like messaging, old-fashioned traditions, and "the American way." This has to change. This book seeks to be an aid in reducing such "class warfare" with history and truth, and defending the true virtues of liberty and capitalism, especially to the next generation.

Ronald Reagan was the defender of capitalism for America's baby boomers. For the millennials, it was Donald Trump. However, despite that, a recent study indicated that two-thirds of those aged 15 to 34 disapproved of Trump's performance as President. The majority labeled him "dishonest," "racist," and "mentally unfit," despite Trump's commendable track record on many practical issues. These include the growth of the U.S. economy, lowering illegal immigration, achieving energy independence, lowering unemployment and taxes for the middle class, securing the growth of blue-collar wages, eliminating ISIS, supporting business and law enforcement, strengthening the U.S. military, making NATO's countries pay their dues, supporting Israel, enabling the "Warp Speed" Project that secured record-breaking Covid vaccine production, bringing trade with China to a more favorable balance, and keeping Putin and other autocrats at bay--just to name an impressive few. If not for Trump's authorized supply of Javelin anti-tank systems--which followed after Obama's supply of mighty blankets post Crimea annexation--Ukraine would have probably been overrun already by Putin's army. As a tribute, some Ukrainians are calling their newborn infant babies "Javelin."

However, Trump's rough-around-the-edges personality and exuberant rhetoric failed to connect with the younger generation in great numbers, in spite of popular movie and music personalities having similar behaviors. Instead, Trump was viewed as a "strict" parent who brings you back to harsh reality and sets a curfew for your own good. In that failure, however, was a lost opportunity to make a better case for the values of free society and capitalism. That opportunity must not be lost again.

While "mean tweets" were somewhat of an issue with Trump, the current social environment takes the focus off a candidate's deeds and sets it solely on words and *"how that makes you feel,"* which is probably not the most practical way to elect the leader of the free world. If the devastation of Biden's policies continues and gas hits the projected $6 a gallon (*at the time of this writing, the average price was just below $4/gallon, so now $6 already looks like a bargain for California at least)*, we will see which "feelings" prevail.

Many of the unique grievances and perceived "hardships" voiced by millennials are produced at least as much by government intervention as by free markets. Millennials may not appreciate it either. Tuition has risen as a result of federal loans and grants because universities have zero incentives to lower prices and compete in a marketplace. The demand for health care is inflated as a result of Medicare, Obamacare, and lack of true competition and transparency in health insurance and medical care. Rent control and land-use restrictions are to blame for much of New York and San Francisco's high housing costs.

There is very little successful messaging focused on millennials to educate them about economics. When markets are permitted to function properly, they continue to perform efficiently and produce innovations that increase alternatives and lower costs. Consumers' lives have been made easier by Amazon, Apple, Uber, Starbucks, and Walmart. The ensuing price reduction and upgrade in service quality should be the focus of free-market proponents. Food and clothing consume a smaller percentage of our disposable money than they once did in the past. Automobiles, televisions, and appliances are all better and more reliable than previous models. Open competition in a free market is the driving force behind all this.

In the end, if economic systems are to last, they must maintain their moral legitimacy. As Ayn Rand noted, *"Capitalism was the only system in history where wealth was not acquired by looting, but by production, not by force, but by trade, the only system that stood for man's right to his own mind, to his work, to his life, to his happiness, to himself."*

It is not enough just to hate and criticize socialism. One must love and understand capitalism with an even greater strength and comprehension. Not just its economic efficiency, but also its higher moral, ethical value, and moral legitimacy.

Capitalism has always had to fight back against its detractors. However, as our society grows complacent and spoiled, capitalism and its fundamental freedom need a better message, particularly toward millennials and Gen Z. Note the very real and stark differences between capitalism and socialism. Capitalism is both economically and morally superior. Capitalism is based on logical persuasion and free-will choices made by the market participants. Socialism is based on ideological coercion and sheer political enforcement— with a particular emphasis on "force." Sooner or later, all people quickly discover they do not like a particular emphasis on "force."

Suppression of Free Speech in the Socialist State

Socialism cannot survive in an atmosphere of free speech. Consider just a few of the core elements of socialism. Complete detachment from reality. Lack of accountability of inept rulers responsible for abysmal outcomes in every sphere of everyday social and economic life. Excessive self-professing praise for non-existent accomplishments. Mass deaths in staggering numbers. The "self-evident proof of the superiority of socialism" presented continuously--a fake reality shining brightly from TV screens and newspapers, as if the message could erase the dismal reality. Freedom of speech in the Soviet Union, if and when dared to live, is relegated simply to "kitchen talk" and "anecdotes"--always with the overhanging danger of being prosecuted.

Life Story Yuri told us a story about the time when he went to the so-called "construction brigade" where students were allowed to work over the summer and make good money because they were paid based on their results. Essentially replacing the inefficient working crews of the regular state workers.

Sadly, there are no Caribbean or Black Sea beaches for most Soviet Union students. Instead, they had to do manual labor all summer in order to make ends meet during the school year. The head of the "construction brigade" was Yuri's childhood friend. As Yuri was listening to the Voice of America telling "political anecdotes"--and since Yuri was rather loose in his political opinions--at least 8 out of 15 people in the crew snitched about his "behavior" to the head of the brigade. They certainly did not realize Yuri was friends with the head! Otherwise, they would not have "relayed" those "warning signs and reports" up the ladder for fear of personal risk or potential prosecution.

It should be noted that not all Soviet citizens were so fortunate to have loyal and stoic friends. As Sergei Dovlatov, a famous Russian writer, wrote "*We endlessly condemn Stalin, and, of course, for a good reason. But I would like to ask you -- who wrote over 4 million donosy [snitching reports] [to KGB]?*" In an ugly turn of social fabric into an unpleasant Stalinist past, "donosy" about those who are against the Putin's genocidal war are taking off like wildfires resulting in hundreds of criminal convictions. A father of a 12 years old girl is sentenced to two year in prison for her school drawing against the war. Ironically, a recent April Fool's spoof about an alleged new app "how to snitch on your neighbor" was not even taken by most Russians as a joke.

Ironically, the pursuit of universal comradery and artificial "equity" actually produced a "new Soviet person," willing to sacrifice his family and friends for the "higher" cause. In reality, it usually morphed into more pragmatic shortcuts in cues for state handouts and preferences. It also culminated in a demonstrable fanatical loyalty to the regime with its mindless "deals" and "causes" as a survival mechanism. In fear of incarceration and retributions, similar loyalty and obedience is now required of Russian citizens in the form of unrelenting support of Putin's war without regard to atrocities or the growing death toll on both sides.

Any public criticism of the authorities was akin to treason. However, at the government level lip service was given to the prevalence of free speech. In fact, the Communist government would claim that it prosecuted only "wrong," "destructive," and "anti-social" speech. In other words, only speech which they deemed "against [communist] community standards." This, of course, would be any speech against communism.*# Furthermore, both Hitler and Putin used the term "national traitors" (German: *Nationalverräter*), reserved for those who go against official policy. In the current case of Putin, this would include anyone who dares to oppose the brutal aggression in Ukraine. Whether such

"matches" occur incidentally or as a Freudian slip, one thing is clear—
—if you follow the same ideology, you are eventually bound to use the same concepts, policies, and insignia.

Again, in an uncanny following of his heartless (though not shirtless) predecessor in pursuit of world domination, Putin's puppet legislature adopted a law banning "discrediting or distributing disinformation about the Russian Army." This comes frighteningly close to Hitler's "fälschungen über die Armee."

|| *Now in America the Left, the movement mesmerized with "colors" and "disadvantaged classes," while losing the battle on substance, tends to cancel and ban criticism, and even the argument itself. Such trends are clearly apparent in the social fabric of the new U.S. society as well, and it is not a healthy trend.*

Such suppression of the people is nothing new. It started at the dawn of the Soviet Regime. Sailors and peasants revolted in the 1920s in an event known as the Kronstadt Revolt, demanding that the Soviet government live up to its promises of giving land to peasants and offering a truly free, open election. The Bolsheviks responded with airstrikes, artillery, and even chemical weapons used against its own people. Throughout the history of the USSR, any attempt at contradicting the government was treated harsher than real crimes, such as armed robbery or murder.

It is most important that you understand why. Because contradicting the government exposed the fundamental flaws of the regime, the fundamental flaws of the socialist ideology itself. It was seen as a direct challenge to the validity of socialism's "core" ideological values. Challengers were branded as "insurrectionists." Not even the vilest of murderers were charged as an insurrectionist. Challenging the government was a more heinous crime than murder. *The ideology was more important than the lives of the people.*

* In other words--the Western "cancel culture" also ferociously fights so-called "misinformation," a concept you won't find in the U.S. Constitution as being subject to restraint. In essence, any opinions that do not fall squarely with "progressivism" become the primary target of all socialists of their 50 shades of red. They do not tolerate dissenting opinions or "dissenting facts," i.e., facts resulting from the application of natural and economic laws and logic, rather than a directive from the state.

As a result of all those policies in a land that promised "free speech," there were 7+million homeless children in the Soviet Union in the 1920s. Not surprisingly, despite the obvious evidence on the streets, that subject was one of many topics out of reach for coverage or any "free" discussion by citizens. Discussions on that subject would lead straight to the "Red Terror" and communists' brutal policies.

Mikhail Bulgakov, after writing his book "Master and Margarita," an allegorical novel about the Devil coming to Moscow in the 1930s, could not get a job even as a street sweeper and was essentially dying of hunger. He forced himself to write an apology letter to Stalin.

|| *At first glance, this seems to be a far cry from today's banning on social media or losing a job in the U.S. for taking an "unwoke" stand. Look again. In principle, is it really?*

In the 1930s, even a slight hint at criticism of the system or independent thinking on the part of ordinary citizens was summarily dealt with by execution or long prison/Gulag sentences. A simple statement by a person, at times, would be a reason for prosecution. Even more drastic, sometimes not speaking at all, as in failing to praise the regime or not enthusiastically joining in the socialist movement, was a sufficient offense for you or loved ones to lose their life. This is similar behavior to citizens being arrested for "not crying enough" when a leader in North Korea dies.

Many artists and academia initially embraced socialism as the new hope for a new, fairer world. But eventually Kandinsky, Chagall,

Malevich, Exler, Baxter, Sautin, Larionov, Goncharova, and Delaunay realized the hypocritical, rotten nature of the socialist ideology, and its even harsher implementation by the Bolsheviks. Their voices, through the medium of art, shared a clear message that humanity and socialism were not "comrades." It's no surprise that most of them were either killed or exiled to Western Europe. In Belarus, in the fall of 1938, over 130 artists, poets, and writers were gathered and summarily executed with no particular crime committed, other than they dared to be independent thinkers.

Of course, as the "directives" from the top changed, so changed the "allowed speech rules." Prior to the invasion of the Soviet Union on June 22, 1941, one could not have openly criticized Hitler or Germany in any way. At that time it was the official position that both "socialist" states, Germany and USSR, were in effect, hand-in-hand challenging and fighting "imperialism" and capitalism around the world. This "comradery" extended beyond anti-capitalist rhetoric and newspaper cartoons. Their joint invasion of Baltic states and Poland culminated in a Soviet-German parade in the occupied city of Brest with alternating swastika and hammer/sickle red flags. Two years later, citizens of Brest put up fierce resistance to the German invasion. Again.

After that invasion, there was an about-face in the Soviet government's positioning on its relationship with Germany and the West. Stalin was "missing in action" for a few days after the German assault, having issued the first directive not to shoot at German soldiers as it was all, in his belief, a "provocation." Meanwhile, German troops obliterated the meek resistance and advanced a few hundred miles within a week, creating millions of PoWs and causing millions of Soviet citizens to live under brutal German occupation for years. My grandparents and my mother lived through that. As you can imagine, any criticism of the commander-in-chief or his generals, who we were sure were concerned with the "root causes" of the devastating losses, was punishable by death on the spot.

|| *When the U.S. carried out a botched withdrawal from Afghanistan and ignored the explicit advice of American generals to keep sufficient troops on the ground for a successful operation, it was wise not to criticize the mess or the deadly consequences of the operation. Lt. Col. Stuart Scheller found that out the hard way and ended up in jail--which could have been justified from the point of view of the military chain-of-command and an officer's duty not to question the superiors. Scheller fell on the sword. But where was the public outcry or criticism? Where was the congressional inquiry with real consequences regarding the U.S. Commander-in-Chief's operational and military incompetence, including failure to heed the advice of his generals, which led to effective collusion with the enemy, the death of U.S. troops, and abandonment of both U.S. citizens and U.S. military equipment worth billions of dollars?*

In 1961, when workers in Novorossiysk took to the streets to strike and protest against a price hike and salary reductions in what were already horrendous living and working conditions, they were met with machine guns and soldiers' bayonets. Hundreds were killed. More were arrested and jailed or executed. No officials or military people were punished, other than one officer for refusing to give the soldiers a command to shoot. That decision, while saving many lives, cost him his livelihood and earned him a court-martial.

In 1968, when a few brave people went out to the Red Square to protest the Soviet invasion of Prague, they were immediately detained and sent to a psychiatric facility. This method was widely used by the Soviet Union in lieu of regular jail as a repression tool against dissidents and political activists. The typical official sentiment to defend the measure was, "They must be crazy to go against the first country of workers and peasants." In essence, such an act was viewed as an insurrection, despite the fact that not one person was harmed, nor any violence ensued.

|| *Pounding on the January 6th events as "insurrection" brings more discontent to the American society as well. Once again, these tactics often serve as a pretext to silence those whose voice is suppressed or distorted.*

The word game and spelling were a big part of the socialist "woke" culture. As a kid, I collected pins with the names of cities, so I knew the names of most contemporary and historical cities. (Many cities in the Soviet Union were renamed after the names of Bolsheviks, most of whom have since been recognized as mass murderers.) When I corrected my teacher on the proper historical spelling of Tallinn, the capital of Estonia (a country occupied by the Soviet Union after the pact with Hitler) as having a double "n" at the end, my parents were called to school for a warning. My crime? I was engaged in an inappropriate activity because that was the "bourgeois" spelling, unsuitable for the pupil who must be focused on becoming a "future builder of socialism."

Wearing long haircuts or inscribing the name of your favorite rock band was "propaganda of capitalism" and deemed a huge scandal. Teachers were free to use scissors to rectify the situation. How do you think long-haired American students of the 1960s would have responded to a haircut against their will by their teacher?

In my stern Soviet world, politically incorrect spelling and "hair" episodes were taken much more seriously by school officials than a dust-up behind the school or students smoking in the bathroom. Remember, the surface "ideological" mantra for the socialist system is much more important than a broken nose or even "regular" insolence.

|| *Do those escapades and spelling priorities remind you of anything happening in U.S. schools and media nowadays? Here are two to consider. First, the Left's persistent attempts at indoctrinating students with CRT, a clearly racist, even fascist theory. Second, school authorities turn the FBI on parents who peacefully but energetically voice their concerns, rather than investigating the cover-ups of alleged*

rapes by a transgender student. These events are uneasy reminders to those of us who lived through them. The Soviet system of oppression permeated our daily lives, particularly the schools. These are actions we don't want to see repeated for American families today.

The "perestroika," a Gorbachev policy meaning "reconstruction," was supposed to make Soviet citizens freer and more open with some signs of private entrepreneurship akin to Lenin's NEP. While in law school in Minsk during that time, a few of my friends and I organized a private venture, "Rock-o-teque," focusing on rock music. However, out of an abundance of caution, we presented most of the bands as the "music of social and anti-imperialist protest against the decay and shortcomings of the Western society as anti-war protests"-- based on the lyrics of Clash, U-2, Pink Floyd, and Sex Pistols. Actually, for a large portion of the 1970s and '80s music, that was true. However, lines such as "Brezhnev took Afghanistan, Begin*§§took Beirut" by Pink Floyd turned our entire enterprise into "anti-Soviet."

Although we didn't even play that song, we were nevertheless guilty. The next day my dean presented yours truly, as the organizer-in-chief, with a clear choice--law school or my "rebellious rock enterprise." Snitching was always was a big thing in the Soviet Union.

So I boldly inquired regarding this reasoning, insinuating that aren't we supposed to be more open and free, like during New Economic Policy? His response was, "You *do* remember what happened to NEPmen, right? This is for your own sake." His answer was a sobering reminder. Most people, including the Americans active in the New Economic Policy (NEP) era, ended up dead or imprisoned.

One of the most important propaganda tools of the communist regime is a "word" game--what you say and how you say it. It's not "mass murders" and repressions--it's "overreaching" or "over-bending" by Stalin. It's not a crisis. It's temporary shortcomings or, using the phraseology of Biden and Psaki, a "circumstance." It's not suppression of free speech. It's the elimination of libelous and "extremist" statements damaging the "higher truth" and the proletarian statehood. It's not a criticism of the shortcomings of socialism. It's inciting hate and conducting treasonous activity to overthrow the most just working people government. It's not protesting the invasion of Czechoslovakia in 1968 by eight brave people on the Red Square. It's a delusional act by a few mentally ill and capitalism-influenced traitors.

* Menachem Begin - Prime Minister of Israel (1977-1983).

The word game continues today. It's not a "war" by Russia on Ukraine and democracy. It's a "special military operation" seeking made-up "Nazis." Imagine that in 2022 you could get arrested in Moscow for publicly using the word "war" or calling for "peace." Both words are deemed as derogatory of the Russian Army. I assume Leo Tolstoy's most famous novel will soon be edited by Putin into the one-word title "*** and *****."

It has been discovered and admitted recently that after the Soviet Union invaded Poland and executed tens of thousands of Polish officers and policemen at a place near Katyn, it erected a memorial at the village called Khatyn. The memorial was dedicated to the victims of Nazi occupation, despite the fact that 200+ other villages met the same plight of being burned with their citizens. So, what was the purpose of the memorial in *that* specific place? Simply to confuse and obfuscate the Soviet atrocities by those of the Nazis by choosing a phonetically similar village.

It was not the "occupation" of Prague or Budapest. It was the "mostly peaceful" suppression of capitalist insurrectionists by tanks. - *||* *'Insurrection' with no weapons on January 6? What was that, a PTA coup d'état?* It was not food shortages in the stores in the Soviet Union. It was "temporary difficulties" on the tough road to socialism.- *||* *Transitory like Biden's inflation?* It was not the disastrous socialist economy and inept management. It was just sabotage by the world's imperialist force. - *||*It's not Biden's policies, it's greedy private enterprises that jack up the prices. It was not Holodomor or famine. It was "lies and capitalist propaganda." - *||* It's not a terrorist act committed by a racist lunatic by plowing his car through a Christmas parade, killing and wounding innocent people. It's an "SUV accident in Waukesha, Wisconsin."

Recently, the German consulate made an exhibition in Russia showing the atrocities of the Soviet regime. Not surprisingly, it was met immediately with protest from the Russian government under the premise that it was inappropriate to equate Communist atrocities with those of Nazis. Why not? According to the Germans, Nazis were killing *"other" people* (other than German Jews), while the Soviet socialist regime typically killed and caused suffering to *its own people*. But is that the main difference? Because there is historical evidence that the concentration camps were invented by Lenin. Then Stalin transported much of the equipment, barbed wire, and even clothing from German concentration camps to Stalin's Gulags after the end of WWII.

As a result, the Dachau concentration camp, liberated by the U.S. forces, was left mostly in its original condition. It remained as the most authentic evidence of atrocities and a reminder for future generations. However, Osventsym (aka Auschwitz-Birkenau), liberated by the Soviet forces, essentially migrated to the Soviet Union for "continued use" in its joyful socialist society against those who failed to subscribe to that path with full passion.

For those of us who grew up in the Soviet Union and other socialist countries--Cuba in particular--America's trend of "playing" with words and applying double standards in assessing events and people are real threats to our freedom.

|| *January 6 "insurrection" versus "mostly peaceful" burnings of cities by Leftist protestors.*

It's not the words or the humor--which, by the way, has to at least slightly offend someone or it's just not funny--which present a threat. It's the fact that the government and technological oligarchs take the stern Leftist "party line" in their law enforcement, censorship, and ensuing policies. This is known as "double-speak." This pattern of "double speak" is reminiscent of the Soviet indoctrination that the Party could not be wrong.

The Ministry of Truth, as perfectly described by George Orwell, is now voluntarily assumed by Facebook, Twitter, and Google. For example, it is not a "crisis" at the border, simply a "situation." People are not "stranded" in Kabul, they are (we assume) simply there at their own will. It's not blackmailing the Ukrainian General Prosecutor by then-Vice President Biden for investigating Burisma (where his son Hunter held a board seat, having no prior or relevant experience), but simply "exercising U.S. policies."

The Ministry of Truth does not act for both parties, however. No similar forgiveness was shown to Trump's phone call simply asking for an investigation into apparent acts of corruption by a government official.

A few years back, when I tried to chastise my Ukrainian friends about corruption in their country, some of them responded with a one-word answer-question: "Burisma?" It is still beyond my comprehension as to how a country, which claims to be the world's leader in law enforcement and government transparency, just ignored the Burisma, "Hunter laptop," and other credible evidence of Russian, Kazakh, and Chinese-related corruption ties leading to the family of President Biden.

It is frustrating to watch when the media, rather than describing "a bunch of idiots headed by a shaman trespassing on the Capitol," continues to report the January 6 events as an "insurrection worse than the Civil War or 9/11." At the same time, burning a federal courthouse, capturing entire city blocks, shooting the police, and looting or burning businesses are portrayed as "mostly peaceful" protests. By the way, as of this writing, no evidence of premeditation, "insurrection-like activities," or any sort of planning was uncovered by the FBI (which could not be seen as sympathetic to Donald Trump) regarding the January 6 events.

Nevertheless, the blown-out-of-proportion description of the unfortunate events of January 6 is now being employed repeatedly in the same way the Nazis used the "burning of Reichstag." An arson of the Parliament building in Berlin, which historians view as an apparent provocation and a setup, was then relentlessly employed by Hitler for suppressing those who opposed Social Nationalism, or "Nazi."

Media and "the Swamp" are quick to exclaim, "You cannot challenge the elections!" (Not even through legal means?) Social media censors the public to that effect.

|| *All this after "the Swamp" investigated President Trump for over three years based on opposition research and falsified documents provided and produced by the Russian FSB. So illegal means are permissible if you can get away with it?*

Suppose you are successful in quashing people's desire to verify the process and secure its legitimacy. Suppose you do suppress the people's voices. In that case, you also succeed in pushing people from the realm of peaceful legal action to pure resentment and mistrust of the system. You force them to search for other means of change. Let people peacefully speak and express their gripes. Let "an ax to grind" remain an expression in a field of free speech. Not a call to action by frustrated citizens. Social or political movements should never perceive violence as the sole remaining method of effective public protest. Silencing voices and deteriorating social institutions only serve to goad and incite people to resort to those means.

By the same token, the rallying cry "Guns kill" (so we have to confiscate them) sounds all too familiar. This is nothing new. Taking guns from citizens was one of the first actions taken by the Soviet government in 1917. Humans have an inherent God-given (Colt-fortified) right to protect themselves. These assaults on the Second Amendment persist. It's interesting when violent events that can be manipulated by the Left to fortify their "Guns kill" rally cry seem to receive excessive media coverage. Don't miss the hypocrisy. While the Left are "defunding the police" and diminishing the protection of citizens, behind the scenes, they are significantly increasing private security for the politicians.

The hypocrisy doesn't end there. "Guns are evil" unless we donate the most sophisticated weaponry to the Taliban at taxpayers' expense. "Trust every woman," unless, of course, a Democrat is accused by a woman of sexual harassment. "Black Lives Matter," except when dozens of blacks lose their lives, including bystanders and innocent infants sleeping in their homes, over a single weekend due to shootings on the streets of Chicago. "Everyone should wear masks" (or you are a murderer), except, of course, Governor Newsom and Speaker Pelosi and those "sophisticated" people who attended Barack Obama's birthday and Governor Lightfoot's events, and except, of course, Biden's visit to a restaurant.

"The law is for thee but not for me" was one of the main reasons for the fall of the socialist system. Judging by the ease with which they ignore their own mandates, hungry-for-power Leftist politicians care very little about whether people are discontented with their inane and inequitable principles. When the ruling class decides to ignore the law which they themselves have written and then enforces it to the letter against "other people," such hypocrisy breeds unstoppable anger and disgust for the government. It also rots the system from within. It's the same hypocrisy.

Whether it occurs in the Soviet Union or the United States, it's the same. Hopefully, as of this writing, to a different degree.

Present-Day Restrictions on Freedom of Speech

While the assault on freedom of speech and freedom of press essentially started with Putin's first day in office, since 2012 the assault has worsened. Russian authorities have intensified their crackdown on freedom of expression, labeling certain types of government criticism as "risks to state security and public order." Considerable limits have been imposed on online expression along with invasive surveillance of online activities. Since the unprovoked invasion into Ukraine began, Putin's government has arrested, expelled, or shut down all independent media in Russia.

Similarly, in Belarus, criticism of the authorities is not tolerated. The attack there has reached unimaginable heights. Any public criticism of the election process or perceived fraud, including social media, is deemed "extremist" and punishable by harsh prison sentences.

Similarly, the U.S. started losing its pinnacle position as a protector of freedom of speech when it designated as a "terrorist" or "extremist" a select group of offenders. The list includes anyone who questions (even by legitimate and legal means) the outcome of the 2020 election. With such designation, the authorities have banned from Twitter this illustrious group: Donald Trump, Nobel Prize laureates, numerous conservative politicians, known public figures, well-known political commentators, and resources, including Russian-speaking American conservative groups. Their offense? "Community (Did they mean Communist?) standards." A nebulous standard previously applied to defining "pornography."

This ill-conceived attack by social media and "progressives" brings back unsettling memories for many like me who have lived through it--Socialist censorship of any speech or thought that is not within the rigid "Party line."

The only "community standards" that have the right to exist in public space in the U.S. are the well-established Constitutional standards of freedom of speech. When the Left-leaning government essentially employs the power of private enterprise and its ingenuity to suppress free speech, that brings the efficiency of strangling personal freedoms to a new level.

The situation was further exacerbated by the Biden Administration when it unleashed the FBI on American parents for voicing their legitimate concerns and discontent with the school bureaucracy's "woke" agenda, claiming it was both useless and harmful for children.

"False speech" is still free speech. And unless it presents some imminent threat of violence or danger, such as yelling "Fire!" in a crowded theater, it is still the right of every American to say it. You do not need to dumb down the American public. The people of this country are more savvy and shrewd than their Leftist leaders give them credit. Most Americans can analyze what they hear and make the right choices without being spoon-fed "convenient" facts. Facebook and Twitter have no business nor expertise, taking a side in political debates, scientific disputes, or any censorship whatsoever, other than clearly prohibited content or calls for violence. It is hard to comprehend the hypocrisy. When the then-President of the country stated, "You must march and protest patriotically and peacefully," that was deemed "insurrection" and prohibited speech. Yet, clear incitement of violence by Leftist politicians, BLM, and neo-Nazi Antifa against police and opposition, rioters burning the federal courthouse, rioters capturing a city block for establishment of "Chad," rioters beating up independent journalists, and "mostly peaceful" burning and looting were all deemed "protected free speech."

It's unfathomable that Trump was banned from Twitter while the Taliban and Putin's warmongers were not. Is this because the Taliban complies with Twitter's same "community standards" while others of higher moral standing apparently do not? Can we review *those* standards? Or should we just assume and take comfort that stoning and beheading–including the beheading of a female volleyball player–were done with correct pronouns?

According to social media and, most recently, the Department of Homeland Security, the true "potential terrorist threat" is posed by those who dare to question ever-inconsistent Covid policies and those who peacefully call for audits of results of presidential elections through a nonviolent legal process. Apparently, offenses like beheadings and taking over Kabul don't make the list of true "terrorist threats." Doesn't DHS have better things to do, such as actually following up on reports of raping of U.S. gymnasts by an abusive team doctor? Or investigating ignored warning signs about tragic mass shootings in yet another school or July 4th parade? Maybe soon, the FBI and the likes will realize they are often being used as pawns in political prosecutions. One can hope they will then go back to performing their essential functions.

You see, doing your job at the FBI would probably mean following up on the spelling of the terrorists entering the USA rather than those being let go through the security cracks. As a reminder, the warning by the Russian FSB regarding the potential terrorist threat came with a slightly different spelling of the last name of Tsarnayev's brothers, who were ultimately responsible for the Boston Marathon bombing. To put it mildly, this was an unmitigated blunder by the FBI. Apparently, a few years back the FBI's spelling disagreed with that of the FSB when Russia made an effort to be integrated into world affairs and security–specifically, whether or not "y" was used–which, of course, led to a wild goose chase unsolvable by allegedly the world's premier intelligence agency.

What's up with the U.S. government's bumbling of spelling Russian words? There are at least 10 million Russian speakers in the U.S. I'm sure many of them would gladly lend assistance. Hillary Clinton, then-Secretary of State, embarrassed herself and the country by misspelling one word on the "reset" button presented to the Russian Foreign Minister Lavrov into "overload." Again, ONE word! Is Mrs. Clinton's typical arrogance to blame? Or is the U.S. government incapable of finding resources to spell one word correctly in a foreign language–even when a high-level theatrical act is needed to symbolize a significant shift in public policy? Or was it a Freudian slip?

Remember the Benghazi debacle when both the government and U.S. intelligence ignored threats against the U.S. Embassy, which led to the public execution of the first openly gay U.S. ambassador? One might ask: "Why does any of this matter?" A review of these gross mistakes, and even misconducts, is needed to hold people accountable and ensure they never hold a public office. Unless, of course, like some in Washington, one holds an incredulous view that the withdrawal operation in Afghanistan was a 'success' and still naively believes that the U.S. "does not leave its people behind."

Within a few short years, the "woke" culture managed to kill humor in the U.S. Jokes are supposed to be funny. Jokes are supposed to poke fun at stereotypes. Jokes are simply meant to entertain and bring attention to issues, calamities, and problems. Not to change people's perceptions. One has only to look at what happened to humor in Russia and Belarus to see the handwriting on the wall for the U.S. Even though the Slavs have an acute sense of humor and wit, anything "humorous" that is made public today is not even remotely funny. All jokes are limited to alcohol and making fun of Western culture. Any humor that approaches criticism of policies or internal hardships within the country or the character of either Putin or Lukashenko is immediately banned and harshly punished.

There are credible stories about the Belarusian KGB being commissioned to kidnap a Belarusian stand-up comic, Slava Komissarov, from Moscow (to which he had escaped) after a few clever jokes about Lukashenko. Fortunately, he escaped yet again into Ukraine, being forewarned by an opposition sympathizer within the KGB.

Look no further in the U.S. than SNL. The Biden administration continues to provide plenty of joke material with its gaffes, duplicity, and blunders. Yet, SNL apparently finds nothing joke-worthy about this administration's dismal policies or "progressive'" lunacies. No mention of the hypocrisies of Newsome or Pelosi-ice cream, anyone? No skits about Biden's brain short-circuiting in his incomprehensible and angry rants. No poking fun at Biden's continuing escapes from meaningful live interaction with members of both sides of the aisle. No reenactments of the softball questions tossed at him by the media or his temper tantrums when journalists dare to ask a real policy question. Maybe one day SNL will open the show with Peter Doocy's inquisitiveness which resulted in Biden's famous locker room "SOB" lingo. I suppose we better not hold our breath waiting to see any of that.

Humor is supposed to be funny. Oftentimes, exaggerating things out of proportion to make them ... well, funny. While Trump's SNL sketches were somewhat funny, excessive like his personality, and clearly one-sided, there are certainly plenty of opportunities for jokes post-2020 based on what people view in daily life now. Then again, I guess the mass media, being the butt of jokes in real life, would not joke about its hypocrisy, dismal prejudice, and abysmal misreporting. Although it probably should after so many Cuomosexual Avenatti-like faux pas and so much brazen over-the-top Leftwing prejudice.

And do they find no humor at all in our cackling Vice President or her complete abrogation of duties, such as the border crisis? But then, the mass media, our U.S. modern-day Ministry of Truth, claims the long-standing principle of the Left since the French Revolution–*pas d'ennemis à gauche*–

"There are no enemies to the Left." With such ease, they give themselves a total pass in reporting real news, providing real analysis or criticism of their tribe, i.e., anything that is "woke" or left-leaning.

Making fun of politicians, regardless of their political affiliation, used to be a long-standing tradition. People on both sides of the aisle laughed it off. Today's media, however, favors holding the

Party line along with the media of Russia, Belarus, and the Soviet Union, abstaining from making fun of "their" politicians.

I could write ten humorous sketches just from one day of political reporting. As an example, the perky clueless wife is off to spend $3.5 thousand on something unplanned and useless by charging the family credit card and then arguing with her sensible husband that it will "*cost them nothing, sweetheart*" because the credit card "*will pay for itself.*" I'd like to see that on SNL one evening. Again, I won't hold my breath waiting for that story to be repeated in real life outside of Biden's administration.

In the Soviet Union, political criticism was legally banned, but people could read between the lines. Artistic and daily assessment of the backwardness of communism was still delivered through jokes or hidden messages. An example of such a joke:

A Soviet and an American argue as to which country has more freedom of speech.

The American says: *"I can go to the White House and yell, 'Reagan is an idiot,' and nothing would happen to me."*

The Soviet says: *"I can go to the Red Square and yell, 'Reagan is an idiot,' and nothing would happen to me either!"*

While critical thinking and the apparent legality of freedom of speech still appear to be prominent features of the U.S. social system today, suppression of freedom of speech and censorship of any critical analysis is way too close to the "dry and objective" Pravda and the single approved "Party line."

It's not really a problem that the Democratic Party wins elections. We sadly concede that it's enticing to be offered a lot of "free" stuff. It's universal to blame the rich when you hear "the top 1% should pay their share." It's also natural for compassionate people to respond with misguided emotion when bleeding-heart liberals easily manipulate that compassion for their own political purposes. The fact that the top 1% earners pay an overwhelming portion of U.S. tax revenues while the lower 50% of income earners pay virtually no taxes somehow repeatedly goes unnoticed.

The blame game, coupled with socialist slogans, leads nowhere, however. Prime examples are the crime rate in cities governed by the Left. The educational system failures go hand-in-hand with crime in those same cities led by the "compassionate" but impractical Left.

The problem is that despite promises of unity and politically centrist positions, once the Democratic Party gains power, whether in Congress, the White House, or school districts, all issues are pushed through their radical agenda. That agenda continues to become increasingly more radical, more anti-American, anti-capitalist, anti-Israel, anti-Christian, anti-God, and anti-law enforcement. That agenda comes with a non-compromising command to "heel" to the most leftist foot of that amorphous centipede, which coyly plays with various shades of red.

History always has tough lessons to teach. It should be noted that the elections in Germany prior to the 1930s did not result in the election of the Nazi Party. In fact, the Nazi Party gained very little in the 1928 elections, winning only 2.6% of the vote and gaining 12 seats in the Reichstag.

How, then, did the Nazi Party come into power? Nazi dominance was secured in the 1930s political arena by ever-shrewd propaganda led by Goebbels, which portrayed Hitler and the Nazi Party as the progressive, new, people-centered movement. "Progressive" can be a *very* misleading word. Interestingly, Goebbels despised capitalism, blaming its focus primarily on individual freedom, while he adored socialism as humanity's purported highest level of development. Not very right-wing of him, was it?

We are now well aware of the consequences of internal and external policies of such dominance and "progress," which was symbolized in the Nazi Party by the swastika. If history were to teach us anything from that part of Germany's regression into a murderous state, it is that people must take fringe populist policies *very* seriously. Why? Because they manipulate and play on people's worst feelings. They breed hatred of success, free speech, dissent, law and order, and any opposition to the "truth."

|| *Kamala Harris travels to Latin America to find out the "root causes" of the border crisis. Isn't it interesting, considering the vector of the flow of immigration, that those countries are now using Donald Trump's not-so-eloquent expression, "shithole countries," to describe the situation? But the United States does not.*

Clearly, Donald Trump could have used different epithets and been more diplomatic when describing other countries supplying illegal or non-verifiable immigrants to the U.S. Such a reference, particularly if you lack the unique sense of humor and irony that is part of Donald Trump, could leave any immigrant feeling a bit insulted about the country of their heritage.

However, those same immigrants, including yours, truly chose where they are living now. They are enjoying the benefits of life in the U.S. rather than returning, for instance, to Somalia. So, the outrage of the squad and CNN, much like the outrage of any person who prefers to live in this country, has no real ground for disagreeing with such a harsh comparison.

Furthermore, there are only two ways to stop the "root" cause-which is that populations of other countries are flooding into the U.S. Either you raise the level of the daily life of those other countries to the level of the U.S. or, alternatively, you turn this country into a "shithole" where people no longer want to immigrate or live. Since this administration's meek handouts offered to governments of those struggling countries aren't enough to move the needle, the latter option appears to be the choice of Left-namely, ruin this country.

Similarly, criticizing a country by assessing its flaws is not the path to improving it. Suppose you choose to come and live in this country. In that case, your constant bashing and assessment of the United States as a racist or suppressive country-without giving credit to its vast achievements, freedoms, and benefits-is nothing but the empty whining of a spoiled brat.

Millions of people of various religions, skin colors, and backgrounds would gladly stand in line, pay a lot of money, and risk their lives to exchange their dismal positions in other parts of the world with people in the United States who complain about their "disadvantages" and "oppression." It is dangerous when people do not know their country's history or appreciate its many accomplishments or shortcomings. The founders' wisdom allowed for this nation to gradually alleviate those shortcomings through laws, statutes, and checks and balances. Nevertheless, it always adhered to its fundamental principles in the pursuit of happiness. The U.S.A. is civilization's greatest experiment. People often forget this is the same country where millions of white people fought and sacrificed their lives to obtain freedom from the Crown-and again years later, fought to end slavery in the 19th century- and again years later, fought to gain equal rights for all citizens during the civil rights movement in the 20th century. All these causes were fought by white people to primarily affect and prosper minorities.

As viewed by the Left media and outlets such as the Soros Foundation and liberal academia, freedom of speech has taken on a different purpose. Today it seems to exist as a tool for the constant bashing of capitalism and the United States as systemically and inherently evil.

Freedom of speech affords every person the right to speak their mind. It is not my intention to deprive anyone of their right to talk or criticize. But there is danger in the constant self-condemnation of the capitalist society and its true world leadership. As a matter of fact, that was the foundation for the Chinese communists who chastised and scolded the U.S. State Department's (filled with liberals) like a schoolchild with its self-inflicting, overblown claims of racism and police brutality.

It is unfathomable to think that the Chinese Communist Party, with blood on its guilty hands from the mass killings of Tiananmen Square and the Uighur concentration camps, would ever have dared to openly chastise the U.S. State Department under Colin Powell, Condoleezza Rice, or especially Donald Trump.

The extent of such nonsensical pursuit of humor is a clear extension of entities like Facebook favoring one political type of free speech over another.

I posted this joke on Facebook: "Payday [a candy bar] is changing its name because it might be offensive to people who do not work." Again, it was a joke! My joke was flagged as "false/reviewed by an independent fact-checker." So, the government and Tech oligarchs apparently think Americans are so stupid that they need Big Brother to explain which jokes are "false" and which are not.

Putin's court gave a 10-day jail sentence to a stand-up comedian who made a joke criticizing (rightfully so!) the bigotry of Russian society. His joke was deemed to be "offensive" and defamatory to the Russian nation as a whole. Recently, Putin's government published a list of over thirty Russian and Belarusian musicians whose performances in Russia are now banned for their anti-war stance. Imagine that Yuri Shevchuk, the leader of the rock band DDT, was charged with a crime for opening his concert with this statement: "Motherland is not Putin's ass that you have to kiss every day." What was the prosecutor's alternative law-abiding stance on that statement? I am not entirely sure. That *it is?* ...or ... that it's wrong to say *it is not?*

One has to wonder, how far behind are the American Left's attacks on science, economy, family, religion, and humor from this same type of intolerance of alternative opinions or inconvenient facts?

New limits on freedom of expression in Russia appear to be directed at political opponents and civic groups designated as "extremist" or "foreign-influenced," but those limits affect all Russians and all Belarusians. If free speech is restricted, anyone disgruntled with the ongoing economic crisis or even moderately critical of the foreign or domestic policy of Russia or Belarus will be denied a voice. Typically, that person ends up in jail on drummed-up charges.

Such was the case with Alexey Navalny, who was critical of the government corruption and every electoral opposition candidate in Belarus (other than Svetlana Tikhanovskaya, who actually won the presidential election in 2020). In lieu of a prison sentence, she was allowed to leave the country due to international pressure. Navalny, on the other hand, was thrown in jail upon his martyr-like return to Russia after a botched assassination attempt on his life and fearlessly facing Putin's ruthless machine. Ironically, the initial leading opposition candidate in Belarus-Victor Babariko-was actually arrested on his way to register with the Electoral Commission! He eventually received a 14-year sentence on preposterous charges, including giving a bribe to *himself*. Now that's an apparent novelty in legal theory.

The Russian government's crucial campaign on suppression of free speech is part of a broader attack on civil society. That attack began after significant protests in 2011-2012, particularly around Vladimir Putin's re-election to the presidency in May 2012. Since then, Parliament passed a slew of laws restricting, or potentially restricting, freedom of expression and information. Among these new suppressive laws, there were prohibitions on insulting "the senses of the religious believers" and insulting the government or questioning its policies. This practice is deemed as "extremist" and "anti-social."

It's not clear why the American Left would want to use re-socialized Russia and former KGB agents as its role models. But with their present degree of intolerance, critiquing their "moral superiority," they are certainly on the foolhardy path to do so.

Many of these new laws have already been invoked by the authorities in Russia and Belarus. Some of the most recently enacted legislation jeopardizes internet privacy and security. Now no digital communication in Russia will be safe from government eavesdropping. Unregulated surveillance has a chilling effect on online freedom of expression.

|| *At the same time, the unmasking of U.S. citizens in the FISA process, sending the FBI against vocal but peaceful parents, fabricating a case against Michael Flynn, and the recently revealed spying on Tucker Carlson are all examples of results when the American Left resorts to using the same techniques against effective political opponents.*

Hundreds of people have been wrongfully prosecuted for social media posts, online videos, newspaper stories, and interviews both in Russia and Belarus. In fact, Belarus was recognized as the most dangerous country in Europe for journalists. As a result of these new restrictive laws, many Russians and Belarusians are increasingly unclear about what actions constitute lawful speech and what actions could result in a hefty fine or even a prison sentence. In Belarus, inadvertent exposure of the LG's TV box (painted in the white/red/white colors of the Belarusian opposition) or drying lingerie of the same colors on the balcony have gotten people arrested for misdemeanors.

Installing and subscribing to opposition chats or "liking" of "extremist" posts (i.e., posts critical of the government) on social media gets you an actual prison sentence. After questioning the veracity of the alleged WWII veteran, Navalny added a few years to his prison sentence for "insulting" a group of people, allegedly the veterans.

|| *Similarly, public persecution of conservative views by the Leftist U.S. social media and mass media, spewing their made-up stories, i.e., the "Racist Kid (Nick Sandmann) versus the Native American," Mr. Smollett's alleged MAGA attack with an attempt to stage a hate crime, the non-existent "nook" at Nascar, supporting the "Russian hoax" which cost taxpayers millions of dollars, and giving credence to other lies and biases have all crossed a line which was previously deemed unacceptable in a free society.*

State meddling in the media has reached a new high in Russia and Belarus since the collapse of the Soviet Union. Subsequent to 2012, the state has drastically extended its grip over the media landscape. With rare exceptions (primarily online), mainstream media outlets have become the state's biased mouthpiece. These outlets employ sophisticated propaganda techniques to elicit patriotic support for the government. State-controlled media encourages skewed reporting and, at times, even outright lies on a variety of topics, including the current situations in Ukraine and the West.

"Whataboutism" has reached its new high. Any wrongdoing in Russia is always covered by commentators and politicians raising questions such as, "How about Iraq?" or "Do you want to live like they do in Ukraine?"

The Belarusian president diverted a commercial airline using a fake "bomb" call and aggressive fighter jet maneuvers, then forced the plane to land in Minsk. For what purpose? Just to arrest an opposition journalist, Roman Protasevich, who later showed visible signs of torture when seen speaking on state TV praising the dictator. Despite established media standards against showing torture victims, U.S. social media, including YouTube, failed to "police" such broadcasts over their channels. As a result, the world had to listen to a forced statement by a tortured journalist about the bravery and fairness of Lukashenko and the size of his balls. In essence, U.S. social media effectively aided and abetted the dictator in his despicable propaganda tool.

One has to wonder. Google's fact-checkers seem very vigilant when it comes to conservative issues and anything related to Donald Trump. Were Google's fact-checkers at lunch at the time when this victim of torture was talking about the dictator's steel balls, or did they verify and "fact-check" this one personally?

While the Russian and Belarus governments have complete authority over state-controlled television and other mainstream media over the narrative on politically sensitive subjects, government critics can still reach the majority of Russians and Belarusians online due to the increased usage of social media.

The majority of independent discourse currently takes place online, particularly via social media. However, there are numerous methods to block, control, or shut down "unfavorable" and "extremist" resources, including the channels of Svetlana Tikhanovskaya. They clearly get the majority of the votes in the presidential elections.

|| *So apparently banishment from social media as a means of communication between the actual elected President and his electorate is something new for America. However, I don't recommend using the totalitarian practices of Belarus as the best role model for a free society. (Note: Even if assuming arguendo Trump was not elected in 2020, he was elected in 2016.)*

Russian and Belarusian authorities have stepped up their measures aimed at bringing the Internet under stronger state control in the past four years, particularly following the revolution in Ukraine in 2014, the annexation of Crimea, the ensuing Russian military engagement in Eastern Ukraine, and the widely reported election fraud in Belarus in 2020.

Some of these actions have to do with the infrastructure of the internet in Russia. In 2016, the Russian parliament passed legislation forcing telecommunications and internet firms to keep the contents of all communications for six months and data about those communications for three years. The bill made it simpler for authorities to identify people and obtain personal data without judicial review. The bill also infringed on privacy and freedom of expression without justification. According to a 2015 regulation applicable to email services, social media networks, and search engines, Russian individuals' personal data cannot be stored on computers located outside Russia. Western social media (other than LinkedIn), as true "champions" of privacy and personal freedoms, quickly heeded the FSB-designed regulations.

In November 2016, Russian authorities suspended access to LinkedIn, a corporate social networking service with over 400 million users globally, for non-compliance with the 2015 legislation. Belarus shut down Tut.by-the largest news resource in Belarus, charging it with "extremist" activity and financial manipulations-a pretext to shutting down independent reporting. Over 50 percent of the country's inhabitants were loyal users of Tut.by.

Most post-2012 Russian legislation governing internet content, data storage, and online conduct is still in the early phases of implementation. The manner and breadth of enforcement are as yet unknown. Belarus is also quickly advancing toward the same principles employed by the Bolsheviks after 1917 and the Nazis in the 1930s-namely, subduing each and every sign of political dissent.

Meanwhile, authorities in Russia and Belarus have been aggressively enforcing earlier laws that criminalized internet speech. As a result, they are increasingly linking criticism of the government with "extremism," particularly on specific issues like the occupation of Crimea, criticism or mockery of the Russian Orthodox Church, and Russia's armed engagement in Syria. In general, any criticism relating to government corruption or election fraud is considered "extremism." The number of criminal prosecutions originating from "extremism" charges has risen dramatically, particularly in relation to expressing views and thoughts online. In Belarus, even peaceful protest was viewed as "extremism."

|| *And these protests were not "mostly" peaceful--using CNN's terminology-as in Portland and other big U.S. cities suffering from mob arson and looting. The protests in Belarus were truly peaceful. The most popular meme about protests in Belarus emanated from a picture where protesters were shown taking their shoes off before stepping on a park bench. Unfortunately, the more peaceful these protests became, the more brutal were the unrepentant beatings and tortures ordered by Lukashenko, convinced of his impunity.*

People in Belarus would take their shoes off when stepping on the benches, cross streets on green lights only, and carefully gather all garbage at the end of the day. This is the character of a nation of people who are now being viewed and punished as "extremists" by their own government. Considering the brutality with which Russia has "helped" Lukashenko and the "oppressed Russians" in Ukraine, I would imagine Belarusians, particularly those fighting alongside Ukrainians, will think twice before taking their shoes off next time.

According to the SOVA Center, a renowned Russian think tank, 216 social media users were convicted of extremist offenses in 2015, up from 30 in 2010. In 2021, the number of political prisoners in Belarus reached over 600. The number detained or fined for peaceful protests or social media posts exceeded 30,000. People were routinely jailed, tortured, and in some instances, beaten to death for wearing a scarf of the "wrong" color (specifically white/red/white) or making "extremist" posts on Facebook. This included posting evidence and facts about violence and government brutality. Approximately 85% of prosecutions in Russia for "extremist expression" between 2014 and 2016 involved online expression. Penalties ranged from fines to community service to prison time. Between September 2015 and February 2017, the number of people imprisoned for extremist statements nearly doubled from 54 to 94.

During Russia's seven-year occupation of Crimea, authorities there have suppressed opposition, claiming they are "fighting extremism." Russian authorities have actively pursued critics, threatening them with harassment, intimidation, and, in some cases, criminal accusations. The number of opposition reporters, including Pavel Sheremet and Anna Politkovskaya, and political opponents who have died under "suspicious circumstances" continues growing exponentially.

|| *The phenomenon of death under "suspicious circumstances" is something the U.S. is also becoming more familiar with, particularly when that person relates, one way or another, to high-level investigations of politicians. Similarly, at least five families of top executives of Gazprom "committed suicide," often with their entire families, in different parts of the world. It's astonishing to me to hear European politicians calling for a softer stance of negotiations to assure that Putin, who many are convinced ordered those suspicious "suicides," does not "lose face." Is that the tenor one would have dared to take against the other mass-murdering fuhrer in 1940 or 1944?*

Rulers in Belarus and Russia do not shy away from conducting assassinations on the territory of other countries, including Great Britain, the Czech Republic, and Ukraine. Most recently, a leader in the Belarusian community in Ukraine who assisted Belarusian asylum seekers in Ukraine was found hanged in one of the parks in Kyiv. His body had been severely beaten before the brutal execution.

|| *And, of course, as in the case of Jeffrey Weinstein, another government hides the truth behind an apparent "suicide." At least a dozen of Russia's Gazprom and former high-ranking military officers died under mysterious Weinstein-like suicides.*

Crimean Tatars, an ethnic minority in the Crimean Peninsula that has publicly protested Russia's annexation, have been hit particularly hard by the government's persecution. Numerous reports detail the most recent examples of persecution of Crimean Tatar activists, attorneys, and others who have spoken out publicly and peacefully against Russia's actions in Crimea. In response, Russian authorities forced the closure of all independent media outlets in Crimea.

Authorities have vigorously implemented measures to now punish a newly-created criminal offense-"offending the sensibilities of religious believers."

// *It is curious that, rather than prosecuting only concrete acts, and even actual violence and corruption, socialist-leaning activists are now bent on "protecting" someone's "feelings" - so long as those "feelings" align with the agenda of the government, in the East and even now in the West.*

Following the highly known unauthorized punk-rock performance by the feminist group Pussy Riot in a Russian Orthodox cathedral in Moscow, authorities added this offense of "offending the sensibilities of religious believers" to the Criminal Code in 2013. At least six people were charged with violating this provision in 2016. As of this writing, at least five more people have been convicted and given punishments ranging from a fine to two years in prison. I have a suspicion these numbers will continue to rise.

At the same time, the Moscow Orthodox Patriarchate has no problem with offending Christian "sensibilities" by foregoing "Thou Shalt Not Kill" while blessing the brutal war, effectively justifying Putin's atrocities in Ukraine.

Likewise, at the same time, Russian authorities also utilized "extremism" laws offline. Their purpose was to outlaw the Jehovah's Witnesses, and target other minor religious groups with a smaller influence in Russia to maintain the monopoly of the obedient

Priests of the Orthodox Church in power. Hypocrisy is still alive and well in the realm of various religious outlets, but in Russia, it's rampant and nauseating. It seems "offending the sensibilities of religious believers" is yet again used as a tool to protect the sensibilities and undeniable "righteousness" of certain people in high places.

While Putin and Lukashenko do not openly proclaim that they follow socialism, they follow its principles of governance meticulously. Both openly praised Stalin and Hitler. There is great religious irony in Russia's history. When the "communist religion" failed, it was quickly replaced by Russian Orthodoxy with its subservient modern clergy in willing total submission under the KGB's yoke. Russia has such "affection" for its "religion" that the KGB (and Putin, since he's the main KGB guy both in and out) were responsible for the destruction of hundreds of churches in Moscow alone, as well as the extermination of over 90% of traditional clergy. The hypocrisy of "offending the sensibilities of religious believers" apparently knows no bounds in Russia.

KGB (ChKa at the time) even used the 1921 famine as a pretense to expropriate religious paraphernalia, such as crosses and icons, and execute anyone who opposed them. In fact, before the Russian Church became a servant to the neo-communist regime, it sanctified two attorneys who helped the church fight the Bolsheviks' despicable policies and atrocities in the '20s. That's a far cry from a lawyer joke!

The contemporary Russian Orthodox Church, while historically retaining a large following, is viewed by many as a corrupt institution. It's seen as being "in the pocket" of the FSB, having transformed itself from a spiritual institution opposing communism to a business and propaganda outlet trading in alcohol, cigarettes, and real estate. In exchange, it had to display complete allegiance to and uninterrupted praise of the current regime, war crimes or not.

In Belarus, true leaders of Orthodox and Catholic churches were ostracized and displaced from their positions by the government. Why? The dictator in power sensed the churches did not accept the fraudulent results of the 2020 elections and rightfully opposed the violence that ensued.

Surprisingly, the Russian and Belarusian Constitutions protect freedom of thought and expression and prohibit censorship. Russia and Belarus are both signatories to several international treaties that require governments to preserve freedom of expression and information. Even if it is on paper only, interference with or limitations on freedom of expression are permissible under international law, but they must be adopted in pursuit of a recognized legitimate objective, have a valid legal basis, be justified as essential and reasonable in a democratic society, and cannot be discriminatory. I guess all limitations of freedoms in Russia and Belarus are justified as essential, reasonable, and necessary for the survival of its brutal leaders?

|| *While violations of those principles are brazen in Belarus and Russia, the slippery slope of events in the U.S. is not a trend that will make our country prosper, neither politically, morally, nor economically. When political debate dies, so dies the democracy. Freedom of speech is one of the most prized possessions of this country. It is now dying a slow death, deteriorating rapidly due to "woke" culture, clear extreme socialist tendencies, political intolerance, and withdrawal of the Left from any meaningful dialogue.*

One of the most important cornerstones of a democratic society is freedom of expression, which applies not only to information, ideas, and lifestyles that are welcomed but also to those that offend, shock, upset, or even "hurt your feelings." (Oh, grow up already!)

All governments should respect and protect the rights of their citizens to freely receive and transmit information, and to express opposing or critical viewpoints. *····

The recent history of Russian media reveals how that country's political "progression" has influenced the media sector. Following the disintegration of the Soviet Union in the 1990s, the Russian media system underwent significant changes. The media was exposed to new realities such as the market economy, the collapse of the Communist Party's ideological control, political plurality, and new public institutions.

This may surprise you, but most of the attributes of the seemingly ideal Western model of the press were acquired by Russian media. These included freedom of expression, private ownership of media outlets, similar legislation, distance from the state, public influence, and a watchdog role. Even a true political debate in Russia-the first congress of the deputies that was called during the "perestroika"-drew ratings that our Super Bowl would envy! Their newspaper, "Arguments and Facts," reached nearly 20 million subscribers. Its popularity has even been recognized by the Guinness Book of World Records. The Russian people, after 70 years of sheer propaganda, were gasping for true debate, free expression, and truthful reporting. The new system thrived for about a decade after the collapse of the Soviet Union.

So what went wrong? The deeply ingrained cultural and professional traditions of Russian journalism hampered the development of the new Russian media system in the direction of the Western ideal. While the state liberalized media economic activities in the 1990s, it was clearly not ready to relinquish control over the content. By the end of the 1990s, the tide had turned. This created an almost unsolvable dilemma for the media, which was attempting to serve as both a commercial corporation and a social institution.

In 1991, following the adoption of the new Mass Media Law, which effectively established guarantees for media independence and freedom of speech, the first stage of media market privatization in

Russia began. The country faced a severe financial crisis in the early 1990s. State support for the media was drastically reduced, resulting in significant reductions in circulation and staff. According to some experts, an entire generation of Soviet journalists was pushed to change careers. Simultaneously, due to market pressures, new private media firms and many traditional media channels were privatized, reformatted, and repurposed.

---

* HRW (2021). *Online and On All Fronts. Russia's Assault on Freedom of Expression.* Retrieved from https://www.hrw.org/report/2017/07/18/online-and-all-fronts/russias-assault-freedom-expression

Even though Russia's political and social institutions experienced significant formal changes during the transition period, informal practices remained unchanged. The country's development resembled more of a "democratic civic charade" than true reform. The new elites fought to redistribute power and economic prosperity. The "masquerade" could be seen in the media system as well. While formal protocols for interactions between media and government were established, those protocols did not impair the traditional informal contacts and direct influence previously enjoyed between journalists and officials. In other words, they were able to "have their cake and eat it too."

Under President Boris Yeltsin's "polycentric" political paradigm, the second stage of media privatization began in the mid-1990s, when the country gained relative political and economic stability. The "polycentric" concept was founded on balancing multiple power centers, including oligarchs, industrial-financial conglomerates, and regional state administrations. During this time, the media enjoyed considerable freedom and independence from the government. Even so, the new owners and managers of the media companies exploited the media to manipulate public opinion in their favor. The media was seen as a tool by both political and commercial leaders. Despite the changes, most of the leaders were still closely tied to the old ways of achieving political capital. They only knew how to operate in an oppressive socialist society. Sadly, they fell back into dictating the "new party line" rather than enjoying a market of ideas.* †††

The media tended to focus more on the likes of an Entertainment Tonight episodes on American television. They offered "clickbait," exaggerating the shortcomings of speech, walk, or mannerisms of Trump (or, at times, pretty silly exercisers of spit-balling) or other conservative leaders. Very little attention was paid to facts, actual political achievement, the down-to-earth concerns of the people, or causation.

|| *The same could be said for American media, which chose to accentuate some of Trump's stupid and silly tweet references to Clorox yet ignored the credit that should rightfully have been given him for spearheading the swift creation and distribution of a promised vaccine. Exaggerations about the crowd size of a rally took precedence over bringing to light a failed promise that "We will not leave any Americans behind in Kabul."*

Meanwhile, during this time in Russia, the fight between the elite clans was frequently represented in the media in the form of "black" and "gray" PR and "kompromat" conflicts. The elites appeared to realize the media's advantages in this conflict and desired to turn these advantages into concrete benefits and power plays. The media had now become the supplier of even more political leverage.

National, regional, and local election campaigns would now be impossible to win without the backing of the media. In the 1996 presidential elections, incumbent President Boris Yeltsin faced off against Russian Communist Party leader Gennady Zyuganov in a runoff-the struggle for political dominance. In this historic battle, Yeltsin came out on top by a razor-thin margin despite initially enjoying a 3% rating.

---

* Drawing a parallel with trends in the social landscape in the U.S.A., those of us who are too familiar with censorship and oppression of thought are scared by the merger of the government acting as a puppeteer with kowtowing journalists that forgot the decency and tenets of their profession—namely, be in opposition to the government, be truthful and objective, and ask tough questions. One could not imagine even a decade ago that the media would become a "yes, man (or ma'am)" to far-left extremists and daydreamers, turning a blind eye on the "mostly peaceful" burnings and looting of the cities, a loony policy of defunding the police, and ever-growing crime.

Much of the credit for Yeltsin's victory was attributed to the new liberal Russian media outlets, which actively backed the incumbent president despite his health issues, policy failures, and well-publicized alcoholism. NTV, Russia's first independent television channel, was regarded in 1994-96 as one of the most impartial and professional television networks, as was Kommersant, one of Russia's first business newspapers. NTV was part of the MediaMost media conglomerate owned by Vladimir Gusinsky, a powerful Russian billionaire. Kommersant Daily was owned by Boris Berezovsky, another powerful oligarch and adviser to President Yeltsin.

As a result, the media played a critical role in swaying public opinion in Yeltsin's favor and ensuring his 1996 win. The critical scare tactics of the media at the time portrayed Yeltsin's competition Zyuganov and his reforms as dooming the people back to socialism. That proved to be the winning strategy. Russian voters had a fresh memory of their abysmal life under socialism and went with Yeltsin.

|| *American voters find socialism winsome and appealing because they have zero real-life experience of its dismal effects. The lure of "something for nothing" is bewitching them. Unless America wakes up and recoups its moral compass and foundational principles, the White House may soon be won by the candidate who proudly boasts of being a socialist. In this changing cultural climate, the conservative anti-socialism candidate may soon be doomed. We must never underestimate that peril, particularly as "progressive" candidates continue to find their way onto the ballots.*

Thus, the media, in an admitted and clear bias, albeit voluntary at the time, pushed heavily for Yeltsin's victory, fearing that the other choice would mean going back to Soviet rule. Even the slogan was coined: "Vote with your heart," playing the stereotypes of the Russian soul. However, such bias and predetermined prejudice did not go unnoticed. If you were manipulated for a "good cause" once, the only remaining task is to find "another good cause."

After dusting off the ashes of the Soviet empire, another "good cause" was unearthed by Putin and Lukashenko. This duo was dangerous, as Lukashenko was nothing more than a rougher but meager version of his "Big Brother." The cause, or the unwritten scripts-("skrepy") as Putin and his followers call them--was a bizarre pairing of opposites. A sandwich, if you will. One slice of bread represents the uniqueness and superiority of the "Russian" way of life solidified by traditional values, mainly staunch denial of LGBT rights. The other slice of bread represents the made-up threat of Western aggression against Mother Russia. The "meat" of the sandwich is the fire of the craving for greatness again. Fanned by the catalyst of his own propaganda, Putin yearns to be something grand, even messiah-like. The Russian media's daily revisionist frenzy blasts over the former greatness of the Soviet Union, which was either allegedly stolen or degraded by the "liberals" or exterminated by the West.

So, Putin's "New Red Deal" mission is to be the one who restores the Soviet Union's greatness at any cost. For this great feat, Putin will force others to "respect him." But "him" is often ambitiously and falsely equated with Russia itself, though from afar. You see, Putin is hunkered down in his secure bunker with a 60-ft. long table for visitors who must undergo a two-week quarantine before meeting him. It's a bit extreme and paranoid, to say the least. Certainly not the comfort and safety the rest of the country enjoys.

To avoid confusion, it should be noted that the term "liberals" is used in Russia to describe those who vie for Western values and democracy, akin to the "liberal movement" against despots in 17th century Europe. The fire for greatness in Russia is fueled by the underlying Goebbels-like war mongering tactic:

|| *"The West still wishes for Russia's ultimate demise." Yeah, right. And that's why the West sells its goods, from hamburgers and aircraft to countless Rolls Royce luxury automobiles, to a Russian population becoming wealthier and benefitting far more from the West's appetite for Russian oil than from Russia's long-term internal reforms.*

The abstract question of the outside observer remains unanswered: If these intentions of Russian demise are true, why did the West not annihilate Russia in the 1990s when it was at its weakest?

Interestingly, the Russian aggressive mix of self-pity, self-victimization, and hatred toward the West as the "bad guys" appears to have come full circle. Putin's wishful thinking for Russia's renewed greatness, evidenced by its current invasion into Ukraine, has Russia perceived by the West now as the world's pariah and global security threat.

In essence, Putin generated, as I would coin it, "Parashism"–a poisonous cocktail of paranoia where everyone is an enemy out to get you-served alongside a helping of arrogant superiority that the poor and undeveloped Russian world that evolved into the modern form of open Nazism toward other nations would place its own nation on the brink of at least regression into barbarism if not extermination. Ironically, the word Rus' (or "Russia") has been in use by Ukraine since the 10th century when Kyiv's Rus (now the territory of Ukraine) adopted Christianity. "Moskovia" (or the territories united by Moscow, a city founded in 1147), on the other hand, was renamed "Russia" by Peter the Great in 1721. It's third grade math and geography, plus a little bit of logic. Which of the "entities" has an earnest claim to a longer "Russia" legacy?

With Vladimir Putin's ascension to power in 2000, the third stage of Russia's media transformation began. Under the theme of improving stability and security, the new Russian president altered the country's political structure from "polycentric" to "monocentric." This move gained widespread public approval. Vladimir Putin consolidated control over Russia's government, parliament, courts, and media system by constructing the so-called "power vertical." In essence, he eliminated any challenges by alternative political forces, thereby ensuring the new regime's "stability."

By the early 2000s, various state agencies had assumed financial or managerial control over 70% of electronic media outlets, 80% of the regional press, and 20% of the national press. As a result, Russian media remained utilized as political control tools, but these "tools" were no longer spread among rival political parties and enterprises. Control had been shrewdly concentrated in the hands of a narrow political circle sworn, of course, to loyalty to President Putin.

Overall, Russia's political discourse naturally deteriorated during this time. Public debate in the media was either replaced by imitative forms, or pushed out of popular media outlets, such as television and large-circulation newspapers, to publications with a much smaller readership, such as Novaya Gazeta, or the internet. After Gusinky's NTV media empire was essentially taken over by the government, Boris Berezovsky was also compelled to sell his stake in ORT to Roman Abramovich, another Russian oligarch who pledged allegiance to Vladimir Putin. All these events occurred under pressure from the new Kremlin elite in 2001. The symbolic climax of the new elite's control of the media occurred in 2002 when the government seized MediaMost, which I had the privilege to represent along with other attorneys.

Simultaneously, Russian media became an integral component of the global media community due to global convergence and homogenization. It was a natural development under the new conditions of Russia's monocentric political system. The state benefited from the ability to regulate political discourse, while the state-controlled media welcomed the influx of money from the burgeoning advertising industry in Russia.

One of the key characteristics of Russia's political system under both Putin and Lukashenko administrations is the informal subordination of both the rubber-stamping legislative and judicial branches of authority to the executive branch, which the President controls. This move echoed the Communist Party's controlling principles in place during the former Soviet Union. With the overwhelming dominance of the executive branch, even termed as the "vertical of power," this framework allows the President to achieve his goal of establishing total control over the entire political process. Putin essentially eliminated both potential competition concerns as well as oversight checks and balances.

Vladimir Putin conveyed a strong message to the business sector to separate themselves from politics by silencing many influential businessmen who didn't conform to executive dominance. Some, like Mikhail Khodorkovsky, were actually imprisoned. Putin now secured his authority over corporate Russia along with the same, if not stronger, choking grip over the private industry. Only those who followed his political line and showed devotion and support were allowed to go about their business as usual from now on, at least with regard to large businesses. This python-like strangulation over the private businesses in Russia was one of the main causes of the embarrassing, less-than-stellar performance by the Russian Army in Ukraine.

In essence, the ruling principles of Putin have very little to do with economic stimulus. Rather, they are a toxic combination of Soviet-style distribution and redistribution of the resources, "Oprichnina," practiced by Ivan the Terrible. Under this redistribution, local vassals were free to abuse and loot the local populace as long as they paid dues to the central power. It is the worst possible version of crony capitalism–abusive power, money-grabbing, unprecedented personal luxury, and self-indulgence.

In this bribe-cemented hierarchy of Putin's regime, some of the lower law enforcement foot soldiers fell out of grace and were punished as "scapegoats", to demonstrate his "anti-corruption" measures. It's hard for Americans to imagine, but in Russia, a major can get arrested with *hundreds of millions* of dollars and literally *tons* of hidden gold. This certainly looks like evidence of midstream "flow of bribery funds!" By the same token, Putin's palace, with its solid gold toilet paper holders, is not seen as out of the ordinary with "Party" line politics. Just another example of Putin's exorbitant stolen wealth pyramid.

Public consensus persists that the Navalny prison sentence and prior attempt to poison him for the made-up "fraudulent transaction" (otherwise a well-documented transparent transaction for profit), was revenge for Navalny's investigative reports on the exuberant palaces built for Putin, and his team's unrelenting reports on corruption.

Certain strategies were used to turn the Russian and Belarus media systems into a restricted homogeneous field in which only state-controlled media outlets were permitted to function on a national scale. The dictatorship enabled-or rather, graciously allowed- limited independent media (press and internet media) to absorb the protest atmosphere in limited ways. Due to the limited political context, Russian media were unable to withstand state pressure, succumbing to the well-known propaganda and conformism pattern they had followed since the Soviet era. With Vladimir Putin's ascent to power, the age of relative press freedom came to an end. Since Russian media hadn't had time to develop into a strong democratic institution/watchdog, their feeble sprouts of free speech were quickly quashed in the best Stalinist traditions.

It is worth noting that the current scenario somewhat varies from that of the Soviet Union. Russia, at least for now, is not a closed country. However, it is becoming more and more so. Russian journalists are aware of the media's role in the free world. Since members of Russian media are exposed to the open flow of information and advancements in the global media market, particularly via the internet channels, consumers of the news have access to independent Western media. Surprisingly, however, the bulk of the Russian media freely chose to engage in corrupt practices by serving as propaganda tools in exchange for state handouts or advantages. In essence, they simply abandon their public duty to report the truth and facts.*

One of the last "nails" in the coffin of Russian independent journalism was labeling, among others, the channel "Dozhd" (Rain) and Medusa, which was already earlier pushed out from TV to the Internet, as "foreign agents."

---

* Index on Censorship (2021). *A Complete Guide to Who Controls the Russian News Media*. Retrieved from https://www.indexoncensorship.org/2013/12/brief-history-russian-media/

Unlike most Russian politicians and lead propaganda journalists who own foreign yachts and real estate, no "foreign" ownership was involved here, at least on any meaningful scale. A designation of "foreign agent" would cause many advertisers to disassociate with an "enemy of the state" in fear of retribution. In a typical "whataboutism" explanation, "That's the law and that's our interpretation of it," the Russian authorities refer to the "foreign agent" designation of "Russia Today," even though it is 100% owned by the Russian government.

As a recognition of the courage of the independent media in Russia, the Nobel Peace Prize in 2021 was awarded to Dmitry Muratov, an editor and journalist, for "[his] efforts to safeguard freedom of expression, which is a precondition for democracy and lasting peace."

Belarus, on the other hand, made a full turn toward the Soviet-style media, serving outright low-grade fabrications laced with biased content and boring socialist reporting. The narratives frequently shift between boasts of an "unprecedented harvest" and denunciations of the "evil grimace of capitalism." Lukashenko has completely banned all forms of independent media, so in that sense Putin is his belated pupil. As a result, virtually all journalists have been imprisoned or forced out of the country both in Russia and Belarus.

You may find what I am about to tell you disturbing. Reporting the recent death of Vitaly Shishov, an activist of the Belarusian community in Kyiv, the state-media anchors gloated about his death, adding their own commentary about wishful deaths of other opposition leaders in exile, actually superimposing their photos with a noose. An actual noose was also hanging from the ceiling during such a "news" report, and a horse's severed head was amiss. Ironically, the program was bracketed by advertisements featuring the products of Western companies such as Procter & Gamble and Mars Candy. Even more ironic, such shocking content was not removed from either YouTube or other social media. It seems the ad-providing enterprises, much like the NBA in China, are slow to harmonize their moral compass with their old-fashioned greed in the lucrative markets.

This is a clear demonstration of when and how capitalism makes a bad name for itself by supporting the terror and brutality of oppressive regimes with a thinly veiled threat to political opposition. Can you imagine companies like Procter & Gamble and Mars Candy advertising a "news" program in the U.S. gloating about a social activist's death with a noose hanging from the ceiling? Why have the standards of capitalists and Western media changed? Have they lost all conscience on the way while crossing the proverbial American border?

Chapter 3
Perception of History

"History teaches us that man learns nothing from history."

- ***Georg Wilhelm Friedrich Hegel***

The above quote goes somewhat against philosopher Santayana's famous observation, "Those who cannot learn from history are doomed to repeat it." Humanity and the United States are no exception. It behooves us to carefully study our past and learn all lessons from history, both bitter and better.

History, as its name dictates, is one of the oldest sciences. It is as old as it is amorphous and imprecise. This is due to the fact that many events and their memories have been erased from humanity's "hard drive." Therefore, the stories that do reach us are likely distorted, from slightly to significantly. This alteration, or bias, in our recapture usually occurs due to one of two factors. First, imperfect storytellers tell imperfect stories. Second, the simple fact that history was written by victors of war ensures that war is the predominant theme of historical events, which naturally ensures that losers are usually relegated to memory's dust.

Unfortunately, history is frequently employed by various social groups as a tool of offense or defense as they pursue the goals of their particular ideology. To prove my point, let's explore how history has been used by social groups, and the Left in particular, to further their aims. We will see two distinct ways history is misused. One way is to ignore it entirely or twist the facts to justify one's actions. A second way is to broadcast a deliberately false legacy.

Proactive ignorance regarding historical events is the response to the first way. Forget it. That helps explain how or why certain policies or choices were made by humanity or society over the course of history. Some historians believe that history doesn't repeat itself. However, in one of his keener observations, even Karl Marx noted that "History repeats itself, first as tragedy, second as farce."

Whether or not history is truly repetitive or follows the path of an eternal spiral, certain events and human choices will still lead to similar consequences. If your goal is to repeat things that were tried in the past but gain a different reaction, you should try to come up with a different action, a different way of attaining your goal. It makes sense to learn what happened and what wrong and right choices were made to cause that result. Otherwise, according to an expression attributed to Albert Einstein, "Doing the same thing and expecting a different result is a definition of insanity."

In the case of socialism, we all hope that humanity at some point will choose to avoid, or at least correct, such a drastic description of its primary *modus operandi*. Again, certain events and human choices will still lead to similar consequences. If over 50 countries tried "socialism," and it worked in exactly zero instances, why would anyone glorify it or try to repeat it? If the result of socialism each time brought on the misery of mass social, political, economic, and human devastation, why would anyone want to glorify or repeat it?

If simple logic applies, would you buy a product-let's say an iPhone- that failed each time for all 50 users? And I don't mean 50 out of thousands but 50 out 50 that tried it? On a much grander scale, it's not logical to choose a way of life for a society that failed each time it was chosen.

One of the essential goals of this book is to show through factual and some personal examples that socialism did not work in the past. Historians have recorded their accounts. Recent history is replete with examples. There is no logical reason to try again–even if you sprinkle it with powdered sugar.

We realize that such a generalization might be too generic to get a 'like' or even register in the minds of young American parents from the past several generations who labored selflessly for an honorable goal-to give their kids a better life than theirs. Those parents succeeded. Today's kids have been showered with stuff. Maybe even spoiled by prosperity and entitlement. Shielded from learning the hard lessons that shaped their parents. Consequently, today's generation tends to make emotionally-based decisions. Many have not worked for what they have been given. They have never experienced horrors. Their primary concern is- How does this affect me?

Our primary concern-How do we get their attention? I think we need to dissect the mistakes and horrors of socialism in a more precise and pointed manner, one they can "feel" on a personal level. The specifics we offer should highlight today's trends in American society. Open their eyes to see that "social nets" provided by the government morph into the "socialist realm" and eventually bring enforced government domination. Socialism brings irreversible devastating effects on a modern free society. Over 50 societies in other countries learned that painful lesson. All of us, from baby boomers to GenZ, must learn from them. Otherwise, America may become 51st on that awful doomsday list.

The traditional isolated nature of the U.S. and Monroe-like political doctrines caused the prior generation of Americans to mock any need for knowledge and perspective based on the experiences of other nations. Instead, their focus was on "our own business." Namely, American exceptionalism and isolationism. With university academia leaning more and more Left, the motivation for students to know and appreciate American history, particularly its positive achievements, is fading. Our entire education system is being infiltrated and overtaken by utopian, ultra-radical revisionist theories. Their determined purpose is to trample capitalism and embellish socialism in the minds of our children, America's next generation.

If you wake up every morning with a view that the world is there to hurt your feelings, and you blame everyone and everything else for your problems, history will never be your friend. History will not bring you comfort. However, history may open your eyes to reality.

*Life Story** One of my friend's daughters in Florida mentioned to other students in a history course that Armenia was the first country to adopt Christianity as its official state religion. She was called racist, of course, because somehow we assume it diminishes other nations, nationalities, races, or countries in their pursuit of spiritual development or even alleged historical superiority. However, beliefs and past history are not a competition–they are facts. Nor are they evidence of someone's superiority. They are simply naked facts. Kardashians are neither evidence of Armenians' spiritual leadership nor a mark of the nationality's religious curse. The history course is a reality of historical development. I am sure your own spirituality depends very little on the fact that your nation recognized Christianity a few years past Armenia. Some historical events "just happened." Some events had a clear chain result of linked events and causation. It's simply a mathematical result that if Armenia is the oldest Christian country, then it would have the oldest traditions, artifacts, and history to brag about.

So, "forgetting" or ignoring mere facts or labeling "provocative" themes as "racist" puts extreme pressure on the teacher to avoid 'inconvenient' facts and truthful portrayal of events. ('Inconvenient' is now a popular designation made by a crazy fringe.) However, most historical points are just facts, whether you like them or not. You don't have to like them. You don't have to view them as role models or pattern your behavior after Napoleon or Nero. (I hope not!) Nevertheless, you can actually learn from facts and use them to form actual fact-based opinions.

To avoid torpedoing contemporary sympathies to socialism, today's academia simply ignores any in-depth study of socialist history. These cohorts of newly-baked progressivism and socialism don't want students to learn socialist history. They don't want to talk about misery, destruction, famine, or the truth that over 100+ million innocent people died because of socialism. So, our young people are barely exposed to the truth. In the absence of a constant revealing light directed at the historical gutter where socialism found its permanent, well-deserved sanctuary, socialism's empty promises of "equity" and fairness continue to be served on a faux golden platter to our students.

In reality, however, if our students were allowed to study history carefully, they would witness that the "equity" promised by socialism always turns into a totalitarian regime. There is only one path toward "universal welfare and equity." That path requires rejecting individual freedoms and natural or God-given rights, including freedom of speech and economic freedom.

Socialism achieves such sweeping destruction of individualism through expropriation–the act of the state or authorities taking property from its rightful owner and declaring it is now for "public" use. In other words, "equity" is achieved by taking from those who have worked hard for what they own and assigning it to others as the authorities decide. Think about that when you decide if you want to be on the "taking" or "receiving" side- or if the "sides" are at all equitably justifiable.

Socialism sees the outcome of one's labor, entrepreneurship, or ingenuity achieved by hard work as "excess results" or "excess wealth." Commonly referred to as Big Brother, the goal of socialism is to tax–and kill–the rich! You wonder how can this be? Once the personal financial freedoms of the people are disposed of, such highway robbery is not only possible, it becomes inevitable. It is much too easy for abusive power to manipulate the "needy" and dependent populace.

|| *No wonder when the Biden administration was criticized for the hardships suffered by ordinary Americans, one of the responses voiced by Biden Advisor Brian Deese was that everything was going "according to plan" (much like Putin's dreadful war efforts) and "[t]his is about the future of the Liberal World Order, and we have to stand firm." Sounds far too much like Lenin's World Revolution. We need to look no further for the "root causes" of the Left's policies or motivation. Biden's administration and the champions of the Left's cause have stated them plainly. Again, this is nothing new under the sun–it's yet another Red New Deal.*

Next, civil liberties, the integral parts, and safeguards of a free society where people pursue happiness as individuals rather than serving state goals, are wiped out. History proves this can happen instantly, as in 1917 Russia or Putin today, as the regime gradually and selectively removes lower hanging fruits. But when our schools and universities avoid any in-depth study of socialist history, our students conveniently never see what they must see. How will they grow to make informed decisions when they are uninformed?

History will also teach us that an assault on civil liberties is just the first step in securing the economic dominance of the ruling class. This is typically done by denying the concept of "property" as a universal right. Instead, members of the "ruling class" and the "great leader" (known as the Chief, Fuhrer, General Secretary, or Great Leader, to name a few) secure untouchable status for the members or "guides" of the "ruling class." These self-professed "rulers" must not be confused with the so-called "ruling class" itself. In fact, socialist "rulers" never intermingle with the masses in real life. Not even with the "ruling class."

Rather, the proverbial "ruling class" exists as a pretext for true despotic rulers to assert the veracity of the source of their power. So, the masses of common "ruling class" people are ruled by their messiah-like leaders who are not in a hurry to stand in line for food with the rank-and-file proletarians. The "ruling class" becomes a group of useful idiots reduced to the role of eternal beggars and immature dependents. They must permanently ask for "favors" and graciously praise the crumbs swept their way from the chosen's luscious tables.

As Russia continues the tradition of Soviet stratification-rearranging people into different classes-a new development occurs. Unlike the former Soviet Union, which functioned based on privilege, now money also enables the ruling class to distance itself from the commoners by their ability to buy luxuries. Their source of power now- is a widely accepted term, "Rashism" (though I prefer my term "Parashism"), a blending of Nazi-like superiority of the so-called "Russian cause" with hatred for the "morally inferior" rest of the world. Now it seems that to justify their ingenuity and hard labor in keeping that balance. Rulers must be vested and "blessed" with unmatched luxury and wealth, which of course is essentially stolen from the rest of the country.

Remember-taking from those who have worked hard for what they own and assigning it to others as the authorities decide. Otherwise known as "redistribution" in favor of those in power.

The pretentious luxury of socialist bureaucrats accentuates their status as being above the law. An example is seen in the seized opulent yachts of Russian oligarchs. Think of it as the "chief's headdresses" with as many expensive and striking "feathers" as possible. Think of it as a mixture of the golden chains worn by rappers coupled with Teflon-like accountability for any legal or social responsibility, tact, or conscience. The only difference is the current Russian elite prefers golden toilets to golden necklaces. Go figure!

For the self-righteous members of the Soviet and now Russian "ruling elite," it is deemed unacceptable and embarrassing to commingle with the plebians that they profess to represent, such as taking public transportation or being seen in the grocery store. So, the autocrats have created two separate worlds-one is drilled into the public psyche through television propaganda that would make Goebbels blush, and the other who enjoys their preeminent privilege totally removed from the miseries of the public.

Imagine, if you will, that Elton John held a concert in Moscow and a bullet-proof box was built right in the middle of the bleachers so the identity of the "main fan" or his proximity to the miserable commoners all around him wouldn't be revealed. This is a far cry from pictures of Sanna Marin, the Prime Minister of Finland, walking around at a rock festival without visible guards (though they were surely there), or numerous European high-ranking politicians actually riding their bicycles to work.

|| *Unlike the virtue-signaling case of arrogant, largely incompetent Pete Buttigieg, who had his bike dropped from an SUV near his office, and took months of vacation or paternity leave while the country's transportation infrastructure was in trouble and needed professional and competent care.*

Putin's distance from reality and his people is even longer than his infamous 60-foot tables.

|| *This may not be that far apart from the arrogance of U.S. politicians in imposing mask restrictions on others and then blatantly ignoring them, including Newsom, o'Blasio, Cuomo, Pelosi, and, lest we forget Obama's famous birthday. And, of course, the pinnacle of hypocrisy is found in Cori Bush. While supporting the lunacy of defunding the police, the two-faced Ms. Bush demanded private security for herself. Her reasoning? "I have private security because my body is worth being on this planet right now." Seems quite self-righteous to me. According to Ms. Bush, I suppose our bodies, or the bodies of our children and grandchildren, or the bodies of innocent kids killed in drive-by shootings in Chicago, are "less worthy ...?"*

My American brothers and sisters, you could not write a better script, even for Trotsky or Lenin. In case you are unfamiliar, they are *remembered for their infamous disregard for the lives of others, so long as the "chosen ones" in the Russian government could pursue 'higher' goals without a care. Ms. Bush's haughty self-importance sounds frighteningly familiar.*

This is a perfect example of exactly what socialism is about. When resources are scarce for one reason or another, the "chosen ones" will not share that scarcity with you. And, believe me, under socialist policies, shortages *always* come. It's just a matter of time.

Since family loyalty means nothing to them and they have absolutely no personal reasons to make things better for everyone else, they never embrace the reality or value of family. You must understand, to Russia's "chosen ones," family is an unnecessary reality thriving in the horrible, antagonist West. Sanctions on Putin's surroundings following the war with Ukraine made it even more difficult. Again, they live essentially on a different planet than their subjects. If they follow any rules, I assure you they are *not* the same rules they created for the masses.

In the socialist world, scarcity of resources actually makes the socialist swamp creatures more valuable. The "chosen" control others by rationing and redirecting resources and favors. Their purpose? To create a subservient eternal circle of grateful masses dependent on their peaceful Big Brother.

Well, it's ... *mostly peaceful,* as Ukraine recently found out.

At the same time, the Left contrived "great causes" such as the Great Revolution, Greater Germanic Reich, Cultural Revolution, Denazification of Ukraine, or the Red/Green New Deal with its $3 trillion "infrastructure" fig leaf. Inflation would probably be approaching 20% by now if that bill hadn't been torpedoed in the Senate. They do this to give the impression they are preoccupied with something of perceived social value for someone other than themselves. Nothing could be further from the truth. These goals are nothing more than "feel-good" slogans, known today as virtue signaling. As we called it in the army, they act as "occupational therapy." It's an old ploy. To make sure you don't get dragged into doing hard work, you make yourself look busy with something that creates a lot of commotion but, in the end, produces no results that can be verified or expected.

I remember the first advice I got from a seasoned soldier in the army. He enlightened me on how to keep myself out of trouble and extra work with this advice: Avoid additional tasks. Never walk straight. Always walk bent or even doubled down. People will think you're either sick or picking up trash!

In other words, if you can't-or won't-do something useful, invent a Sisyphus type of labor for yourself and display the utmost effort at it. If anything, those socialists must always resort to creating vain artificial problems, such as (mis-)use of pronouns and overblown isolated events until they become problems, i.e., "systemic" racism or sexism in the 21st century Western world. It was exactly that *modus operandi* that elected Barack Obama as U.S. President and set the long-dormant racism issue afire again.

Due to the Left's innate inability to understand causation, combined with their arrogance toward the "boring" daily stuff that causes misery for the masses, actual social issues such as rising crime and war-like casualties in inner cities do not ring a bell with the BLM movement or its supporters.

They are equally indifferent to economic failures. As an example, watch for the exodus of frustrated citizens from California and the lack of reaction or compassion from authorities. These hot-button topics, such as growing crime, homelessness, and out-of-control costs, simply do not matter to the elite. Thus, issues do not register on their radar until it's too late to fix them.

Putin is another prime example. With inherent selfish and vain ambitions, he believes he is building the Third Roman Empire.

Instead, in the view of the civilized world, he has ended up trying to resurrect the Third Reich.

Obviously, we do not deny the existence of racism or sexism. But it begs an important question: Is the nebulous "white rage" represented by fringe and marginalized groups really a greater threat than tragedies such as hundreds of minority murders in Chicago, hundreds of thousands dead from fentanyl infiltrating through our porous borders, or the terrorism and atrocities associated with Islamic religious fundamentalism? Can we really assert in good conscience that "white rage" by a few crazies is our greatest threat?

Using similar tactics, when Soviet leaders were asked questions about any actual human rights or social issues in the Soviet Union, the typical diversionary responses were: "What about the suppression of black Americans?" or "Freedom to Angela Davis!" Ms. Davis was a black activist arrested as an accomplice to murder, which then made her a martyr of the socialist cause. Putin and Lukashenko have employed the exact same tactics in both civil and war management.

|| *A carbon copy of those same tactics is frequently employed by the current Biden administration. As an example, when President Biden is asked about any problems at the border, he answers by diverting attention to the disproven and non-existent flogging of immigrants by border patrol agents. In this way, he avoids the intent of the question— uncontrollable migration, lack of vaccination, and the surge of illegal border crossing.*

When gas prices go up 40%, the Biden administration blames anything and everyone, including predictably Trump, and now Putin's war. However, he happily accentuates and makes a flashy visual graph showing a miraculous 2-cent decline. This diversion hides the fact that the Left completely ignores real issues.

This tactic is the heart and soul of "big state" governance and the sole operational mode by incompetent and impractical socialists. At the time when Biden was supposed to be the "adult in the room," his administration vigorously denied even the existence of the problem, let alone taking any effort to suggest a meaningful solution.

Pay attention to what you are seeing. The Left is demonstrating the attitudes and results of "big state" government-pursuing "deals" while covering them with exalted but empty rhetoric.

No wonder another leftist comrade, Vladimir Putin, spent hours and hours at "town halls" answering calls from all around Russia. By listening to complaints about mundane issues such as broken water pipes (which were typically heroically fixed at the President's steadfast direction), Putin was able to ignore systemic social issues of corruption, fraudulent elections, failing economy, encroachment on liberties, and total degradation of social institutions. While the common people were fooled and thrilled about the appearance that someone actually cared about their mundane issues, their very lives were being threatened by devastating social issues. Still, they eagerly relied on the phone call at the next public stunt.

The parallels between such charades once exhibited and boasted by former Eastern Bloc Communists and now exhibited by the "Sovok-style" President Biden occupying the White House are uncanny. And it should be disconcerting.

Curiously, when Alexander Lukashenko was slammed with European sanctions, he instituted a state scheme of flying Iraqis and other Middle Eastern refugees to Belarus. Acting in spite of the European authorities, he even made money along the way. I personally witnessed the organized process while flying to Belarus through Turkey. Then he shoved them through the northern border to Lithuania, an EU territory. In this way, he made money coyote-style, to the tune of $3K to $8K per person. As an extra bonus, this was an explicit means of retribution against the EU for sanctions.

After a few hundred illegal immigrants successfully crossed the border in such a manner, Lithuania declared the situation a "crisis." They built walls around the borders with barbed-wire fences, and heightened their security personnel. It's ironic that in the U.S. when hundreds of thousands of illegals pour across the border, the Biden administration refers to a real crisis as simply a "situation."

After the Chernobyl nuclear disaster, when Soviet officials discovered their meat in the Soviet Union was contaminated with radiation, Communist rulers decided on a plan by a secret directive. Failing to meet their "production plan" due to a shortage of meat was not an option. Rather than destroying the contaminated food, they secretly decided on an alternative plan. They would "dilute" the effects of radiation poisoning by redistributing the contaminated meat "equitably" around the Soviet Union regions. You see, in a socialist society, you equitably share the miseries with the vast majority because society is seen as the army of builders of the (very distant) bright future.

There was, however, one region excepted from their secret plan. No poisoned meat was redistributed to residents of Moscow. Their plan specifically excluded that region. Are you wondering why, or have you figured it out? That's where all the "chosen ones" lived.

Similarly, nowadays, a Russian family receives about 1 million rubles (about $20,000) in the case of death of their relative in the war in Ukraine. However, if the death concerns a family of the "chosen ones" from Moscow, then you get 3 million. Well, according to George Orwell, all animals are equal, but some animals are more equal than others.

Putin certainly pursued a policy of genocide against Ukraine through a clear directive to erase everything and anything Ukrainian. However, he also essentially implemented genocide against various minority nationalities of the Russian Federation, which represent more desolate and poor areas. In fact, people from Buryatia or Tuva are now 80 times more likely to die in the Ukrainian war.

|| *Does that "more equal than others" attitude remind you of the situation in the U.S. with illegal immigration? Texas was forced to suffer the brunt of the ramifications of illegal immigration. But when they bussed a few hundred illegal immigrants into so-called "sanctuary" cities in Washington and New York, their Democratic mayors cried "wolf" and called the Texan move a "political stunt" that placed undue pressure on the social systems. So, in essence, these "sanctuary" cities are in name only. Yet again, they are not ready to live up to their virtue-signaling, socialistic declarations. That seems to be the most distinctive feature of socialists where lip service prevails at all times and all costs.*

When the Democrats support illegal immigration, that support only applies while they are insulated. When large groups of illegal immigrants actually show up on their doorsteps in their neighborhoods, suddenly, they lose their affection for the cause. America obviously welcomes immigration. But it has to be legal and controlled. We can't expose our country to an uncontrollable population increase and invasion led by drug dealers and human traffickers.

One of my friends ended up working for the Environmental Prosecutor's office. An office of this kind was established in the aftermath of Chernobyl in Belarus. Seeing firsthand "socialist equity" in action, my friend was kicked out of work when he punched a driver who was redirecting poisoned meat from a restaurant to a state-run kindergarten. Wisely, after the Chernobyl disaster in 1986, most newly-created private establishments in Belarus acquired radiation detectors. Sadly, that wisdom did not extend to protecting children. Neither state schools nor kindergartens were able to acquire radiation detectors. Socialism shows no favoritism to children or the weak. Only to those who are privileged by their own self-declared virtue signaling or "selfless service to the high cause." Remember that.

|| *In the same clandestine manner, the Biden administration hauled illegal immigrants on red-eye flights around the country, imposing a huge burden on local communities which were forced to absorb the brunt of the social impact.*

Imagine the impact on your community if hundreds of illegal immigrants suddenly arrived secretly in the night and found their way into your public services, hospital emergency rooms, grocery stores, etc. It's interesting they were not hauled to any communities where politicians or their generous donors lived. And all this fuss for a simple "situation" not even deemed a crisis.

Americans are passionate people, but America has limits as to how many illegal people it can absorb before being diluted to a third-world country itself. There are certainly legal ways of immigrating to the U.S. One has to wonder why illegals get priority simply based on the proximity of our southern border to their path while people from other oppressed or poor countries who happen to live across the ocean do not receive such favor.

The agricultural land in the Soviet Union was so heavily contaminated by pesticide overuse that the Soviet government imported shiploads of "clean manure" from foreign countries. This clean "fertilizer" was to be used on the farms where food was grown for the Party's "apparatchiks." Of course, the masses were not included. Literally, the Soviet Union, the country boasting its first space flight, was not even able to produce good "crap." Thus, the good manure was not redistributed for its equitable effect around the country.

Ironically, the only good "crap" the Soviets could distribute to the masses was in the form of rotten TV propaganda produced by then-Soviet authorities and now by Putin and Lukashenko. This is particularly true during the current war with Ukraine and the suppression of peaceful protests in Belarus following fraudulent elections. Any dissent against the war is severely punished.

By now, you are seeing the pattern. In a socialist society, suffering and the consequences of socialist disasters are always laid upon the common people. Never will the immoral individuals who make those stupid decisions feel the painful effects on their bodies. Much like the arrogant Cori Bush, they consider their bodies to be "more important." Surely we common people see the value in this arrogant perspective. If anything were to happen to those chosen bodies, who would be there to conceive, contrive, and carry out the immoral secret plans designed to ease the plight of the helpless and destitute commoners? After all, aren't we the bright future builders of communism?

One of the most recent examples of how one leader can move a people away from freedom to total dominance of their economic and social life by the ruling few is modern-day Russia. After the fall of the USSR, Russia went from a seemingly free society into a backward slide, right back to a socialist or even a fascist-like country. All during Putin's 20-year reign. One leader can indeed move an entire people into misery and also threaten their neighbors and even the entire world with extermination, or at least old-fashioned feudal submission.

Similarly, Belarus went into full "purge-like" socialist suppression mode in every aspect of its society. In August of 2020, when it became clear that the current ruler of Belarus could not win a free election and was incapable of staging any resemblance of a vote count beyond an eventual shameless self-proclaimed win, all remnants of the rule of law were set aside. Yet another leader can indeed move an entire people into misery. Lukashenko treated his country Belarus similar to the purge-like times of Stalin where any form of protest rewarded you with a long prison sentence. What shocked me during my last visit to Belarus in 2021 was the sense of hopelessness and despair in the eyes of the young people. Once upon a time, in 2020 in particular, they really believed their vote could matter, could change their country, and could even end its tyrannical path.

While proponents of socialism try to portray it as cozy, "fascism" is, in fact, still used as a derogatory term. Despite being rooted in the same principles as socialism, fascism is often mischaracterized as a far-right-wing ideology–one of the most misleading falsehoods of the 20th century. The Italian term "fascism" refers to "fascio," or a "bundle of rods." This symbolizes common goals and power through unity and supremacy. Hence, "common goals" take precedence over individual interests and freedoms.

Can you see the symbolism in the "community/communism" of fascism? And the dominance of the state over an individual is the core of any left-wing ideology to varying degrees. Whether it is named socialism, communism, or fascism, at its core is predominance of the ideological goals of the state over personal liberties and economic freedoms.

Certainly, fascism (and its extension Nazism, or *National Socialism*) got its unquestionably bad reputation due to its association with Hitler. Remember, the victors write history. Hitler's ruthless and raucous policies, his insatiable appetite for war, and his explicit and undeniable racism against Untermensch–a term for *under-humans*, which included Slavs and Jews and resulted in the Holocaust and mass murders–strongly influenced the extremely negative perception and attitude toward fascism.

Hitler hated the freedoms of capitalism with the same passion as Stalin. That seems to be a commonality amongst ruthless socialist leaders. As history shows, Stalin and the Soviet Union eventually fought Nazism and defeated it.

Another commonality is death of innocent people. Tens of millions of people were lost due to the military and economic incompetence of the Soviet rulers. It seems this fact turned an evil victor, Stalin, into somewhat of a positive character in the eyes of

Western liberals while keeping the loser, Hitler, in eternal disdain. By their evil core beliefs, however, these two proved to millions of suffering people that they were two sides of the same coin.

Considering that Hitler was pure evil for the entire world, the reputation of Stalin (and Soviet socialism by association) for fighting such pure evil appeared to create for him a more favorable image. This was particularly aided when he joined Western democracies in the fight against Hitler, considering that the Soviet Union and Nazi Germany were allies for the first two years of WWII. The Germans later admitted their guilt and charged Nazi criminals, who were then either jailed or executed. The German nation repented for the sins of their grandfathers, with the next generation of children taking mandatory school trips to view the concentration camps.

After the war, the German nation went on to embrace Western-style democracy, but not without the benefits of the Marshall Plan. They became one of the most advanced modern societies. This closed the prior chapter of their history, hopefully for good.

This is not the case with the Soviet Union or Russia, however. Perhaps because they neither recognized their sins nor repented for them. In fact, it is illegal now to do so publicly. I guess this is the Russian version of cancel culture. The big difference is that it's not about canceling or criticizing socialism. Rather, punishment from Belarusian and Russian authorities only comes for critiquing or drawing parallels between Soviet socialism or despotism and its German alter-ego.

Imagine that a high school student named Victor Savinykh and several of his classmates were convicted in 1940 and sent to Gulags to serve a 10-year prison sentence. Their crime? "Counter-revolutionary conspiracy." They simply wrote a letter to Stalin complaining that sending grain to the Nazis was inappropriate when the Soviet people were suffering from famine. It seems surreal to us. However, voicing your opinion against German fascism–even by teenage students concerned about their country–was a crime in the Soviet Union up until the German invasion, much like voicing your concerns about neo-Nazism raising its head in contemporary Russia.

The Nazis certainly deserve a bad name. These types of repressions and atrocities against their own people are both openly and silently hailed by Putin, Lukashenko, and other contemporary communists. Even in the context of opposing assistance to Nazis, shouldn't they be similarly condemned?

No NKVD/KGB "karateli" ("executioners") were convicted or even deprived of their pensions. While Lenin was the main perpetrator of bloody terrorism on his own people, his statues are still everywhere. Lenin's mummy is actually in the mausoleum on the Red Square, though Stalin's mummy has been removed. Even in death their atrocities are still celebrated. There are Russian and Belarusian cities and streets today that still bear the names of people guilty of genocide against their own people.

Why is it important to rehash all that disturbing past history? Because the chilling truth is that Lenin's ominous evil and disturbing influence is alive and well right now in both Russia and Belarus. A clear example of that influence is Russia's war waged mercilessly and purposelessly against the innocent people of Ukraine. Current opposition to the civilized order and achievement of the Western world is challenged by Lenin's notions and principles. Most people do not realize that the term "concentration camp" was Lenin's idea. The concept of gathering dissenters behind barbed wire was Lenin's idea, later perfected by Stalin.

All those concentration camps were built as an opportunistic endeavor for a "happy" society and equity. That was the biggest Left-wing misnomer and scam, to label the fascist societies of Germany and Italy as "right-wing" societies. Perhaps "*National Socialism*," or Nazi, should have been the first clue.

If you were to compare the main characteristics of fascism and socialism, particularly as implemented in real life, you would discover they are virtually identical. Consider their so-called "benefits"– suppression of free society and liberty, elimination of free media, supremacy of state interests over those of individuals, subversion of elections, vertically-integrated cronyism, corruption rampant ultra-nationalism, aggressive militaristic patriotism, obsession with security (which results in over-empowering military and law enforcement to commit atrocities with impunity), and searching for enemies within and outside as the core unifying cause.

However, all was not equal. There were two discernable differences between Lenin/Stalin socialism and Hitler/Mussolini fascism. First, Hitler/ Mussolini fascism declared war on certain nationalities–Jews and Slavs in particular. In addition, fascism recognized that state ownership was inefficient. So, they technically allowed private property, but made sure it was under complete control of the state and the party, thereby creating a relatively efficient pre-war economy. Hitler favored economic Darwinism against "bureaucratic management of the economy." Well-known companies such as Krupp, Porsche, Hugo Boss, Volkswagen, Audi (which was called Horch at the time and renamed after the war into a loose Latin version of the German word), and the like bloomed under Hitler. Ultimately, they became the engine and foundation of his war machine.

It should be noted that even though socialists have a similar disdain for "upper" classes, entrepreneurs, and intelligentsia, their hatred is not directed at "nations." Socialism, as well as Nazism, hates a way of life–individual freedom and autonomy.

The current Russian and Belarusian regimes, with their rulers overstaying their posts for at least two decades, both evolved from relatively promising but unstable free societies into full-blown Soviet-like systems. In essence, after short-lived free societies in the 1990s, they crept back, evolving into full-blown fascist societies, complete with an inefficient state-run economy.

Indeed, in building his version of the neo-Soviet Union, Putin effectively wiped out both differences between Stalin's and Hitler's societies. First, he substituted Hitler's efficient economy with the riches of an oil-driven economy. Second, he slapped a nationalistic sentiment on top of it, culminating in a clear demonstration of disdain for Ukrainians and their innate desire to live in a free democratic society.

Supported by his lapdog lackey from Belarus, Putin directed his military aggression against a free sovereign state and did so on a very specific date- February 24, the birthday of Hitler's Nazi Party in 1920. (NSDAP - National Socialist German Workers' Party). The symbolism was not overlooked by the Ukrainian people who are the current targets of his 2022 military aggression. It was they who quickly coined the term "Rashism," a Russian version of fascism.

The Jews could not have even conceded to the ideology to become the representatives of the Arian nation simply due to their "wrong" heritage. It should be noted that the current Leftist *modus operandi* of identifying themselves as someone they are not was not even available at the time of the Nazi regime. In other words, due to the size of their nose or the color of their eyes, one could not just say to Gestapo, the Nazi secret police, "I identify as a German woman or a straight Arian man." Arbitrary "tests" were used by the Germans to determine who had the right "heritage" and who did not.

Ukrainians were appallingly degraded to second-grade sub-human status by Putin. Yet, they steadfastly refused to shed their identity, language, or pride at the whim of their aggressive neighbor, who single-handedly assumed the role of the ultimate eastern make-believe genealogical "historian." Ukrainians, led by heroic President Zelensky, essentially defended Western civilization, countering Putin's insatiable craving for ever-expanding power.

Putin's craving for world superiority is coupled with his bloodthirsty obsession–no matter what the price–to bond or even merge former subjects and colonies of Moscovites under one incoherent, poorly managed formation of the "Russian World." Remember, 25% of Russian homes do not have toilets with running water! With his aggressive xenophobia, bashing of homosexuals, and imitating fascism and socialism in the worst possible manner, this reincarnated "creature" has no underlying public-spirited principles of operations, no redeemable human value, no economic coherence or governance structure. His claim to conservatism and defending traditional values is virtually limited to promoting traditional Russian family structure and values.

In the words of Russian propaganda by the devil himself–the Western culture of "Parent Number One and Parent Number Two." The critique of the conservative movements in the West is often mixed with a "Putin-like" defense of the traditional family. However, unlike the conservatives in the West, Russian propaganda actually denies the values of individualism, human liberties, freedom, and even life itself. Remember, in Kremlin propaganda the lives of Russians are "overvalued, which makes Putin's alleged "conservatism" pretentious and phony.

By the same token, you cannot be deemed an ally of Hitler just because you, like Hitler, are fond of beer. Thus, fighting for "traditional family values" cannot be the single unifying factor of "conservatism" since Western conservatism is deeply rooted in individual freedom–the element that all socialists, and Putin in particular, loathe. Add to it an even fuzzier "moral superiority of the "traditional Russian world," coupled with the strong-hand of the righteous Big Brother. What do you get? Modern day merciless hordes of Hun that must be halted by the civilized world.

When I try to argue with Russian "whataboutists" (who stress Western hypocrisy) about its ill-designed military conflicts, they are typically stumped by this question: Other than hatred toward the (hypocritical) West, what does the "Russian World" bring to the world? Could it be social progress? Perhaps a booming economy? Education? Medicine? Wealth? Internet? Ballet? At least vodka?

The true answer is virtually nothing of value beyond the efforts and ingenuity of individuals who work hard and desire to be integrated into the contemporary world--even the famous Stoly is produced outside of Russia. The contemporary Russian state, having an aura of oil-driven wealth for its elite, brings nothing to its neo-colonies in terms of economic or social development. It doesn't even bother to make promises or design any semblance of social or economic plans or benefits--other than the proverbial middle finger to the evil West. It simply boasts the same old story. Russia's ultimate justification for any of its aggressive, vicious actions is its vague proclamations of "self-righteousness" and contrived "historic necessity" and the hypocrisy of the big bad West.

Why would Ukrainians, who have known and enjoyed true freedom, ever willingly trade their freedom and future for slave-like submission, turning themselves into obedient vassals of an authoritarian egomaniac? Naturally, and quite heroically, Ukrainians are putting up a fierce fight at great sacrifice for the very things that many Western people take for granted. Even worse, these Westerners, who sadly take their abundance of freedoms for granted, are *willing to relinquish them voluntarily*, without a fight or a second thought, for the sake of socialistic virtue-signaling "common purposes" repeated endlessly by Leftist leaders. Sounds to me much like Putin's "historic necessities."

To be fair, in our comparison of the two systems, however, while Nazis weren't exactly known for being frugal, the yachts and palaces that Putin, Lukashenko, and their loyal cronies have built for themselves are probably worth at least two formidable Wehrmacht's armies. So, such Russian corruption indeed served as a blessing-in-disguise for the Ukrainians. You see, their courage and valor **are** now strongly "supported" by Russia's abysmal corrupted "Potemkin-village" army, headed by a former deer shepherd who rose to be Minister of Defense due to his loyalty to Putin.

While Germany and Japan atoned for their past sins by painful confessions, Russia, on the other hand, continues protectively hiding, twisting, and changing its past, particularly everything that relates to the brutalities of socialism. Russia's intention is to avoid drawing damaging parallels with the present cruel regimes. Ironically, the horrendous atrocities of its present are killing its future. No wonder the archives from WWII and the "purges" of the 1930s are still classified. This silence and concealment of facts effectively contribute to the "beautification" of the Soviet regime and socialism, which are now followed as direct role models.

Just as an example, Svetlana Aleksievich, a Belarusian writer, was awarded a Nobel Prize for literature. However, her achievements and works are not taught in Russia or Belarus nor mentioned in any textbooks. Why? Because her writing revealed the horrors of socialism forced by the Soviet Union upon Eastern Europe during and after WWII.

It's no surprise the accounts of atrocities leaking from Ukraine today reek of the same horrors. No surprise that they are denied as "fakes" by Russia with the same audacity as WWII atrocities described in Aleksievich's books or the facts gathered by the Memorial Foundation created by Dmitry Sakharov. It's no surprise Putin subsequently shut the foundation down.

Just imagine if the children in Russia were taught actual history, allowed to see the bad things that happened in their country's past, and inspired not to repeat them. Just maybe this merciless war on Ukraine with its gut-wrenching consequences of destruction and death, especially of children, could have been averted. And any subsequent horrors yet to come.

Contemporary society loosely and jokingly uses the terms 'Nazi' and 'fascist.' Remember the famous 'Soup Nazi' in Seinfeld, a popular American comedy? The expression, "This is a fascist contract!" describes the rough-natured message or demeanor. These humorous and sarcastic references can be somewhat excessive. They're rarely done in good taste. It's certainly painful for those whose families suffered under fascism. Belarusians lost one-fourth of their population due to fascist aggression. Therefore, unless its use is truly justified, as in describing a craving to exterminate the Ukrainian nation, you would not hear the word "Nazi" in jest from a Belarusian. The massive losses caused by Stalin are still uncounted, but certainly no less painful and no less consequential.

However, what is more troublesome is the fact that the media and academia describe someone like Trump and his followers as "fascist" or "worse than Hitler," etc. That means they consider all right-leaning voters to be "fascists." That should worry many voters. Despite the typical over-the-top tendencies and required hyperbole of mass media in broadcasting their messaging, there is a key point here that must not be ignored. Those who defend capitalism and America's freedoms–typically right-leaning voters-- are on the opposite end of the spectrum from those who want to propel the state toward overwhelming control--typically left-leaning voters. We must do a better job of educating our children to realize and truly comprehend that.

In simple words, a child could understand that those who want America to run freely under capitalism are at one end--and those who want America to be run by fascism or communism are at the opposite end. They remain worlds apart.

When colleges are unwilling, from a historical perspective, to show the historical "excesses" of the Left, the natural defensive mechanism is to blame the other side for the sins that *your socialist side* did. Socialism. Fascism. Nazism. They are evil triplets born to the same parents. We could think of it this way--their father is the supremacy of the state, and their mother is shrinking personal liberty. They are a perfect genetic blend of their parents.

These lessons were taught to the American public once upon a time. They need to be taught to our children today. Even ten years ago, labeling someone a "socialist" was deemed a derogatory remark. And rightly so.

All the efforts of the leftists to destroy capitalism and whitewash the social plague of communism have brought about dangerous changes in perception among some Americans, particularly the younger voting generation. Fancy socialism "packaging" has caused a dangerous growing infatuation in our land. Socialism now seems acceptable. Even desirable. This is exactly where we must focus our education and our fight for the souls of our youth.

Again, studying history in our schools would shed a bright revealing light on socialism that our children must see. It's no wonder the Left has held captive our school curriculum. Sadly, America's children are historically and, for the most part, logically illiterate.

Our next generation would learn the inherently evil nature of socialism in a broad social sense. Hopefully, they would see through the media "packaging" and realize that socialism inevitably brings misery to the daily lives of the innocent. Just ask the millions like me who lived it and still remember.

Capitalism has given hope to millions of people since its inception, with America as its pinnacle. But its history has not been flawless. Two primary examples of its blemishes are the mistreatment of Native Americans and slavery. There are numerous reasons why America and its flag became the symbol of freedom and success for people worldwide. That symbol continues as a beacon today, despite its rising disrespect among the Left.

Again, a critical study and view of American history by our students is an absolute must. Teaching an appreciation and gratitude for America's vast achievements and how they are freely enjoyed in the daily comforts of her citizens is as important as revealing the atrocities of socialism. We owe it to our children today, and the next generation of children that will follow them.

Historical "memory loss" is both shortsighted and dangerous. It deprives this new "participation trophy for everyone" generation of valuable knowledge that would otherwise enable them to operate and succeed in a fact-based, result-oriented society. Success requires reasoning, merit, ingenuity, and effort. No one rewards you for doing nothing. "Free stuff" always comes with a price. In real life, everyone doesn't get a trophy. Only the winner. Everyone else is forced to work on improving their skills and getting better--unless they got a trophy anyway. In other words, losing is inevitable. Losing is also healthy. We deal with it and work at getting better. Our loss is not everyone else's problem. *It's our problem.*

When you know the actual history of America, you know that the trespassing on the Capitol on January 6, 2021, while pointless and irrational, was not "worse than the Civil War." Hundreds of thousands of Americans died in the Civil War for the primary purpose of abolishing the horror of slavery. In simple words, they died to make someone other than themselves free.

When you know the actual history of America, you know that people who refuse to vaccinate, including due to natural immunity or religious beliefs, are not "terrorists." You understand that such a reference should be reserved for true terrorist activities. What are terrorist activities? Torture and murder of innocent victims around the world. Mostly "peaceful" burnings of buildings in American towns like a courthouse or police station. Violent destructive looting of American cities. "Terrorist" references should be squarely reserved for American modern history events such as 9/11 or the Boston bombing.

I was on an airplane approaching New York on September 11, 2001. While I was obviously not on one of "those" planes, the pain and anguish that my family and I felt on that horrendous day still lives with us. For security reasons, we were not told what had happened while we were on the airplane. We didn't learn that until we landed a few hours later in Gander, Canada. However, feeling your plane make a 180-degree turn and fly toward the northern pole to "nowhere" causes anxiety. When our Virgin Airlines flight attendants were suddenly visibly distraught but silent, I knew something terrible had happened. I made the (logical at the time) conclusion that we had been hijacked. After writing a farewell note to my family, I pulled out a knife. Yes, you could still fly with a knife then. I was ready for the worst.

Luckily, all 38 airplanes that landed in Gander, Newfoundland that day with over 8,000 passengers were greeted with gracious Canadian hospitality by five thousand of Gander's inhabitants.

That experience was unforgettable for many reasons. Bear cutlets brought by the locals, along with warm clothes. Showers in the hockey locker room. There was a wide selection of hockey gear at Walmart, which was unusual for the U.S. (well, hockey is a religion in Canada, Eh?). Sleeping on the floor in the biology classroom using posters as pillows. Having been in the air during that catastrophic time made the tragedy more relevant. Truly, a somber reminder of "Russian Roulette" so close to home.

However, not all the people in the world had a similar reaction. Some countries cheered along the lines of "America, the world's bully, deserved it!

Even among our allies, compassion was clearly lacking. The airlines were busy trying to send their aircraft home back to Europe, along with us, claiming that this was required by law. That statement was a total lie, easily established in a Canadian school library with the Internet. Talking to a representative of Virgin Airlines, I did lose my temper. I mentioned to this UK airline that I am an American and Belarusian. I might have reminded them that if it wasn't for America, the Brits would probably be speaking German today! A weary British member of Parliament who faithfully stayed with us at the library's floor commented on my zealous efforts, "No wonder [Bela]russians were revolutionaries." But that day, when Americans were in need, all the airline cared about was jacking up the prices in London's hotel. By some reports, considering thousands of Americans were stranded on the other side of the pond, prices skyrocketed from 300% to as much as 500%. They cared only about their stupid airplanes.

My perception at that time was that we were on the brink of a new war. Traveling by land from Canada to reunite with family (potentially a 70-hour trip) still appeared to be a better choice than joining stranded people in Europe. So, indeed, I bought tickets all the way to Montreal-a two-day trip from Gander, assuming I could get from there back home to Virginia. The tickets were never refunded.

Frustrated by the airline's stubbornness and heartlessness, I collected signatures of the passengers who "wished to reunite with their families" and faxed them to various news outlets. There were a few of those 20 years ago. After that, the airlines took note and appeared to heed our demands. Five days later, when the airspace opened up again, we were sent home to the United States.

About 12 hours after it happened, I finally saw footage of the two planes hitting the World Trade Center. It took that long for the people of Gander to move all the passengers from the planes into the city. I was probably one of the last people on Earth to see the heartbreaking footage. But I can tell you from first-hand experience that there are very, very few things in life "worse than 9/11."

It takes some courage to name a specific group or ideology as radical and evil. The recent attack on Salman Rushdie certainly points in the right direction--a threat, despite the radical Left failing to condemn radical Islamism. Again, "no enemies on the left."

Similarly, the term "racism" should apply squarely to actual racism. Today, it's casually thrown around for anything that is hard, unreachable, unpleasant, disagrees with one's perspective, hurts one's feelings, works to one's perceived disadvantage, or may have an unequal outcome due to various social or economic factors, even personal efforts or merits.

From a historical perspective, keeping the Taliban (or, as Biden calls them, a "professional business-like" organization) on Twitter while removing President Trump follows a typical pattern of prosecuting and censoring political opponents. They did it in Fascist Germany, the Soviet Union, North Korea, Putin's Russia, and Lukashenko's Belarus. Now, news outlets effectively merging with the Left have begun to practice similar harsh and biased censorship.

The burning of the Reichstag in Berlin in 1933 (which many viewed as a provocation by the Nazis) was, in historical fact, similar to the January 6th events. The U.S. media and the government have conveniently used the events of January 6th as an excuse to go after those who dared to ask questions about the irregularities of the 2020 elections or point out the utter incompetency of the Biden administration.

It is unfathomable that the people who looted and burned cities during the riots were released from prison. Many politicians, including Kamala Harris, actually bragged about their assistance in the bail process. Yet, the participants of the January 6th event were held without bail. While the actions that took place were stupid, irrational, and senseless, they were certainly lacking the violence exhibited by "mostly peaceful" protests. The charges actually brought against the participants of the January 6th event were "parading," and "trespassing," and "destruction of property." However, shooting an unarmed Air Force veteran, Ashli Babbitt, as much as CNN gloats about it, can hardly be described as necessary and may be viewed, in fact, as an example of excessive use of lethal force.

It is a curious parallel that 600+ people are deemed political prisoners in Belarus now for their protests against fraudulent elections, and similar numbers have resulted from the January 6th U.S. apprehensions. I find it interesting that when the threat comes to politicians, when there is a challenge to their corrupt or malfunctioning system, when their "house is on fire" (even figuratively, not literally as the case with Portland), then politicians take it seriously.

There also appears to be a typical propensity and appetite among the Left for disproportionate vengeance against anyone who dares to disagree with government actions. It doesn't matter whether or not any actual harm or damage is done. We do not condone any type of violence. However, if one were to look at the world's history of organized assaults or coups, these typically are armed and well-planned, with the intent to bring the results expected of "insurrections." The unruly protests on January 6th fell far short of such historical "insurrection" goals or results. Perhaps that's why no one was charged with insurrection. Perhaps that's why the FBI found no "conspiracy."

Actual "insurrections," particularly in light of the percentage of armed conservatives, would likely involve weapons, coordination, and projected outcomes. A spontaneous riot of angry citizens is something different. It is not an insurrection. Even though not always justifiable, such protests are typically the logical consequence of the suppression of people's voices and disregard for transparent legal processes.

The anger boiled over on January 6th when discussion and challenges to irregularities in the 2020 elections were suppressed. Social media and liberal channels rigged the elections by predetermining who should be the next president. Then, they carefully censored and subdued sensitive information capable of damaging candidate Joe Biden. This information included the story of Hunter Biden's laptop, as well as his shady Chinese, Ukrainian, Libya, and Russian dealings. At the same time, all social media deliberately suppressed conservative voices.

When we forget history, parallels will not be recognized. This is dangerous. For instance, the Christian Church and numerous prominent German scientists and philosophers embraced Nazism and Hitler. Today, the majority of Russian society recently welcomed Putin's bloody aggression on their peaceful neighbor Ukraine.

Let me explain why that happened. The Christian Church and prominent German scientists and philosophers believed and asserted, in an act of wishful thinking, that the adverse and inhumane consequences of Hitler's election and his regime *just could not happen in Germany*. Why? Because humanity had been so deeply rooted in German society for centuries through art, philosophy, and literature by works of Kant, Goethe, Hegel, Schopenhauer, Schiller, Wagner, and so many other intellectuals. Therefore, the German people expected that humanitarian history and traditions of civility would act as internal checks and balances against the abuse of power. They could not have been more wrong.

Similarly, many Russians, both the less educated and upper-class people, turned a blind eye to evident facts that would have distanced them from the war crimes and the pure evil of looting, annihilation, and torture. Why? Because they believed *or wanted to believe* Putin's psychopathic pseudo-history and his make-believe fairy tales about Ukrainian "Nazis." Again, the works of Tolstoy, Dostoevsky, Gogol, and Tchaikovsky deeply rooted in Russian society appeared to bear no influence on the sharp turning away from humanity, empathy, or compassion. Rather, the Russian people desired to be associated with pretentious plans to satisfy a moral void. Inflated egos ruled the day. Putin's fairy tale obliterated all of Russia's glorious past. It destroyed any hope for a Russian future that wouldn't be marred by the stigma of atrocities and war crimes. Perhaps saddest of all, it resulted in an inevitable embarrassing defeat at the hands of Ukrainians fighting fiercely for their country and freedom. And, frankly, for the rest of Western civilization.

Unfortunately, relying on history is not enough. Lessons learned from history require us to think rationally and act affirmatively. Russian and German historical philosophers and writers did not stand on the bloody paths of Hitler, Stalin, and now Putin. If anything, they were often used to justify their "higher calling," as with Freud, Kant, Mayakovski, and numerous contemporary Russian artists, pop artists, and classical musicians. Russian and Belarussian rock musicians, for the large part, stay true to their conscience and integrity. Yes, rock musicians lead again!

Another way history is misused is the twisting of events, traditions, and motives of historical figures and events to show a distorted version of history's course. From that distorted view, it is an easy leap to illogical connections or justification for wrong actions. As an example, the same strategy is used to put the blame on someone in contemporary society by making an attenuated connection to the past. These tactics are the mainstay of the Critical Race Theory curriculum the Left is trying to force into our schools today. Why teach accurate history that doesn't serve our agenda when we can simply twist history and teach students our version of truth? Which is really no truth at all.

The biggest weaponry of today's Left movement is the supposed "morality" of socialist ideology. That's an oxymoron if ever there was one. That is also one of the reasons that fascism gets a bad name for its explicit policies, while socialism is still seen as "cozy," so its atrocities are hidden.

Let me ask you a question: How do socialists really see you? Buckle up because this will sting. First, they view your entrepreneurship as self-indulgent. Yes, you get up every morning, work hard, and sacrifice to build a business. They say you are just indulging yourself. You are driven by your inferior materialistic desires.

Next, they view you as greedy. Yes, you desire to take care of your family, so you provide nice things for them. They say you're just greedy for more.

Next, you are an egotist. Yes, you work hard to pursue a better life for you and your children. Socialists see your pursuit as egotism.

Get ready for this one. They view you as a bigot. Your chivalry, punctuality, good manners, patriotism, willingness to open a door for someone, to say "Yes, ma'am" and "Yes, sir," and defend your rights are all evidence of being taught proper social graces. Socialists see this as pure bigotry.

Finally, perhaps the most cynical description in modern Leftist terms falls on your business savvy, your education, and your drive to succeed. Socialists hit that hard with a broad stroke of their cruel brush. "You are a racist!"

The key to their indoctrination of Americans is to convince you, the average law-abiding citizen, that you are actually a victim. Despite all your hard work and sacrifice, you have no control over your life, no responsibility, no matter what you do. And it's never your fault. *Nothing is ever your fault.* So, with no reason or incentive to do anything, you are a loser with a cause! A loser who needs someone wiser to take control of you.

Thus, it is prudent for you to surrender now and hand control of your life over to "Big Brother." After all, as you will discover when you "see the light," he knows much better how you should run your life "from the cradle to the grave." And he has the ever-growing state enforcement machine behind him. He can tear down anything or anyone who dares to go against the state. One very effective weapon used by the Left is to launch trends of repression, subduing people by force. Then, before you know it, a socialist society turns into a vicious circle--or a circular firing squad, if you wish. Turning brother against brother exacerbates those feelings of being a victim.

Before you know it, the people themselves are doing the work for Big Brother.

Americans are the largest charity donors in the world. We take care of those who are unable to take care of themselves. We strive to do our best, be the best, and give our best to others. This system encourages everyone to be the best and the brightest. Socialism, on the other hand, is a meritocracy. This means a select few of the most prophetic, most ruthless, and most successful in the political loyalty game run the country. It's the survival of the fittest mentality.

Rather than raising others up through charity, achievement, and good works, the socialist mindset shoves everyone down to the lowest common denominator. Once everyone becomes embittered as a victim and stops taking responsibility for their actions, the downward trend stifles society's actual progress. Socialism has a paralyzing effect on personal initiative. Rather than encouraging everyone to be their best, it encourages the worst behavior in humans. Character traits such as true patriotism, diligence, persistence, and honesty are replaced with snitching on others, tribal mindset, hatred toward outsiders, disdain for success, contempt toward personal freedoms, laziness, envy, passivity, and a doomsday mentality.

People gave birth in the Nazi and Lenin-style concentration camps with the hope that the next generation would survive and have a better life. Despite the high human price paid by that generation, their children indeed had a better life. The hysteria of that new generation in the 21st century caused a very different perspective. Some of that next generation, now grown-up "educated" adults, were so disenchanted and disgusted by the behavior of other humans that they actually expressed the desire not to have children at all. Why? Although they, too, wanted a better life for the next generation, they didn't see how that could happen. So they chose to avoid having children at all rather than placing children in the "terrible world" around them.

That is the result of victim mentality. People have no hope. They see life as nothing more than misery followed by the inevitable environmental apocalypse that has been predicted at least every 12 years for the past half century--and we are all miraculously still alive! As I think about it, in light of socialism's exaggerated meritocracy and Darwinism, maybe stupid people should not have children!

Naturally, the cult of a victim is being nurtured. We see it all around us today. We're encouraged to find some reasoning, logical or not, to be offended rather than making your life better through hard work or education. Marketing slogans such as *"You deserve it!"* and *"I'm worth it!"* contribute to the lunacy. It's so much easier to be offended.

There's always someone available to blame for the bad stuff. Just ask today's teachers. It used to be that if you got in trouble at school, you would be in trouble again when you got home from school. Your job was to go to school, learn, and make your family proud. Today, when a kid gets in trouble in school, no one believes the teacher. In fact, today, parents blame the teacher! The disrespectful kid is never held accountable. After all, they are now the eternal "victims." The kids have learned that lesson well, even if they learned nothing else in school. We can see where this kind of mindset has taken our schools.

The media has shrewdly used this mindset of being offended to push forward, among many other notions, its gender agenda. If you believe in actual science--and biology is science--there are more than 2,500 biological features distinguishing males from females. It is a scientific fact that the male human body cannot naturally get pregnant. It is also a fact that the female human body has no prostate and, thus, needs no prostate exams. There is no scientific reason for people to be offended by these simple biological, historical facts.

The science of sports is heavily based on physics, perseverance, and effort. When a child wants to do a triple twist in gymnastics, their ability to do so depends on their weight. Imagine a typical situation when the parents torment the gymnastics coach: "When will our kid be able to do the triple twist?" The coach *knows* that the kid is severely overweight. Unfortunately, even an attempt by an obese kid to do the jump is dangerous. The physics of some elements are such that extra weight would make them scientifically impossible. This explains why we don't see obese figure skaters doing quadruple jumps. We all know there are many hard-working people who struggle with extra weight. But extra weight only breaks legs. Not sports records.

There needs to be some accountability to reality, even though the child might be predisposed to obesity through genetics. Nevertheless, any coach who would vocalize the reality that the child is obese will be crucified in today's mindset. The coach cannot, dare not, simply state, "Your kid is fat." Somehow the coach has to be able to deliver the message that the child is overweight, and for the child's safety, the coach *will not* even teach the jump until the kid loses 15 pounds and stops chugging cokes and pizza. All this, of course, without being fired, chastised, or sued for insensitivity by offending either the parents, the kid, or both.

Here is another reality of today's "woke" sports. After a tumbling attempt, the kid lands on her head.

The coach approaches the kid and asks, "Do you want me to tell you what you did wrong so you can make it the next time, or do you want me to just tell you 'good job'?"

The kid replies, "Just tell me 'good job!'"

So, the coach exclaims, "Gooooood job!"

The kid goes home with a trophy clutched tightly in her hand, and she still can't do the tumbling routine.

Is that the society we want to live in? What are the long-term results when trophy kids grow up and become trophy airline pilots or trophy doctors? In accordance with Darwin's law, that society is doomed to be eliminated.

By the same token, however, the media continues gushing, "Good job, President Biden! Good job, Vice President Harris!"

We learn a great deal from a study of history. From studying the history of the women's rights movement, you learn that Ruth Bader Ginsburg was not only a Justice of the Supreme Court but one of the most prominent human beings and champions of women's rights. She was also instrumental in eliminating actual systemic discrimination against women in contemporary society. The masterminds of the ACLU do not think the movement for women's rights was important. Instead, they have now twisted Ginsburg's quote to read: "The decision whether or not to bear a child is central to a [person's] life, to [their] well-being and dignity."

So, from a historical perspective, when the ACLU replaces the word "woman" and female pronouns in RBG's actual quote with a neutral ["person,"], that is indeed appalling from both a historical and evolutionary perspective. It is degrading to women and to all who fought and often died, for equality for women. It is a dreadful demonstration of social insanity to imply that anyone but females can actually give birth naturally. It also implies that the ACLU thinks women are incapable of achieving this on their own and need some kind of social "booster seat."

Does the ACLU think Ruth Bader Ginsburg's words needed a helping hand from the enlightened "woke" movement? This undermines the fight for actual equality rather than made-up injustice over "hurt feelings." This is so close to Facebook fact-checking of Nobel Prize laureates that, who knows, one day they may even think the ACLU and IT Left-activists oligarchy follow the same Marxist playbook!

No wonder professional women and athletes, with the silent approval of the "woke," have now become "under people." In today's culture, in addition to the humiliating process of nominating people for positions because of their woke qualities rather than skill, the Left is killing women's athletics with their transgender agenda. The reality remains that those transgender "women" still carry male chromosomes--at least if we are talking about *actual* science and not the "pretend" science debacle.

Twenty years ago, if a biological male, as in the case of Lia Thomas, were nominated as "Woman of the Year," feminists and human rights activists would have lost their minds. And for good reason! Unfortunately, in today's world, losing one's mind has become much more widespread. Today, honoring a biological male as a woman is relatively normal--although it should not be.

Similarly, Katie Couric, a so-called journalist, decided to take it upon herself to censor RBG's speech because she spoke against 'kneeling.' Such haughty behavior is dangerous. It propagated the lies of the Left, belittled a beloved American heroine, and denigrated U.S. history, facts, and truth. More importantly, it solidified the division that already threatens our society. In Washington's partisanship culture today, "crossing the Party line" or extending a hand across the aisle is deemed treacherous to the "great cause."

For many of us who lived through it, this all sounds far too much like an overriding theme in communism. Rather than engage in productive discussion searching for harmony, and finding ways to unite, let's just tear our nation apart.

The history of humanity, particularly the social and economic discoveries, was not advanced by the stupid or frail. It was the daring, the bold, the bright who struggled and sacrificed for success. Today's environment is exactly the opposite. We encourage sheer stupidity, a narrow keyhole cultural perspective. We kill any initiative toward brilliance in academics by canceling and diminishing the roles played by math, homework, tests, or other academic performance criteria.

This is the exact opposite of Asian "Tiger moms." Their culture results in an overwhelming dominance in science by students with an Asian heritage. However, the "scholars" of liberalism in elite U.S. universities have instituted measures and regulations that discriminate against the admission of students of Asian descent.

Unfortunately for the "Reds," even the most learned Leftist "woke" proponents cannot attribute any such advances of Asian or African students to "white privilege." This type of so-called artificial "regulation" through discrimination against advanced students of the "wrong" color causes an imbalance in the social equilibrium. It also produces a chilling effect on education, including widespread discrimination against the achievements demonstrated by Asian American children. Reliance on government handouts breeds immaturity of thought and action and a lack of personal responsibility. The more severe the imbalance, the worse the adverse implications on a society that already expects a "free ride" rather than a merit-based reward.

Socialists, communists, or other so-called "progressives" have very little respect for reality. Instead, they invent an issue, blow it out of proportion, and then try to apply their perceived "morality" to solve it. Imagine that one were to apply the principle voiced by AOC that "[it's improper to be] more concerned about being precisely, factually, and semantically correct than about being morally right" to a surgeon in the medical profession or an airline pilot flying a massive airplane. While morality should be the underlying reason and guiding light for all human actions, a surgeon cannot perform surgery by being "factually incorrect" but "morally right." I doubt even foolish AOC would submit herself to the knife of a surgeon who is "morally right" but totally "factually" untrained.

That logic is absurd and dangerous. Our purpose is to attack thoughtless and dangerous policies and, by association, those people who conceive, put forth, and defend such unsafe and detrimental policies without any regard to real-life consequences for Americans.

Why, then, do voters keep electing politicians who use this nonsensical norm to govern our society?

To preempt the typical short-tempered response of the Left to any critical analysis of their so-called "progressive policies," let me be perfectly clear. I would dare to assert that neither I nor any conservative believing in the true American way are "sexually attracted" to any members of the Squad, as suggested by AOC as the primary reason for our critique. Frankly, there is very little appeal for us, sexual or otherwise, to Trotsky with lipstick.

When socialists cannot reach the intended result they desire, whether due to factual and causation reasons, they lie about it, or they impart new meaning to standard meanings or concepts. No revolution or progressive reforms ever started with promises like: "We will tax you to oblivion!" or "We will kill half the population and take their stuff and give it to you so you can live better!" No, my friends, it's much more subtle and devious than that.

Sadly, innocent people do not realize until it's too late which side of the equation they will fall on. Their mantra has always been "Tax the rich!" ... not "Kill the rich." And yet now ... .

The modern version of that underlying socialist dogma from years ago is reduced to a simple paradigm from a socialist leader: "I will declare the moral purpose, anything from Communism to the Green/Red New Deal" or the alleged "Denazification (of Ukrainians)." But the means of achieving it will not affect me personally. Since you elected me, I am the chosen one. You, however, will have to suffer a bit and, more likely, a lot. But it will lead to a better and more moral tomorrow for everyone."

The Bolsheviks, who brought about the fall of Tsarism and Imperial Russia, used the alleged virtues of "equity" and the immorality of the monarchy rule to turn the country upside down. In an unprecedented feat of incompetency and sabotage of reality, they scorched the entire economic and social system. The socialists were blinded by their ideology. They cared very little if they were throwing the good away along with the bad.

Their self-centered ideology turned Russia into a miserable and poor country for decades.

Consider this: In Tsarist Russia, 20 years before the October Revolution, the length of roads built was twice as long as in the next 40 years under Communist rule, notwithstanding the advances in technology. Similarly, Putin's highway development is less than one-tenth of Chinese construction during that same time. No one involved in socialist revolutions explicitly boasts with this slogan: "We will make you starve and stop building roads!" Yet, they always end up killing the economy and making people miserable.

However, the slogans of the populist Bolsheviks' or Nazis (and now today's Z Army of Putin) can be summarized in a simple notion: "It's not your fault. It's the fault of the Tsar, the Jews, greedy capitalists, antirevolutionaries, NATO, or Ukrainians." This type of language always finds fertile ground in socially immature masses throughout history. They are eager to place blame on someone else. They tend to believe in simple solutions that do not require much effort or personal responsibility on their part.

// *The recent voices blaming "greedy capitalists" for high prices are yet another lesson that the modern Democrat Party is borrowing from its historical antecedents. It's easier than admitting its own socialist nature, its failures as seen in abysmal economic, international, energy, and monetary policies in the United States following the booming and record-setting successes prior to the 2020 elections.*

As Margret Thatcher once noted, "There is no government money; it's people's money." This simple truth is the reason for one simple fact. Socialism always brings misery and catastrophe. Why? Because, in the Iron Lady's timeless and wise words, "Eventually [you] run out of other people's money."

So when the Presidential administration of Joe Biden, with a serious face, declares that spending $3 trillion will "cost us nothing" and "will pay for itself," the liberal mass media lackeys echo and kowtow to an outrageous lie. It's a lie. It defies any and all laws of mathematics and economics. If those claims were true, why is the administration hiring extra IRS hounds so that they can snoop on the $600 transactions of every American citizen?

This is exactly how the Soviet Union "paid by itself." It robbed the Soviet people of the results of their labor in pursuit of its numerous utopian projects, the military arms race, and industrialization. They even arrogantly attempted to turn Siberian rivers backward and built "nature-centered" projects for the happy future of the Soviet people. Those grand pursuits resulted in many natural disasters. Two of those disasters include the drying out of the Aral Sea and the virtual extermination of fish in the Volga River.

Nevertheless, I will give them credit. At least the moral and futuristic pretext for those ill-advised, grandiose Soviet failures of previous days had a bit of pomp and circumstance. Today, the Left's "infrastructure deal" or their monotonous "Green New Deal" are simply mundane and tedious. The Left almost appears as if they are pursuing the destruction of civilization's achievements, such as energy, food sufficiency, and security, for no other valuable reasons than spite and ideological stubbornness. Simply a wholesale opposition to the Western World's achievements.

This self-mutilation of society by the rich and educated could also arise from their unresolved internal sense of guilt. This is likely the case with billionaire George Soros. Despite being a Jew and the marvel that he was able to hide from the Germans, this wealthy robber-baron admitted he then cooperated with the Nazis during World War II. In his uncanny display of self-guilt and thinly-veiled protest against Western society, Soros is set on destroying the pillars of modern civilizations. He openly supports radical prosecutors who make victims of crime insignificant while exonerating the real criminals.

Soros views criminals as the true victims of society's inherent "inequities." It's ironic that after escaping the powerful Germans who tried to destroy Western society, Soros became rich and powerful through the freedoms of that same Western society. Now, he seeks to use his wealth and power to destroy it himself. Who is the true criminal?

Sometimes, even oftentimes, criminals are simply criminals, particularly the ones who commit numerous violent crimes. For the good of society, they must be isolated. That has been the tenet followed by human society for thousands of years. Until now. Today's socialist "root causes" dogma turns away from personal responsibility toward a predetermined destiny.

Numerous " alternative energy" and "clean harvest" projects brought numerous disasters and turmoil in Third World countries of Africa and Asia. As an example, Sri Lanka's people revolted when they faced famine due to "clean" energy and the elimination of fertilizers and pesticides. Dutch farmers came out into the streets with similar protests against radical "green" (or should we say "red"?) policies that destroyed their livelihoods. These "clean" ideas pushed by international organizations resulted in the critical reduction of their agricultural harvests.

It is difficult to imagine that catastrophic events are the genuine goals of those who propagate socialism. So what are their true intentions and motives? Seeing the glass as half full--as I am an eternal optimist--I will admit that people can have good faith motives even when they are mistaken in their intentions. For example, those who believe in socialism lack fundamental knowledge of economics, human psychology and, most importantly, an understanding of history and its value. Therefore, while their motives may be good, they are sorely mistaken in their expected outcome. There is only one possible outcome of their good intentions. And it's not good.

From the communal "New Harmony" project in the United States in the 19th century to the more recent brutal experiments in China, North Korea, Germany, and the Soviet Union, the practice of socialism has no economic sustainability. It also has nothing akin to human progress. Rather, it touts military advancements or borrowing/stealing the tools and methods learned from capitalists.

Imagine that the KGB had a department whose sole role was to purchase foreign goods so those goods could be replicated and distributed within the Soviet economy. Hence, from automobiles to cameras to washing machines and even cartoons such as Winnie the Pooh, all were shamelessly "borrowed" with no pang of conscience. Details such as copyrights and trademarks do not appear to have bothered Soviet leaders. Did I mention they once stole a nuclear bomb? But no worries, this "borrowing" didn't cause much trouble. It merely enabled the Soviets, and now Putin, to blackmail the "morally inferior" world.

Let's take a closer look at Soviet morality. What would you call a society, free medical care withstanding, where an ambulance will not even be dispatched when they are informed the person in distress is over 60 years old? That particular practice is prevalent (though not official, of course) in Belarus, although there are similar stories about Russia's cities as well.

To give you a personal example, I had to pull some strings among clients to get my Covid-positive mother, over 60 years old, to the hospital. The Russian society has over 300,000 children in state orphanages, and at least 75% of those kids have a living parent.

You guessed it. This is the "moral" Russia. While parents in the evil U.S. stand in line for decades and spend thousands of dollars to adopt a child, Russia stores children like chattel in orphan houses. That is no way for a child to live. It has been reported that children who go through the brutal system of state orphanages in Russia have virtually no chance of going to college. Furthermore, the criminality rate of those children is several times higher than the general population. Those children dream of being adopted by American families. I know at least a dozen such Russian orphans happily living in their new American families. My children helped some of those Russian kids in our neighborhood to adapt to American life and overcome the language barrier.

What was shocking for us was how anti-social those Russian kids were when they were first brought to the U.S. Imagine a five-year-old girl who curses like a drunken sailor, does not know how to use toilet paper, and instinctively steals and hides food and staple items. Over the years, I witnessed those kids turning into delightful, fully functional, kind human beings under the care of American families.

So, how did Putin respond? In retaliation for the sanctions imposed on his regime, he banned all American adoptions of Russian children by introducing the law nicknamed "Law of Bastards." (The nickname referred unsympathetically to the people who voted for it, not the children.) This law effectively doomed those children to miserable lives and deprived them of their last hope.

It gets even worse! In their fight for "morality," the socialists have a bittersweet victory. Soviet Russia was the first country to legalize abortions. Another "W" in the win column of socialism. Although Socialists have proven yet again they have very little concern for "humanity" or human life.

Regarding the Soviets and their stolen nuclear bomb, I offer something to consider. For those naïve enough to believe that Kalashnikov, a guy who only finished 7th grade with no engineering or mathematical background, was able to create one of the most advanced battlefield weapons, I might encourage them that it's time to stop believing in Santa Claus. If they were to read about the German engineering PoWs who were forced to work in the Soviet

Union after the war and see the similarities of AKs with German engineer Gugo Schmeisser's Sturmgewehr, the fairy tale about a virtually illiterate peasant creating a matchless assault rifle would seem highly implausible.

So the visions and theories of socialism, looking down from their higher moral ground, declare "Flying is great." Then they push millions of people off the ledge, hoping that flight occurs even though there is no knowledge of or preparation for flying. They hope flight miraculously takes place simply because it is morally and logically justifiable and generally "virtuous." That is not logical. That is a desire that they lie to bring about. They label themselves as "pilots," but they are rarely eager to jump with two feet. Instead, they hide themselves under the title "traffic-to-future" controllers.

AOC's comment that "[it's improper to be] more concerned about being precisely, factually, and semantically correct than about being morally right" is taken right from the pages of socialist visions and theories. She is prepared to push Americans off the ledge, hoping flight occurs simply because it is morally and logically justifiable and generally "virtuous." Not to mention that in her arrogant sense of entitlement, she *wants* it to happen and *expects* to get what she wants without regard to the price other people will pay. Make no mistake--the price of the "deals" will be high. It is much higher than simply kicking that capitalistic, greedy Amazon out of New York, even though it would have created tens of thousands of well-paying jobs.

The historical repeated failure of socialism does not stand in the way of the naïve. However, it is far more dangerous in the hands of those who have learned history's lessons. They know how to use Leftist theories and methods to grab power in a ruthless and Machiavellian manner. This is power for the sake of power itself. Many historians believe that wealth and luxury sometimes move political activists less than the lust for power. In other words, power is more alluring and corruptive than even wealth and luxury.

However, throughout history, socialists have almost always lived by the principle that strictness of the law and suffering is "for thee but not for me." We see that today in our forced mask mandates and lockdowns, while Pelosi and others in government are frequently seen with no masks. Lenin felt he was above the law, too. He did not move to a hut after the revolution. Instead, he lived in the luxurious amenities of the former nobility. He even had a fleet of cars that once belonged to the Tsar.

Whether in the 1920s, 1930s, or during the German blockade of Leningrad, where almost a million people died of hunger, the famines that occurred were of little concern to the "apparatchiki." Their diet did not lack the required calories, nutrients, or diversity, while the common people starved. There are numerous historical documents mentioning the luxurious feasts enjoyed by the Communists, who were also prone to exchange food as payment for expensive art or other "personal" favors.

Let's look back again at history to see the patterns and the predictable events that resulted. We can foresee the future by watching Putin's actions as he repeats the past. While the Russian Army should undoubtedly be given foremost credit for the victory over the Nazis, the failure of Russia to declassify Soviet materials related to the 1930s and 1940s caused the corruption, depravity, civilian atrocities in Europe, and Soviet government incompetence to remain concealed. Those failures extended to societal, economic, and military matters. Concealing those failures resulted in alignment with Hitler and then the near obliteration of the Soviet Army and several millions of Soviet PoWs in the first few months of the war.

Recently, at the Valdai conference in October 2021, Putin yet again chastised the West for equating Stalin with Hitler and Communism with Fascism. In addition, Putin bragged that most German losses during WWII were made by the Red Army. No one chastised the Soviet regime for killing the Nazis. After all, they started it. However, the Soviet Union was criticized for massive civilian losses, atrocities and occupation of Eastern Europe following the end of the war and the use of its own people. That doesn't include the Soviet Union's pre-war mass murders of their own people as "cannon fodder". To a large degree, this was due to the incompetence of Soviet leadership and the backward nature of the socialist regime. The loss was a national tragedy, but Putin saw it as something to brag about. If anything, the Soviet regime with its internal and external tyranny, inhumanity, and devastation, was the number two villain then, right behind Hitler. That was definitely not something to write home to your mother about.

As I think about it, who but Putin would publicly 'compare' the two regimes (I know, we're doing that here) other than those in Russia who measure all their actions through the "whataboutism" lens? Russian politicians are always seeking someone or something worse than what they do or have done. If anything, such a claim is a Freudian slip and an admission of the fairness of such a comparison. Particularly in light of Putin's own "fundamental" likeness to Hitler's actions, i.e., aggression, xenophobia, and atrocities, as well as superficial cues making Putin "the Hitler of the 21st century." These cues would include the insignia adopting a Z similar to the SS insignia and swastika, "Blitzkriegs," rhetoric repeated verbatim regarding "national traitors," "Western influence," "saving of [German/Russian] population" (through invasion and bombing, of course), the solution of the "Ukrainian" issue (which used to be the "Jewish" issue), and 100 shades of Western and victim "provocations."

In this book, it is my intention to indeed compare and equate many of the characteristics of German fascism and Soviet Bolshevism, as well as their inhumane and ominous natures. The world was happy when the Soviet Bolshevism, seen allegedly as the lesser evil, prevailed over the greater evil-- namely, the Nazis. However, the main relevant difference between the two was the fact that, by and large, the world cured itself of German fascism. Bolshevism, on the other hand, is a social metastatic cancer that continues to spread, often without detection or treatment by society.

The Left likes to rate and rationalize issues. But to say Charles Manson was not as bad as Ted Bundy because Manson killed less people is foolish. Monsters are just as evil on their own terms. A gratuitous comparison doesn't make a monster less horrible because he killed fewer people. By the same token, just because the Soviet people fought the Nazis does not justify the atrocities committed by the Soviets at the end of the war, as recounted in books by Svetlana Aleksievich. Horrendous acts were committed by communists against their own people, as well as other Eastern European and Asian countries who were already effectively enslaved by socialism.

President Putin considers himself the extension, the uncanny lawful heir to both the Tsarist and Communist thrones at the same time. Along with his followers, Putin savored the vastness of the Russian Empire destroyed by the Soviets. An unsuspecting listener may interpret that Putin himself stormed Berlin personally 75 years ago. That event was the greatest Soviet glory, namely the defeat of the Nazis. Putin actually considered those attacks on Stalin years ago as personal insults, a concerted attack on both the victory itself and the role the Soviet Union played in the victory. Putin's dichotomy and contradictions are uncanny.

For example, on the one hand, Putin condemns Hitler and Nazi atrocities. On the other hand, he venerates the ChK's leader Dzerzhinsky, a similar killer but of a different nationality. ChK was the predecessor to NKVD/KGB. The ChK was responsible for mass murders of others, as well as mass murders of its own people committed by Bolsheviks.

As another example, on one hand, Putin declares himself the moral and territorial heir of the Russian Empire and its nobility. On the other hand, the legacy and memories of the old-country glory were systematically wiped out and slaughtered by people like Dzerzhinsky, Lenin, and Stalin. Therefore, Putin's admiration of the Soviet Union and Russian Empire is strange at best since Lenin tried to exterminate anything and everything tied to their prerevolutionary past, both the bad and the glorious. After Lenin's revolution, people were prosecuted just because of their noble blood or surname. All statues signifying the great wars (including the war against Napoleon) and scientific or geographic victories, were dismantled.

As a third example, Putin ironically declared his warring feat for "Greater" Russia, partially blaming Lenin for dividing Russia into federal republics, giving them a hint of independence. On the heels of that, Putin promptly renamed squares of occupied Ukrainian cities and changed the name of their beloved Liberty Square to its new (old Soviet) name, Lenin Square. Upon their unwelcomed arrival, Putin's army also immediately "liberated" Ukrainian cities of any and all symbols of national pride, namely the statutes of beloved Ukrainian heroes and national celebrities.

Putin's admiration for Lenin and Stalin and their evil methods is apparent. Putin's insatiable contempt for liberty and democracy is more than apparent in his actions and deeds. Let's use a more modern example to make my point. You may remember that John Hinckley was convicted for his assassination attempt on President Ronald Reagan in 1981. At that time, Hinckley claimed allegiance to every facet of ultra-Leftist policies. Imagine your bemused reaction if Hinckley then, upon his 2016 release from attempting to kill Reagan, suddenly claimed his undying devotion to Reagan and Reaganomics!

By the same token, Putin causes bemused expressions as he "talks out of both sides of his mouth," claiming adherence to both Tsarist and Lenin legacies. The bemused expressions are on the faces of people who know their history--the two legacies are both historically and morally antagonistic!

|| Wouldn't removing American flags and the statues of heroes like Columbus or Jefferson follow the typical mode and spirit of the Bolsheviks or Putin's agendas? One of the targets of the 2019 attempts by race rioters at removing American historical figures was the statute of Tadeusz Kościuszko, one of the monuments in Lafayette Park, Washington, D.C., in front of the White House. You might ask who is Tadeusz Kościuszko? He was born on the territory of contemporary Belarus but is considered today by the U.S., Poland, and Belarus as a hero. He was also one of Jefferson's friends and comrades in arms who fought for American independence.

Connecting the life of Tadeusz Kościuszko with contemporary events, it should be noted that he fought and successfully defended Kyiv against the Russian army and greatly contributed to American independence as a military strategist and commander. Furthermore, Kościuszko's will provided that his American estate was to be sold to buy the freedom of black slaves, including Jefferson's own slaves. It also designated that part of the funds were to be used to educate former slaves in the art of crafts and prepare them for independent life.

Kościuszko's mindset was certainly ahead of his time and even more enlightened than those of the American founders. In addition to the good faith expressed in his will, he emancipated his own serfs in Poland. This act was disallowed by the Russian Tsar.

So, the lesson is, wouldn't it be worth reading the history before rioters rush to remove the statute of yet another "white guy" whose only "privilege" was to bravely fight tyranny, free slaves and serfs, and extend his unmatched goodwill over two continents?

To protect this weird salad of Soviet and Russian legacies, many laws were adopted in Russia by Putin recently, punishing various "insults" of the state and defaming the victories. Defaming, of course, includes anything that reports the facts, which thus "defames" the Russian army's current actions in Ukraine. In other words, if you tell the truth that Russia invaded innocent Ukraine or report about the war anything outside of state propaganda, you just committed a punishable crime. Simply calling it a war is a crime. Even more astonishing, if you dare to sing or post a Soviet song about how the Nazis were bombing Kyiv at 4 o'clock in the morning (which was the exact time the Russian war machine started shelling Kyiv), the authorities will know exactly what you actually "meant."

All this wholesale glorification of the past does not square well with the fact that the Soviet Union entered WWII on September 17, 1939, as an ally of Germany. The Soviet Union stabbed Poland in the back in the East while Polish troops defended Hitler's attack on the Western front. Of course, in the view of whataboutists regarding Stalin and Putin, it's all the fault of Western democracies and the Poles, and now of course, Ukraine, for appeasing and then "provoking" Hitler and Stalin. All this "historical" talk by Putin about "provocation" by unsuspecting neighbors is, of course, just a pretext, a "moral" justification for his assembling Russian troops at the Ukrainian border and then starting a heinous war.

The declared goal of all Soviet leaders has always been the Communization of the world. Their dream is for all nations of the world to submit to communism. Unfortunately, whether in pursuit of this global goal or to appease the Brown Plague, the Soviet Union entered into a Molotov-Ribbentrop non-aggression pact. This pact was also known as the Stalin-Hitler pact. However, once the war with Germany started, Stalin did not wish his name to be associated with the document. The pact contained a secret addendum (that's no surprise!) regarding the "sphere of influence." In other words, the agreement as to how to divide and conquer the European theater and enable the Soviet Union to invade Bessarabia, Poland, Lithuania, Latvia, Estonia, and Finland. Of course, Stalin saw this and proclaimed this was for the sake of "liberating" those nations from pesky bourgeois governments upon the call from local proletarians. Copies of the addendum were obtained by various governments.

However, the document was so atrocious and treacherous for a civilization that until Gorbachev's "glasnost" period, when some historical documents were made public, even Western historians could not believe the document was authentic.

The Soviet Union unscrupulously invaded its neighbors. My mother was born in the territory that was then Poland. Yet, no document reflected such a fact. The Soviet Union trained German soldiers and officers, including the pilots of the Luftwaffe, who performed so well at the Battle of Britain. Luckily, they were not able to overpower the British Royal Air Force, losing over 2000 aircraft. The Soviets also supplied food, oil, equipment, and metal ore to the Germans.

The United States provided military assistance to the United Kingdom under the Lend-Lease. This policy promoted the defense of the Western World through the utilization of industrial production and supply of weapons, medical goods, and other products from the United States. Lend-Lease was quickly extended to the Soviet Union when it fought against Nazi Germany. Many, including my grandfather, who fought in Stalingrad, believed for sure that Lend-Lease was critical to the Allied forces' victory.

Now, in an amusing twist of irony, we see the new Lend-Lease being designed to help Ukraine, which stands in the way of Putin claiming the world for his soon-to-be-bruised ego. Despite the Lend-Lease having already been signed into law, the Biden administration continues to delay putting it into operation. Sadly, Ukrainian cities continue to be burned to the ground and innocent children are killed by Russian missiles.

It was a gruesome irony, however, when Soviet and Nazi troops held a joint military parade in the city of Brest after jointly defeating Poland, which was doomed once the two monsters joined forces. Clearly, it doesn't matter which monster killed the most people. And it's certainly a poor excuse that the other monster killed more. Both are monsters. That fact will haunt the people of Russia until they recognize it and vow not to follow again in the footsteps of either monstrosity--Russian or German.

Unfortunately, the power-grabbing tactics of Putin and Lukashenko inevitably involve resurrecting the Soviet monster and selling it to the gullible Russian public as a piece of bygone glory.

All in all, historical perspectives matter. But facts and principles of civility, reason, and humanity matter more. Trying to bury something in the historical ash or revive a long-gone heritage mummy to justify one's actions by placing history in questionable high moral ground is absurd, reprehensible, and counterproductive.

Generalizations and comparisons at times lose important details. In my view, the best comparison between the fascist and communist regimes was given by the main character in "Spark of Life" by Erich Remarque, a book about a Nazi concentration camp. The book was, of course, banned by the Soviets. The book included a conversation in which the character, a German man imprisoned for his resistance against the Nazi regime, was approached by a communist.

The communist who led the resistance in the concentration camp asked the German man why he was not joining the communist resistance.

The German man, the main character, responded with a key question: *"How long after you, the communists, come to power, will people like me end up back here in the concentration camp?"*

The Communist responded: *"Not too long, but probably at least a few months, but our cause is righteous."*

It's no surprise that "Spark of Life" was banned in the Soviet Union, probably due to this one revealing and prophetic exchange. I was able to read it only after coming to the United States. It's not likely this book is a favorite among contemporary unwary socialists and is probably considered "degrading" of Stalin's role in the great victory.

DMITRI I. DUBOGRAEV

Chapter 4
Fundamentals of Society

We have highlighted some of the many subtle dangers of socialism and communism upon a society. Now, let's examine their dangers for a government. Any discussion of the potential virtues of socialism and communism is futile without touching upon two points: the function of the government and the delineation of private initiative vs. social community.

The oldest and simplest justification for government is as a protector, protecting citizens from violence. Without a government to offer the safety of law and order to safeguard citizens from each other and foreign opponents, Thomas Hobbes' *Leviathan* depicts a world of continuous insecurity. Among the world's many unstable states and essentially ungoverned territories, the miseries of having little or no functioning government are on display. It is interesting to note that when the chaos of conflict and disorder becomes unbearable, citizens will prefer autocratic and extremist governments like the Taliban and ISIS to no functioning government at all. It appears that submission to predictable terror is better than vulnerability to the ravages of fighting bands.

The concept of government as a protector necessitates imposing taxes upon the people to cover the costs necessary for the said protector to protect the people. These include funds to pay, train, and equip an army and a police force, to construct and run courts and jails, and to elect or select politicians to pass and enforce laws that citizens dare not break.

In terms of external dangers, the government's role as protector requires the ability and willingness to engage and negotiate with other governments, as well as the power to battle and defeat them. Our American Republic followed this minimalist concept of government in its early days.

The Power to Protect and Provide

Among the duties of the government as a provider, we must include providing goods and services that individuals cannot provide for themselves. In this view, the government provides the solution to collective action difficulties. Citizens use the collective action process as the means to generate public goods that benefit everyone. As expected, when dealing with the public, collective action is also prone to free-rider problems unless some form of collective pressure is available.

This category includes both the physical infrastructure through which humans connect, such as roads, bridges, and ports of various kinds and the increasingly virtual infrastructure of human connection, such as broadband. All this infrastructure can be provided by private capitalists. They see the chance to build a road at their expense, then charge users a toll, for example, to recoup their costs. But the capital required becomes so large, and the public benefit becomes so evident the government must take over.

Government is not only required to provide citizens with tangible infrastructure, such as roads and bridges. Another more expansive idea of government as a provider is the social welfare state. Social welfare allows the government to cushion people who are unable to provide for themselves, particularly in vulnerable situations such as youth, old age, sickness, disability, or unemployment. In all these situations, the inability to provide is the result of economic causes beyond their control.

As the welfare state inevitably expanded, critics began to perceive it as either a shield against the harsh effects of capitalism or a way to shield the wealthy from the political wrath of the dispossessed. At its best, however, if carefully implemented, social welfare provides a care infrastructure that allows citizens to thrive socially and economically in the same manner that a competitive infrastructure does. It offers a much-needed social safety net that allows citizens to enjoy some economic stability.

Another main function of government protection involves the integrity of the country's borders. This includes implementation of sensible immigration policies that are applied consistently. The United States and its citizens are empathetic and welcoming to others. In recent decades, they have admitted over one million immigrants per year. Nevertheless, the reality is that America can absorb only a limited number of people coming in from outside, especially those entering illegally. Unfortunately, no nation can afford to take in everyone who wants to come. Not even America. There is certainly an abundance of people worldwide wanting to come to this country at any cost.

|| *Ironically, despite hearing the narrative of Leftist pundits, who repeatedly assert that the United States is "systemically racist" and incurably flawed with inequities, the number of people wanting to come into this country at any cost continues to increase every year.*

The Biden administration, which many criticize as inept, has continually failed to control its borders. This failure became more pronounced after the 2020 elections and the removal of Donald Trump's influence. To minimize the flow of criminals and illicit substances, there is a need to vet those wishing to come in. An unrestrained flow of illegals strains local and federal resources, causes an unprecedented spike in overdose deaths, and substantially strengthens the powerful influence of evil cartels in smuggling and human trafficking.

Politicians on both sides of the aisle, and President Biden's administration in particular, should put a stop to the endless dishonest rhetoric and admit we have a problem. More than that, a "crisis." This is not simply a "situation." This is a "crisis." When the Biden administration finally recognizes it as such, our government will have taken its first step toward a solution.

Practical steps must be taken with strict and humane measures to protect the border and protect law enforcement. Certain actions of the current Biden government, including the distribution of smartphones, the threat to lift the application of Title 42 restrictions, and the creation of "honey pots" and actual incentives for foreigners, have only emboldened illegals to disregard U.S. laws and violate our borders. Why? Because the current administration looks the other way. Our government, whose job it is to protect its citizens, instead offers violators impunity with no adverse consequences. And make no mistake, even the most illiterate of illegals recognize that.

While protecting law enforcement is vital, there is another aspect that must also be addressed. Enforcing the law is equally important for the members of society, particularly against police officers who exceed their authority. Members of law enforcement, like all of us, are human beings who perform a tougher job than most of us. The great difference is that while performing their job, they are in danger, literally in danger every single day. As human beings in very stressful situations, they are unfortunately prone to mistakes. At times, those mistakes are grave--with life or death results.

There is very little evidence to support the Left's cries that the police "get away with murder" or are not otherwise punished for their mistakes. These mistakes and even deliberate crimes are, in fact, isolated occurrences. Statistically, they are almost inevitable on a large scale, particularly in today's environment with the Left calling for defunding police. Any reduction in financing law enforcement also reduces opportunities for training. Considering that police are forced to make split-second decisions, many times while taking fire from madmen wielding guns or knives, and considering the real-life risk of failure to them personally in these life or death situations, defunding police would be the least effective way to handle "police abuse." And yet, the abuse and disparagement of the men and women in Blue by the mass media continues.

Various social movements and politicians have joined the media in calling for disbanding or defunding of police. This concept goes against the very tenet of societal development over the past thousands of years. Remember, one of the main functions of government's protection is public safety and crime prevention. One would think an increasing police role would be paramount to the normal progression of any society where citizens naturally value their safety and life. Rational law-abiding citizens expect their government to protect that. For generations, we taught our children to look up to and respect police officers, just as we had been taught to do. Police officers were invited into classrooms and introduced to students as their friends, the dedicated civil servants they could count on and run to in times of trouble.

However, all that has changed in today's "woke" society. Oftentimes, distinct or conspicuous failures, particularly failures of the police, are artificially inflated by the media as systemic or racist problems of the entire society. Such mischaracterization with broad strokes ignores years of statistics. The reality is this-- the number of alleged legally punishable incidents of "systemic brutality" by police are isolated, numbering in single digits. In contrast, the staggering toll of violent deaths committed by citizens against citizens in just one American city, Chicago, exceeded 800 murders in 2021 alone.

One has to wonder. If the scarce number of police crimes are continually painted by the media as "hate crimes," do we then depict the other thousands of murders of young black males in inner cities as "love crimes"? Shouldn't society and the politicians adjust their focus based on the raw numbers and the story those numbers tell? Wouldn't it be prudent to be heartbroken over the loss of so many young lives and focus on rectifying the "low-hanging fruit?" Isn't that one of the jobs of government and politicians, to guard and protect the public? Even a small percentage point improvement would mean saving the lives of hundreds of young citizens.

If black lives really matter and the BLM movement truly wants to live up to its slogan, wouldn't those lives matter regardless of the source of the violence? Wouldn't the sheer numbers of casualties and virtual impunity of those inner-city murderers matter? Should the Left finally admit that their "progressive" measures of maintaining subsidized ghettos, coupled with degrading and defunding the police, have only exacerbated the problem? Then multiply those dismal results by their "revolving door justice," which fails to prosecute crimes. Now, you will discover the main causes for the jagged upward spike in crime rates we face in our country today.

One could also wonder why the systematic war-like causalities of minorities in our inner cities are not a cause for concern from the loudmouthed social movements and the Leftist mayors and governors. Maybe it's because we have an even greater problem. Creating political dependency for the needy provides parasite politicians the meal ticket to endlessly leech off this "problem" for the duration of their political careers. This endless meal ticket has become far more important than actually helping the people they were elected to serve or solving the problem.

And this, my friends, is an example of socialist principles at their finest failure. This is essentially how everything operated in the Soviet Union. Leaders declared one usually moral, virtuous, and selfless thing but then did exactly the opposite. They denigrated the government and its functions (or malfunctions, take your pick). The lip service simply increased as things inevitably got worse.

I am reminded of a particular childhood memory. This illustrates how the Soviet system operated. It was a Communist Party event and our elementary school choir was invited. After the performance, we were handed a huge bag of candies and headed to the bus. There was enough candy for each of us to fill our pockets. Suddenly, one of the "important" ladies who organized the event rushed onto the bus and grabbed our candy bag out of my hands. She chastised us for being greedy and selfish. She went on and on about some "other people" who deserved candy more than we did. We had no idea who those "other people" were. We were the only ones performing on the stage!

I tried to argue and resist this "robbery." We did end up with one measly piece of candy for each of us. As a nine-year-old kid, I was left with an innate feeling of unfairness and powerlessness. I was determined to both loathe and fight them as much as I could. Since then, I have viewed every encounter with authorities through the lenses of my spat with that "candy witch."

I am no longer a nine-year-old kid, but my loathing of arbitrary application of the law, rampant crime, unfettered biased partisanship, and attempts to destroy this beautiful country still give rise to those same strong feelings in me even today.

It is unfathomable that thousands of people, particularly minorities, innocent bystanders, and little children, are being gunned down in inner cities. The majority of these are "black on black" crimes. Such atrocity goes virtually unnoticed by click-bait media. They fail to show the grieving mothers or grandmothers in their newscasts because it happens too frequently to be news.

However, there is an even more sickening reason why these crimes don't make the hourly news. These crimes do not follow the narrative and talking points of the "Party line." Politicians are unwilling to raise "tough issues" for fear of being labeled as "racist," clearly one of the worst labels in today's environment. Out-of-focus media are frantically looking for issues where there are virtually none. Then, they broadcast such contrived "issues" on the hourly news. This sad combination is a significant reason why these problems continue to exacerbate. Our society can no longer concentrate on real issues and practical solutions. I wonder if it even recognizes them anymore.

Could it be that they are afraid to recognize them as solutions? It draws much higher ratings promoting the overwhelming difficulties proclaimed by corrupt politicians. Could the merry-go-round "solution" be the "problem?" Exposing the corruption and ineptitude, actually solving the issues, would cut the flow of funds to fight it.

Isn't that one of the reasons the media and Swamp hated Donald Trump? As extravagant and abrasive as he was with some of his rhetoric, many issues were indeed placed by his administration on the path of resolution. To mention just a few: reduction of illegal crossings, slashing overregulation, crime reduction, achieving energy independence, dealing with lackluster financing by NATO countries, boosting military funding, signing Abraham Accords (that alone is worthy of the Nobel Peace Prize), going head-to-head with China over trade imbalance, allowing school vouchers, creating real jobs and taking away millions of food stamps programs, replacing unfair NAFTA with the USMCA, placing a full stop on starting stupid wars, and obtaining the first-ever reduction of the carbon footprint by the U.S. That's an impressive list. Well deserving of hatred in the eyes of the media and the Swamp.

Yes, yes, there were some childish tweets. But when viewed against the actual deeds Trump accomplished, looking back fondly at our once flourishing economy, minimal inflation, and unemployment rates, were they really so bad? I'll take childish tweets along with a powerful economy any day.

Public safety through policing, as Americans have done for generations, is a simple but somewhat "boring" issue for today's enlightened politicians. Apparently, today, it's much more virtuous and enlightened to simply proclaim that all people are "good." Once all people are pronounced "good," we can move forward with our enlightened plans to close all federal prisons in 10 years. This insane proposal by Rep. Rashida Tlaib (D-Mich.) was actually echoed by other politicians, particularly in New York. Now, there's a brilliant way to secure public safety from leaders of that bastion of safety, New York City. Simply let all the criminals run free on the streets of America. It's sad that even the "lighter" version of those so-called "criminal reforms" is already turning New York into a modern version of Mad Max.

If America's leaders had any sense of history, they would have known that Lenin did exactly that in 1917. Then, he wholeheartedly welcomed the ensuing lawlessness that ravaged Russia. He saw it as his way of fighting for wealth and success. No wonder Soviet Russia faced numerous famines, hardships, and virtual stoppage in social progress, except for the military, of course (though Ukrainians appear to be determined to refute that exception).

The abysmal situation with public safety is further aggravated by a dramatic reduction of prosecution of crimes, due most particularly to the recent election of many progressive "Soros" prosecutors. They ignore their main function, which is to prosecute crimes as defined by the Legislature, not what is defined by George Soros or "progressive" politicians. This is accomplished by softening the definitions of "prosecutable crimes." For example, the $950 benchmark in California and $250 in New York. They also implemented reckless, ill-advised revolving-door "bail reform." These new "reforms" simply allow violent criminals to quickly roam our once-safe cities again and commit more crimes.

There was an anecdotal story about one of the Soviet bureaucrats complaining to Leonid Brezhnev, who was head of state at the time. He complained that the salaries of Soviet people were so small that people could barely make ends meet. Brezhnev is said to have replied, "But everyone is stealing..."

What does that say about a society when the head of state essentially acknowledges theft as normal behavior, a way of life and survival for many in an allegedly high-level civil socialist society? And even if the story is not true, it does reflect the overall mood and mindset of the Soviet rulers and people alike. Theft was not only socially acceptable, but it was also widespread in the Soviet Union. Even worse, theft was not deemed morally wrong.

For people living in a Western culture, that may be difficult to understand. A large part of it was the ideology itself. You see, you were not really stealing from someone because, per the Bolsheviks, it's all "yours" anyway. You had the right to whatever others had. Similarly, cheating in school, both high school and university, was condoned, not condemned. Furthermore, if you declined to share the results of your mental labor with the lazy or stupid ones--still known today as cheating--most Soviet students would call you selfish and greedy. Despite that, I never once cheated. It was a matter of principle to me. I was a straight A student in school and university. I must confess, I did cheat once on the eye exam, memorizing the last two lines of the optometric letter chart so that I could make it into a "drivers ed" class and get a commercial truck driver's license in high school. That feat almost made me a shooting-without-glasses draftee, eligible to become cannon fodder in the Soviet war in Afghanistan.

Another popular notion in progressive justice is the issue of "non-crimes" such as "smash and grab." These new "reforms" create yet another incentive for criminally-inclined individuals. Petty thefts such as this are rampant among city gangs. The effect is devastating to large and small businesses alike, including minority-owned businesses. For criminally inclined or unscrupulous individuals, the "broken window" phenomenon causes a domino effect of larger and more serious crimes.

Speaker Pelosi recently described the "broken window" phenomenon as a general "sense of lawlessness." However, despite spending over 50 years of her life as a politician charged with the safety of the citizens who repeatedly elected her, Pelosi found herself not "able" to identify its causes. In any other occupation, failure to do your job or identify causation after 50 years of trying would never happen because you would have been terminated long ago! However, in America's politics that doesn't seem to be a worry.

Of course, no one on the Left is willing to recognize their own drastic fiascos which have turned some American cities into virtually dystopian societies--societies where there is great suffering or injustice. Perhaps that's because they are too busy looking for "root causes" or Nancy's ephemeral "sense of lawlessness." Or just blaming every imaginable problem we face on Covid-19. And if not Covid, then Putin. While Putin is much to blame for many wrongs, he is not responsible for the rising crime rate in U.S. cities or the fact that some cities are now turning into a version of Somalia.

One thing is certain. Until these failures are addressed by someone, emboldened criminals will continue ravishing our cities with this massive spike in burglaries, looting, and organized "smash and grab."

Public safety chaos also enables activists, in a RICO-like fashion, to publicly threaten a mayor-elect of New York City for his intentions to crack down on crimes. Now, there's an oxymoron in today's society–threatening the public official for wanting to crack down on crimes against the public. Such threats are made with impunity, of course. You'll also notice there is very little outcry from the mass media. These racketeering media-like demands to ignore crimes come from the "Left," the BLM organization. We are to assume it's incitement of only "righteous and mostly peaceful violence." But that analogy doesn't fly, not even in the eyes of the Left when threats of violence are made against Mr. Eric Adams, a black Democrat, New York mayor, and former police captain, as well as other conservative activists and politicians.

Condoning real violent crimes while prosecuting "ideological" crimes which threaten the ideological creed is exactly what happened in the Soviet Union and Nazi Germany years ago. That's exactly what's happening now in Russia and Belarus with the same, if not greater, intensity.

Imagine that the Belarusian government has declared that hashtag #freebelarus is extremist. The government and its propaganda focused on the "Western Threat," or other contrived "ideological" hazards, and promoted the idea of guaranteeing so-called "protection and security" in exchange for people's freedoms.

Let's put this into a modern-day example. Imagine this Russian reality: a person who sold poisoned alcohol, which caused the deaths of dozens of people, is released on parole after serving just a few years in prison. A father who murdered his two-year-old daughter gets two years in jail. But a journalist who wrote "No to War" is convicted to serve seven years for "spreading derogatory information about the Russian Army." In essence, the first two guys actually killed people. The other one, the journalist, simply "hurt the feelings" of the military.

Ironically, if anyone is "hurting the feelings" of Russian invaders today, it is the brave Ukrainian soldiers fighting for their country's freedom.

It is an upside-down world when "words are violence," and violence is justifiable because it is "mostly peaceful" or because of some paranoid historical pursuit. A similar dichotomy of words vs. feelings has now been suddenly adopted by the Western Left in their warfare against dissent and reason. It reads like a sad fairy tale. "Once upon a time, the happy inhabitants of Earth relied on reason and logic. But now they are becoming scared because their world is upside-down. All reason and logic are gone."

Putin, Lukashenko, and other socialist leaders judging by their brutal internal policies and the largest war waged in Europe since World War II, are effectively employing the same game plan of magnifying non-existent threats. They are such good pupils of their Communist predecessors. What makes this "racketeering" tactic particularly appalling and sad is that the despotic and dictatorial governments of Nazi Germany and the Soviet Union then, and Russia and Belarus now, continue to be the main source of all the damage, misery, and atrocities.

"*But their thoughts are pure!*" Communists on all continents like to reiterate. "*As your hands are red in blood,*" opponents of socialism reply. In an expression referring to future fascism, Huey Long noted that it would come "under the guise of anti-fascism." That is exactly what's happening in today's so-called "Antifa" movement and the repulsive excuses for Putin's despicable war.

Providing for and protecting its people are the solid cornerstones of a government's future. However, such functions should not be so overbearing that they trample upon the individual liberties and economic freedoms of the very people they are called upon to protect. When that occurs, it has a chilling effect on a free society's entrepreneurship and ingenuity.

Citizens need to be protected by their government from violence and the harshest vagaries of life. The governments of developed countries will, of course, continue to deliver public goods at the level required to maintain a globally competitive economy and a well-functioning society. However, the government's first responsibility should be to safeguard individual freedoms and invest in citizen competencies whenever possible. When the government meets that responsibility, individuals are empowered to provide for themselves in quickly changing situations.

The perception of the need for overwhelming power by the government comes at a price. Especially when that power is abused or expanded beyond the government's primary necessary functions. Friends, this is the main danger from the proponents of socialist theories and the ever-growing call for socialist trends in Western society. When the government grows to the level of interference, a functioning market is no longer a viable mechanism. To prevent society from falling into the socialism quagmire, the right balance must be established. That balance includes the government abstaining from areas in which the government does not belong.

Marxists of all colors put their primary hope on the government to run every aspect of societal life. Private business in such a Marxist scenario becomes a fringe phenomenon. The pursuit of government-set goals takes precedence over the individual's pursuit of happiness. *Every socialist society has failed miserably.* Let me say that again. *Every socialist society has failed miserably.* Why? Mainly due to the government's overwhelming power at the expense of individual freedoms and responsibility.

Declaring the "goodness" of the government and its striving for "common goals" cannot overcome the practical shortcomings and inevitable failures of Marxism. Allow me to take you on a proverbial salesman's trip. This is the typical strategy of socialist propagandists and their rise to power. Their strategy is nothing more than selling proverbial "social snake oil," like a door-to-door salesman, to a willing vulnerable public. Then, they use those same fake prophecies and false cures as a pretext for some other more malevolent or selfish government goals. In the end, those goals usually taste like snake poison.

The biggest examples of this would be fascist Germany, the Soviet Union, North Korea, Cuba, and today's slightly modified variations in contemporary Russia and Belarus.

Communist China was able to create and accumulate substantial wealth, particularly due to its well-timed recognition of the effectiveness of market practices copied from Western societies. Nevertheless, its overwhelming socialist ideology still severely limits people from enjoying true freedoms and the fruits of that wealth. Despite its Western gadgets, fashion items, and fascination with fast food, Communist China continues to be an oppressive Orwellian society. Clearly, China's government has omnipotent powers, particularly in financial and budgetary strengths. It could do a lot of good, protecting and providing for its citizens in such important and critical areas as caring for the needy, building stronger infrastructure, and providing safety for its citizens. However, Communist China chooses to ignore those goals and needs.

It appears Communist China may not be the only one. The current Biden administration also chooses to ignore the needs of America's citizens, i.e., staggering crime numbers and the border crisis, just to name two huge problems. It seems failure to protect its people is a detriment of governments today, whether ruled by communism or capitalism.

Instead, reckless spending and irresponsible monetary policies are expressed in the latest Biden offering, the Build Back Better legislation, and the infamous Inflation Reduction Act of 2022, which offers the same hypocrisy and word twisting as Putin's "protection" of Ukrainians. Policies like these threaten the foundations of American society. In reality, these policies bring hardships of inflationary taxation to the middle class in particular. Constant lying and redefining the meanings of economic concepts are thinly-veiled attempts at covering an administration that governs with sheer incompetence wrapped in wishful thinking.

Furthermore, the excessive inflation above 9%, which we are experiencing in 2022 (as of this writing), is a direct result of imprudent government choices. This is the highest inflation seen in America in 50 years. Its damage is real. Just ask the average family of four trying to put food on the table and gasoline in the family SUV. The world's faith in the U.S. dollar is undermined. American leadership is undercut and weakened in all spheres of world affairs.

This damage is especially concerning since the U.S. has been the solid foundation and beacon of the world's monetary and political stability, coupled with economic freedom, for over 200 years. That shining light on the hill is growing dimmer.

Belarus was once the primary example of a society where all functions were solidified in an unassailable center. Once the government promulgated numerous "common-good" spending policies, however, the wheels began to come off. The government declared, of course, that its measures were designed to bring prosperity and security to its citizens, even if the goals were at the expense of people's economic and personal freedoms. The opposite occurred. Reckless spending actually brought the country's economic life to its knees as its currency lost eight zeros over just 30 years.

Here's a staggering comparison. Imagine that 25 years ago, your savings account was worth $100,000,000. That same savings is worth only $1 today. And you have your government's "common-good" spending to thank for your loss. Governments do not print money to loot the savings of their citizens, at least not openly. No, the printing is always done under the guise of government "good deeds" and deals. That does not make the results less devastating or painful in either scenario.

Just 15 years ago, my father used to go to the clerk's office to get his salary with a large backpack that could hold about $300 worth of his monthly wage. My family in Belarus hurried to pay its bills that day because the next day, that money could lose half its value. There were times in Minsk when you would offer to pay for your dinner in a restaurant before you ate. Why? Because the exchange rate was likely to change before you finished eating your meal! That's a good way to get indigestion. But it saves some money for the family!

Of course, no nation "intentionally" devalues its currency and its purchasing power. But when the government acts with reckless disregard for the science of economics--yes, economics is a science--the results are the same whether they occur in Belarus or Venezuela. And now, such irresponsible and careless policies are threatening the well-being of Americans.

Investing in Talent

Education is, without a doubt, the essential priority of the government as an investor. This education continues from the cradle to the grave. The first five years of a child's life are critical, as their brain development affects how well they will learn and process information for the rest of their lives. As a result, the government must invest in or create a foundation for private-public partnerships in a comprehensive infrastructure for child development. Each aspect of that foundation, including formal schooling, child nutrition and health, parenting training, home visits, and developmentally-appropriate early education programs, holds a lot of importance.

At the same time, in addition to the role of government, the role of parents, as the 2021 Virginia elections proved, is critical to making educational choices for the future of a child. As you may know, the Virginia election largely resulted in a GOP sweep, countering the Democrat comments denigrating the role of parents in the educational process. Unfortunately, judging by the failures of our over-budgeted inner city schools, the government has not shown its prowess in reaching realistic goals in education. Many schools, despite hefty financing, are failing miserably in every aspect of education, with basic math and reading skills being virtually non-existent.

Sadly, this explains why the United States ranks so low in education compared to other countries, which place great value on teaching actual skills rather than gender and sex education studies and "participation trophies" of all kinds. America, unfortunately, ranks much higher in the amount of money spent (or wasted) on such non-educational nonsense as gender studies and sexualization of children, which include classroom dialogues that would get you fired at any workplace.

It came as no surprise when American parents had a chance during the Covid lockdown to find out what's *really* being taught to their children in the classrooms, that millions of children were pulled out of public schools in favor of private schools or homeschooling. Despite the Left's claims, many American parents showed *they* will decide what their children learn in school.

Let's compare the disadvantaged urban areas with the cultural and social phenomenon of "Tiger Moms," a title attributed to mothers of Asian descent. "Tiger Moms," often from immigrant families of limited means, are known for focusing, at times excessively, on the careful selection of school districts and school choice, homework, discipline, and actual achievements of their kids. In such instances, despite immigrants having no silver spoon or other inherent "privileges," "Tiger Moms" do not accept the "we-were-disadvantaged" excuses. Instead, they defeat them through hard work, righteous pressures from the family, and parental supervision. As a result, Asian and immigrant kids, in large part, excel in academic disciplines to the extent that many American universities effectively introduced reverse discrimination quotas against Asians.

American schools and universities were once respected for their dedicated teachers, high standards, and excellence in education. So what went wrong? Much of the educational indoctrination in the United States misses the point of actual education and teaching useful, actual "down-to-earth" skills, such as STEM subjects. These skills prepare our kids to be competitive in the real world. Instead, the new liberal trend in education is to ignore achievements, ignore scholastic knowledge, and instead place exceptional value on diversity and "equity" (whatever that means). In the process, they have dragged student knowledge down to the lowest common denominator.

What has resulted from ignoring knowledge and highlighting diversity? We have given the proverbial American child, already coddled and entitled, yet another excuse not to do real homework or pick useful classes. Or learn anything meaningful. But then, in the Left's America, they don't need a solid education. Living in mom and dad's basement until they are well into their 20s doesn't require even a diploma. In a recently revealed scandal, the school authorities in Fairfax County hid the national merit awards from their high school recipients. That act of misguided "equity," for the sole purpose of not making other kids feel "bad," reduced the chances for acceptance into better universities for those students who asserted themselves and worked hard. Obviously, the "progressive" approach punishes hard work and encourages complacency and laziness. If we continue on this path, we will eventually stop awarding Olympic medals or playing events like the Super Bowl so as not to hurt the feelings of the losing team.

Such misguided priorities result in a trend toward today's educational environment supported by liberal professors and mass media, where grammar, math skills, punctuality, public speaking, and discipline are frowned upon. Even worse, they're painted by "progressive" activists as some remnant of "racial privilege"--again, typically white. But that's a tough argument to make in light of the successes of "Tiger Mom" kids and other immigrants.

In the desperate search for excuses or someone to blame for our failed nuclear families and bloated unsuccessful academic outlets, we miss the true demand. Kids need the skills necessary to function successfully in society with other humans, regardless of color or social status. This need is universal, regardless of whether the child functions in a capitalist or communist society. And the degree of that need is neither dependent on nor defined by the color of a kid's eyes, hair, or especially their skin.

Curiously, after the Russian Revolution, proper speaking and writing were also stigmatized, perceived to be "bourgeois" features contrary to the spirit of the proletariat. The humiliation was so extensive, one could be reported to the NKVD for exhibiting such contemptible "virtues."

Killing one's social life in the United States for exhibiting critical thinking, skill, merit, or humor (even if in bad taste) is not actual "killing." And yet, I wonder, if Antifa or BLM were given even greater latitude, would such social attacks on dissenters be elevated in principle to a higher level? After all, isn't speech, especially on our college campuses, now deemed "violence?" And aren't looting and actual violence now painted as "mostly peaceful?"

I wonder again, will it soon be the norm on college campuses, and society in general, that being smart, striving to learn and excel will be deemed insulting to stupid people? What civics class would ever teach students such nonsense as to degrade science and the pursuit of actual knowledge? Is this nonsense "coming soon to a school near *you?*"

Despite such an approach taking a strong foothold in the upbringing of the next generations, one reading of George Orwell's "1984" will bring back the perception of what is normal and what is utterly irrational.

"War is peace. Freedom is slavery. Ignorance is strength."

As noted earlier, it was the move to belittle and defund our police based on a very limited number of unfortunate incidents, supplemented with so-called "bail reforms" and decriminalization of crimes, which caused a spike in lawlessness around the United States. When a woman is raped on the train in Philadelphia and her fellow passengers fail to interfere, one could blame this inexcusable behavior on the moral degradation and carelessness of contemporary society. One could also blame it on the apparent slow death of "chivalry" or constant attacks on a "male-dominated/macho" culture where the father figure is usually portrayed as a buffoon in need of rescue himself. The brave and courageous men typified in old Hollywood movies would come in handy in today's horrendous display. For those of us whose parents chastised us as young boys if we did not act like a gentleman, that term was not derogatory once upon a time. We only wish acting like a gentleman would be enough to come to the rescue of our country today.

However, there is yet another recently acquired factor that contributes to such inaction or indifference. The villains have now become our media heroes and role models--from Michael Avenatti to Epstein to Josie Smollett --and they are certainly not gentlemen. Our perception of wrong is skewed, and everything is now racist. For example, mowing down a Christmas parade in an SUV is dismissed as just a "car incident." If you believe CNN, the car simply "drove through" the crowd. It had nothing to do, of course, with the career criminal with racist, anti-white propensities sitting behind the wheel.

The once-honored police function has been dishonored and diminished to an "eternal racist oppressor."

In American culture today, if anyone dares to step into the shoes of a "vigilante" or "Good Samaritan," they run an instant risk of being thrown to the PC media jackals, where they will be painted with the same degrading broad-brush strokes as the police. And slapped with a frivolous lawsuit for trespassing on their way to rescue a fellow citizen.

The situation exacerbates if there is even a hint of a skin color factor. Suppose a person is a convicted rapist or wife abuser participating in a "racial justice protest." By the way, that is the new progressive term for a *riot*. I'll let that sink in for a moment. In that case, he is given a martyr status with a free pass to loot, burn, beat other people, and destroy property, and no one can dare to oppose him. And should another person dare to cross the state lines or defend himself strictly as the law intended, according to the mass media that person must be hanged!

Don't miss the irony. An American citizen crossing state lines is now considered questionable by our media, and they continue questioning it as if to prove it illegal by sheer will. But thousands of illegals pouring over our country's border and crossing state lines daily raise absolutely no concerns for the government.

It matters not that the law of self-defense is as old as civilization. The fact that Kyle Rittenhouse might not have exercised the best judgment by placing himself in a precarious position is irrelevant. That sentiment did not register with the liberal media. What mother would let her son go to active riots with a weapon anyway? Hypocritical athletes turn a blind eye, or rather their blind pocket, to Chinese atrocities and Leftist politicians. A young, scantily clad girl who gets drunk and then raped at a party may be guilty of poor judgment, but that's the extent of blame in the scenario. Unless, of course, you subscribe to the liberal media's theory that she "asked for it," much like Kyle Rittenhouse "asked for it."

If that is the mindset, why did the media and Leftist politicians, including Joe Biden, immediately convict Rittenhouse based on "appearance" and then unequivocally deny him the right to defend himself? Why did they prejudge the circumstances and legal evidence? The young man was smeared as a "white supremacist" with absolutely no other evidence than "he should not have been there." Says who?

Consider this: if the police are not there or are told to stand down when they are, whose job is it now to protect the community?

|| *The right to self-defense is as old as human society. One type of society that is denied or virtually extinguished is socialism. Hence, the position of the Left is very consistent with the Communist approach. Fearing people's revolt against the abuse of the system, the Soviet Union banned virtually all weapons. Even your bare-handed ability to protect yourself was extremely limited. To ensure this, karate was outlawed. You would go to jail for simply practicing martial arts, whether as a teacher or a student.*

In the Soviet Union, the law was such that if you found yourself in a situation where "self-defense" was required, you were required to use a defense "means" that was not greater than that of your assailant. For instance, we studied a case in law school in Belarus about a potential rape victim who hit the assailant with a photo camera, resulting in his death. She was convicted of murder because the assailant "was not armed with a similar weapon." Hence, she was denied exoneration by self-defense. Even worse, no consideration was given to her disadvantage in size or strength or the fact that she was the target of the unprovoked assault.

Similarly, a young lady was recently convicted of murder in Russia without being afforded self-defense. She used a metal comb and struck an artery of the assailant's leg, killing the taxi driver who had parked in a narrow passage, blocked the car doors, and attempted to rape her. Under the socialist approach, where only "ideologically righteous" and "equitable" violence is permitted (unless applied by the state, of course), the proper action would have been for both girls to essentially let their assailant perpetrate their crimes.

|| *This exact ideology was mirrored by the Kenosha prosecutors and Leftist media when they insinuated that seventeen-year-old Rittenhouse should have let the convicted felons and mob attack him because "everyone gets beaten up sometimes." That's the real difference between a free society, which values life, and the society the new American Reds are so eager to build, which does not. We can only hope that one day soon Americans will wake up, recognize that they do not want "to be beaten up sometimes," and stop allowing themselves to be treated like punching bags in pursuit of misplaced justice.*

Such a failure to recognize the right of self-defense is prevalent in the attacks on Israel by progressives. Israel is the only Middle Eastern country with a Western-style democracy. Despite being surrounded at every historical turn by religious zealots and ideological enemies bent on the destruction of Israel as a country, still this tiny nation has enjoyed unparalleled social achievements.

Sadly, enemies of Israel are not confined only to their geographical boundaries. Unprovoked attacks by anti-Israel proponents spill into social life in the United States today in the form of defending terrorism and excusing crimes of anti-Semitism. That naiveté, coupled with virtue-signaling, brings to bear destructive policies such as the one being pushed by Rashida Tlaib. When she is not busy attacking and sabotaging Israel along with her comrade Ilhan Omar, she is pushing to shut all federal prisons over the next ten years. For what reason? To cause yet another spike in violent crime waves.

Unfortunately, there are many "bad guys" scattered throughout the world, as we can see particularly with Russian aggression and ensuing atrocities. While rehabilitation and social reforms focus on creating conditions that will reduce the root causes of crimes in general, criminal law and incarceration are the inevitable "counter-incentive" social phenomena that will prevent crimes.

War crimes, however, take evil to a new level. One would be insane to think that "social reforms," "root causes," or rehabilitation would be effective against Putin or against those who tortured and butchered civilians in Bucha. Similarly, the wave of electing Leftist state prosecutors who are soft on crime, combined with decriminalizing felonious behavior, such as raising the limit of felonious theft to $950 in California, is causing a spike in crime. The evidence plays across our TV screens as well-organized mobs rob the high-end stores with impunity in broad daylight.

While revising the sentencing guidelines for non-violent crimes is long overdue, letting the convicted violent felon who ran over his wife's leg with his car walk out on a $1000 bail is sheer insanity. Granted, we're reminded that he used the car to "touch" the woman's leg. Yet, if that were a hand touch, the "Me Too" movement would have been all over it. No wonder businesses such as Walgreens are closing their stores, and people are fleeing the blue state and its crime-ridden cities.

It's also a glimpse into the mindset of the Left that, while one is hard-pressed to find any derogatory epithet that was *not* used to describe Rittenhouse, ramming an SUV into innocent participants at a parade is not described as a terrorist act, but rather an apparently benign "car incident." The truth is the circumstances and "proletarian nature" of the perpetrator did not fit the Left's predetermined narrative. Therefore, the "incident" quickly disappeared from endless play on our TV screens. The worst consequence of this hypocrisy was evident when some left-leaning commentators described the horrendous act and death of innocents at the parade as "karma." Were they daring to imply this was God's repayment for the Rittenhouse not-guilty verdict?

Education and Career

Let's return again to the importance of our government's role in education. The American education system provides students the freedom to be smart or stupid, to learn math or skate through gender studies. Students are dependent upon parents and teachers who strive for basic education and critical thinking to guide them in how to appropriate this freedom. It is essential to teach kids to make the right choices, persevere, take responsibility for their actions, and develop the maturity of delayed gratification, particularly in the early years. Students are dependent upon the bureaucracy to spend education funds wisely. Senselessly spending money on education is a misguided priority. Our students benefit when the focus of educational efforts, including spending, is to create a school environment that rewards effort and merit. Unfortunately, today's education system focuses heavily on promoting a "victim" mindset rather than a "victor" mindset. Our families and society, in general, all benefit when students learn the value of effort and merit leading to success.

The Soviet education system was relatively advanced, particularly in areas needed to advance the Communist state in the arms race against the West. Upon graduation, however, merit and educational achievement meant very little for your future economic or professional well-being. In the socialist society, "social belonging" and loyalty to the regime were paramount to your job placement and career progression. As an example, in Belarus during the Soviet era, there were about 360 judges. Every judge was of the right "color," namely "red."

// *One would draw a clear socialist origin to Biden's way of choosing the most recent Supreme Court Justice. Biden announced he would unequivocally make his choice based on color and gender rather than merit. This rings a bell from a passage of a famous satirical*

movie made in the Soviet Union during Gorbachev's time--"The civilization that ceases distinguishing its citizens by the color of their pants is not worthy of existence." Maybe there actually are more important distinguishing human traits and qualities than just the color of pants or skin?

In the Soviet world, to advance in your legal career you must belong to the Communist Party. Becoming a party member, however, was not easy. Members of the intelligentsia, because of their "wrong" inherent "privilege," per Lenin, were apportioned only about 10% admission to the Communist Party. Workers and peasants were given a free pass on admission. Education, activism, and free critical thinking were not welcomed in the Communist Party. Lockstep obedience to the Party line was undeniably the only trait required of "soldiers" of socialism by its "generals."

Membership was an explicit prerequisite for foreign travel, promotion, or the privilege of occupying any important government position. Another Soviet government tactic was to hold the family hostage. This practice stemmed from the early revolutionary years. I actually experienced this "tactic" firsthand. My father was a prominent decathlete. He was tapped to train the track and field team in Seychelles to enable Moscow to increase the country count for its 1980 boycotted Olympics. Although neither of my parents were communists, I was not allowed to travel to Seychelles with them. I was forced to remain in the country with my grandparents for the two years my parents were gone. To the Soviets, I was held hostage as a "security" that my parents wouldn't immigrate to the West.

You should remember that in the Soviet world everything was government. Each and every institution was government. Therefore, this was a prerequisite essentially for advancement in any career.

While I was in the army, a friend of mine applied for membership in the Communist Party. The army was one of the avenues for becoming a card-carrying member of the Party. His reasoning was that membership would give him "a leg up" in life. While the process overall went smoothly, he later confided to me that he was called to meet with the political officer, who suggested that he "report on" officers and soldiers in the battalion. In other words, my friend was strongly encouraged to be a snitch. When he refused in no uncertain terms and slammed the door, his Party application was "lost," and the process ceased. After the Soviet Union subsequently fell, membership in the Party became irrelevant. It turned out my friend made a wise career move after all.

The ideology or "thought" officers in the army, known as Zampolit or Deputy Commander for Political Matters, were much like fact-checkers in the social media in the U.S. They held a huge influence and discretion over the personnel operations of the army. No important decision in any military unit would be made without their input, particularly when it concerned a soldier or an officer.

// *The permeation of the "thought" police in the U.S. in every aspect of our life is not only scary but also dangerous. It will have far-reaching consequences with chilling effects on freedom of speech. In addition, failure to resolve social issues, rising social tensions, undermining political checks and balances, and diminishing people's participation in political and social life are also concerns. This is what happens when you disenfranchise people through censorship and imposition of the single acceptable "party line."*

The current trend in the United States to choose employees or government nominees based on their skin color, gender, or membership in certain groups is very communist-like. Ironically, per the Left, gender itself no longer seems to matter since they've chosen to disregard the science of biology. Even in private companies, some are *banned* from hiring white males without specific permission from the board. Arbitrary selection has far-reaching consequences. It breeds and encourages incompetence and class warfare.

It places unrivaled value on feelings, perceptions, and groupthink, rather than on the actual achievements and merit of employees.

Some may remember that Gorbachev perceived alcoholism as one of the main "chronic" reasons for the decay of the Soviet system, particularly the educational system. He tried to fight it, although his methods were at times excessive. For example, 200-year-old vineyards were destroyed under the guise of "set policies." Every university during that time had an official in charge of broad student body authorities for implementing anti-alcohol policies.

So, the biggest drunk in my law school class was that person with real power. Many aspects of our daily student life depended on him. What was his virtue? You guessed it--he was a card-carrying Communist! To give you a sense of the irony in all this, imagine nominating an Antifa activist to be responsible for freedom of speech at a university's campus. Imagine placing Governor Cuomo in charge of the well-being of assisted living facilities, especially if one of your loved ones lived there. Oh, wait, that's not a good analogy because we've already done that...

Perhaps you're wondering, apart from loyalty to the system, how did someone advance in the Soviet Union or have access to amenities, good food, or other attributes of life back then--things Americans take for granted today? Hopefully, I do not offend people working at the DMV or the U.S. Post Office, but have you seen many employees at those institutions who seem happy to serve you?

I am sure there are many dedicated, honest, and hard-working people in both entities. However, the stereotypes of poor customer service certainly have some basis there. And the reason? Because their livelihood, salary, and career have zero dependencies on their customer. They have absolutely no incentive to be efficient or even pleasant to you.

In any privately-owned store, restaurant, or other private establishment, everyone who works there, especially the owners, approaches each customer with the perspective that their income and business reputation depend on providing satisfying service to the customer. Serving you is their primary focus. Serving you well pays their bills. That type of customer service became an American trademark. Rarely would you be treated with such customer service in other countries, particularly when people are secure in their employment and have absolutely nothing to gain by satisfying you.

Let me put this in perspective for you with two stories. I was walking in a store with my 3-year-old son. I got distracted by my kid, accidentally backed into a shampoo pyramid, and knocked it down. Bottles went crashing. It was completely my fault. I felt totally embarrassed and wanted to make amends. However, the store owner *apologized to me!* He wanted to make sure my son and I were okay. I think he even gave my son candy. That owner understood customer service. He cared about the satisfaction of his customers.

In stark contrast, I had a store incident in Brussels, Belgium, a few months later. (Belgium is not a socialist country yet, but they're working on it.) When I pulled a bar of chocolate from a display, the whole shelf crashed down on me. It was totally not my fault. Rather, it is a combination of a broken shelf and poor stacking of products. That store owner *yelled at me!* As he screamed in a mix of French and English, it transported me back home in a bittersweet way to life in the Soviet Union. You see, yelling at the customers was not only customary, it was almost an ingrained feature of the socialist shopping experience.

How do store owners get away with that behavior? In both Belgium and the Soviet Union, it is almost impossible to fire an employee, even if they are rude or inept. The perspective of socialist policies is the "security" of one's labor. There is no incentive to please the customer. Socialist policies benefit only store owners. *No one cares about the satisfaction of the public or even his or her manager because the ultimate master is the nebulous "state."*

That is why being employed by a government establishment is principally different than working for a private enterprise. And that mindset is what happens when employees are hired by arbitrary selection and have absolutely no incentive to be efficient or even pleasant to you.

But do we really want to live in a society like the Soviet Union, where every person providing us services, from plumbers to doctors, views us as a nuisance? Do we really want to work at jobs where there is no incentive to succeed? Whether we are the unappreciated customer or the disinterested employee, it is dismal on both sides of the counter.

Ronald Reagan retold a famous anecdote about a person buying a car in the Soviet Union who was told he needed to pick it up in exactly ten years.

"Morning or afternoon?" The perplexed purchaser asks.

"Ten years from now, what difference does it make?" replies the salesperson.

"Well," answers the car buyer, *"the plumber is coming in the morning."*

Americans were likely the ones who created this anecdote because a joke about a Soviet person *buying a car* was already a stretch compared to the average American's luxurious lifestyle and limited understanding of socialism. However, the joke accurately portrayed the defeated mindset of a person living under socialism--an acceptance of scarcity in everything along with a complete lack of all government services tending to the needs of its people.

Suppose the recent debacle with the supply chain in the U.S. was caused by socialist-like over-regulation. Can you imagine living in a society where you have to wait, on average, 12 to 15 years for a basic apartment? Are you willing to constantly "hunt" for basic things such as baby food or toilet paper? As a young parent, you might think that having a toddler is tough. Well ... you haven't raised a toddler in a socialist economy. As the saying goes, you ain't seen nothin' yet.

In the Soviet Union, by the age of 10 months, most children were potty-trained. Most kids in America achieve that feat when they are two-three years old. Do you wonder why we did it to our young ones? We had no disposable diapers. Yes, parents washed and ironed cloth diapers! In case you wondered, no corporal punishment was involved, of course, but there was a lot of effort and patience on the parents' side. For a good reason! I have many late-night memories of ironing diapers during my son's first year. As young parents, we also had to spend several hours each day "getting" baby food for our little ones. American parents have it easy, so no parents in their right mind would want to switch from that parental luxury to socialism's cloth diapers and baby food lines. During the abysmal economic policies of the Biden administration, some of the parents in America got a taste of the baby food shortage. Wasn't that enough of a warning?

Imagine this scenario in America one day. A frustrated young mom stands in line with her one-year-old son balanced on her hip, waiting for butter. But butter is rationed, so that weary young mom receives only 200 grams, enough butter "for one person." Do you wonder why one? Because her son "does not count." Really? He has to eat, too ... doesn't he? Let me assure you that's not an anecdotal example. That happened to my wife and son while I was away.

People in the Soviet Union learned to make do in the "natural" exchange. You had access to some resources. I had access to others.

So, we exchanged. This was not bribery. It was the only way to actually survive.

Let me tell you a story that I remember vividly. I spent time with my aunt in a remote village, and I needed a dental procedure. My aunt took about a half-gallon of homemade sour cream along with us for my appointment. She instructed me that when I entered the office, I was to put the sour cream in the refrigerator in the dental office without asking any questions, then take a seat and wait my turn. Which I did. I remember noting that the refrigerator was already full of fresh produce, sausage, meat, and other foodstuffs.

It dawned on me, only a child at the time that this was the way of the "natural" exchange–You help me. I help you. The government only stands in the way. The "mutual dependency" enabled me to get the service I needed while providing a decent living for a good dentist. Although the system was always ripe for corruption, on that day the dentist's daily salary was about the value of the half gallon of homemade sour cream I brought.

One time, we were picking plums with my 7-year-old brother, who asked loud and clear from a tree: "Where does Aunt Asya work?" My dad replied: "At the sausage factory." To which my brother exclaimed: "No wonder they have all that sausage in their house!" It was clear, even to a 7-year-old, that in the Soviet Union's supply shortage, access to goods and government handouts was everything.

In the Soviet system, a highly educated engineer, biologist, or doctor earned a salary of about 120 rubles. This would be about $150 at the official exchange rate, or about $20 on the black market. A street sweeper, at the other end of the social ladder, got about 90 rubles; an engineer got 120; a factory worker about 200; and a coal miner probably double that. So, the entire education system, medical system, science, and many other serving industries were held up by sheer enthusiasm, people's compassion, and personal relationships.

"Socialist-focused" industries, on the other hand, particularly military-related and anything having to do with propaganda and government positions, received hefty handouts and privileges from the government.

The system was designed to increase dependency on Big Brother. Read that again, and think about the U.S. today with government handouts, economic impact checks, etc. The system is designed to increase dependency on government. The lesson to be learned is that when unscrupulous politicians vie for "equity" in socialism, this "leveling downward" brings with it the death of incentive and aspiration for excellence.

Agriculture was not considered one of the advanced industries. It was in such decay and depression that literally every university student and professor would be summoned by the government and sent to collective farms for the first two months of each school year. To study on site? No, to pick on-site. Students and professors manually picked up potatoes or carrots in 17th-century style. Don't miss the irony here. Socialism provided so much "progress" over 70 years that oppressive Tsarist Russia went from the largest exporter of food in Europe to a country incapable of feeding itself. Even Russian vodka was largely made from imported U.S. grain.

As the saying goes, be careful what you wish for. Those in the United States who vie for socialism may just be getting a taste of what they foolishly wish for. Judging by the shortages already caused as a result of socialistic interference in the economy in 2022, more socialistic influence will bring more shortages. Americans may find themselves headed into the potato fields for a few months. It's "a deal they cannot refuse." Hard work for no pay. Helping farmers who may eventually end up in real or virtual Gulag. And that's the best-case scenario. It could get worse. In North Korea, which now faces a real famine, citizens are forced by the government to relinquish their beloved dogs to be killed and used for food.

My parents were somewhat fortunate regarding their wealth in a communist society. My mom was a famous javelin thrower. Club Dynamo, sponsored by the police, enticed her to change clubs by giving her a "luxury" 310-square-foot apartment. That's not a typo. Two young people enjoying 310 square feet! You must understand that 310 was exorbitant by Soviet standards. The minimum allowable was a mere 50 square feet per person. Our family grew to six people before my parents were even eligible to be placed in the queue for "expansion." The average wait was at least ten years.

Propaganda is a mainstay in Russia as a way of continuing the Soviet legacy and promoting the benefits of Soviet life. At least half of the population believes the political garbage. Shameless propaganda justifies the senseless aggression in Ukraine. Shameless propaganda promotes the dream of reincarnating the Soviet Union in some shape or form, regardless of the human price to be paid. One should not underestimate the role of education or the effectiveness of constant propaganda. One example is the contrived stories about Ukrainian "Nazi" and "existential NATO threats."

// *It pains us to draw yet another parallel to the Western Leftist's propaganda. Consider their contrived "single largest threat of white supremacism" and overblown "existential environmental threats." The Leftist's propaganda has not yet caused the same suffering or deaths as that offered by more senior and experienced communists, such as Putin. We should be concerned, however, because the form, substance of thinking, and modus operandi of the Left follow along Putin's propaganda path.*

The recent raid on Trump's house appears largely as a prosecution of a political opponent and a massive overkill and abuse of law-informant powers by the ruling party. This is virtually reminiscent of the Stain-style "purges." We can only hope it is in appearance only. We hope there is an actual underlying legal foundation that justifies such excessive saber-rattling. If not, this should give serious pause to everyone, regardless of political affiliation. We might be much closer to socialism, with its abuses, and even clear traits of forceful fascism, than we could have imagined.

Education and personal growth must have both practical application and a scientific foundation. The liberal arts approach in the U.S. is used to prepare students to analyze and apply information by viewing several sides of the same issue. In other words, they study both the good and bad sides of a social phenomenon. It is also valuable to study failures and inequities, whether historical, scientific, or personal, for these are stepping stones to advancement and achievements.

The liberal U.S. approach is vastly different from the Russian approach to indoctrination. Whether it be Russian or socialist-driven Western academia, one party line determines everything. The Soviet education system featured a mind-numbing indoctrination into Marxist theories from the cradle to grave. Students were subjected to vomit-inducing copying and memorizing of convoluted, long-winded justifications for the socialist regime.

Sorely lacking in this system were logic and causation. Consequently, these studies made no logical or practical sense. It didn't help that students of this system endured a miserable standard of living under what they were told was the "most advanced form of society." While socialist theories had no practical or intellectual application, these "gospels" of socialism were to be reiterated and repeated as prayers in every scientific research paper or any social event.

One-half of all Ph.D.'s in the Soviet Union were in the distinguished and ever changing field of *History of the Communist Party*, a practice thoroughly learned by Putin. In America's current education system, this lightweight degree would carry equal weight with "gender studies," bearing the typical massive student debt backed by the U.S. government. And now, of course, using other people's money (that would be yours and mine), the government offers yet another bailout in the form of student loan forgiveness as a reward for thrift spending, making poor decisions, choosing useless vocations, and price policy abuses by many universities with the government's blessing.

That colossal waste of time and human capital known as the Soviet education system did its damage-producing people with no understanding of important concepts like democracy, self-governance, private property, actual human freedoms, creative thinking, economics, or, apparently, what genocide is. As a result, a large part of the Russian society was, and still is, incapable of analyzing current events from the point of view of the horrendous experiences of Stalin's and Hitler's deeds. At the same time, they were mesmerized by made-up "Nazi" labeling, as well as Western society's empty use of "racist" labels. In other words, in order to justify your actions or war atrocities, all you needed to do was label the other side "Nazi" or "racist," regardless of whether there was any logical or factual justification.

Human freedoms are akin to that familiar expression: "Use it or lose it." If you don't use freedom, you will lose freedom. That's the valuable advantage that Americans take for granted. On American soil, we can live, experience, and advance freedoms that are ingrained in American society. Other nations, in their feeble attempts to advance liberty for all, might not be as fortunate.

On the other hand, if you've never had freedom, you don't know what real freedom is. Think of it as playing the piano. You must practice the piano, or you will lose your abilities. And if you've never played the piano, you have no real idea of the exhilarating feeling of playing a lovely Chopin melody. To put it bluntly, you don't know what you are missing.

Let me give you a Belarusian example. One of the reasons that factory workers in Belarus were afraid to strike or protest against the stolen election in 2020 and the ensuing brutal treatment of protestors by the government was because they did not really know the value of freedom. They only knew life under the dictatorial rule of Lukashenko. *They were afraid their miserable life could become even worse.* To specifically prove my point, they were afraid they would lose their measly $200 per month salary.

One of my clients and close friends is a programmer. He was receiving at least $5,000 per month in Belarus when the average salary was below $200. He told me this story. Earning $5,000 a month in Belarus, you can live a lavish life. For instance, rental for a two-bedroom apartment in the center of the city runs about $200. My friend was arrested for participating in the peaceful protests against the fraudulent 2020 elections. He was ultimately thrown in jail. One of his cellmates was a factory worker, and the rest were also young, highly paid IT professionals. After hearing the stories of all the IT cellmates, the factory worker was visibly frustrated. My friend asked him what was wrong. You may be surprised to hear the factory worker's answer.

When he realized that those young people, like my friend, who were familiar with the Western way of life and had comfortably rich lives, went out on the street, the factory worker was shocked and exasperated. The young people protested so that people like him, the simple state factory worker, could also live a decent, free life and have a little money for his family. However, that factory worker was also discouraged. He recognized that most state workers were so afraid of losing their meager $200 per month that they cared little about their freedom, even when others with more to lose were willing to fight.

It's tragically simple. The intrinsic mind of a slave does not vie for freedom. Instead, he dreams of his own slaves–and if not, at least a kinder master. Unfortunately, the Soviet Union, as now continued by Russia and Belarus, essentially raised entire generations of such inherent slaves to the system, content with a "kind" fatherly dictator. It is as misguided as the proverb about the abusive husband--"If he is beating you, that means he loves you!"

No wonder, in response to demands to give up power after losing the election, Lukashenko's propaganda asserting his right to rule came up with this maniac-derived slogan--"You don't let the loved one go."

In Belarus, school teachers are usually forced to play the role of voter station monitors in the rigged elections rather than being role models for the rising generation of free people. Therefore, in a twist of irony, a vast majority of teachers were active participants in the 2020 Belarus election fraud, all the while clutching their measly $150 per month salaries. Meanwhile, their colleagues in neighboring Lithuania or Poland, who value freedom, are living much wealthier and happier lives. However, in those polling stations where courageous teachers refused to succumb to the political pressure, Svetlana Tikhanovskaya won with overwhelming results.

The role of American teachers, and the teachers' unions, in particular, appeared to take somewhat of a reactionary turn as well. Teachers were not in favor of reopening schools after the pandemic. In fact, they were united in staunch opposition to the efforts of parents to eradicate CRT, gender fluidity, and sexually explicit writings. They even promoted various PC agenda items in elementary schools. It is a sad irony when America has reached the milestone that materials or conversations with sexual undertones that get adults fired in the workplace have now become acceptable for children in the elementary school classrooms.

When prefaced with "socialist," the term *democracy* and every other social phenomenon degrade the original concept of *democracy* to its actual opposite.

"Socialist democracy" is the rule of one self-perpetuating unaccountable virtue-signaling party of privileged self-anointed oracles. Socialist "freedom of speech" is the freedom to praise your leaders, their flawlessness, and their godlike destiny. A recent example would be the shirtless insane leader riding a proverbial rabid bear into the Ukrainian territory. "Socialist economy" is a space rocket made a decade before toilet paper was produced.

The turn in the U.S. from its practical, down-to-earth, well-rounded, once highly respected educational system to today's socialistic disciplines disregards the true virtues of liberty and capitalism. They focus feverishly on overblown "righteous causes" coupled with made-up "systemic problems." There are few practical implications or attempts at rational solutions. Rather, they blindly follow the senseless, degrading, and self-destructive patterns used by other socialist countries. No wonder experienced teachers are exiting the classroom.

// *A mother of a 4th grader transferring from a private to public school in Virginia was informed by the discouraged, experienced teacher that the child would be the only student in the class who had been taught phonics. Our students learn to read without any understanding of how to combine vowel and consonant sounds to form words, but they know the gender pronoun list.*

Government investment in education must recognize and respond to the changing needs of its people, both individuals and industries. This includes providing platforms to assist them in obtaining the specific resources they require. Government involvement should also envision a whole set of public goods provided by education's diverse components, as well as carefully crafted policies that draw on foundational components of our American society. These concepts include personal liberty, historical achievements, initiative, pragmatism, traditions, and equality. And yes, this is a laundry list of many American strengths that would-be socialists in our country strive to destroy.

It should come as no surprise that there are distinctions between a free society government and a socialistic society government. In a free society, the government performs functions that private citizens are not capable of accomplishing on their own, such as defense, security, monetary policies, policing, and justice. The government of a truly free people pursues the implementation of a *system* that assists people in their "pursuit of Happiness" as designated in the first sentence of the U.S. Constitution with a capital "H."

In contrast, a socialist government is always obsessed with "goals" that have very little to do with the real desires of the people. In fact, you can think of them as a "government with a purpose." Their "goals" are always under a veil of some future "goodness" (equity) or "threat" (existential threat) to the Russian world, not the people. Freedom and the "pursuit of Happiness" of the people have no place among socialist "goals."

It is telling that Putin's propaganda now asserts that life is "overvalued." Though obviously not his life, judging by the size of his table set for visitors. Putin commented to widows that it was honorable that youth are dying in Ukraine as "heroes"--although most of the world sees them as murderers- because "otherwise they are doomed to die of an overdose or a car accident in Russia." It's appalling how Russia's rulers, being true to their new-Stalinist ideology, respond to the plight of their constituency by shamelessly revealing their own loathing and detesting of their people.

Ironically, the true function of a socialist government always deteriorates in the pursuit of what could be called "equitable" goals. Thus, if you see a rise in lawlessness, crime, arbitrary justice, and reckless government actions to destroy the economy, along with diminished protection of the country's borders, these are indicators that your omnipotent government is occupied with other "goals." And make no mistake, those "goals"--such as grabbing power for power's sake--are usually not good.

What can citizens in a free society do when they begin to see these things taking place? They must be socially and politically active and cast their vote accordingly. The responsibility rests on each individual citizen.

"Your price for not participating in the political life is that you will be governed by idiots." That wisdom is attributed to Plato. There's nothing new under the sun. Unless you want that to be prophetic of America, you must take a proactive and informed stance. Your freedom and "pursuit of Happiness" came at a very high price. Get out and vote.

Natural Rights vs. Legal Rights

Philosophy and religion are linked to natural rights. Natural rights are based on the belief that our humanity (our distinct nature above all other living creatures) endows us with inherent rights. Among those are the right to life and property. Scriptural or theological teachings, philosophical teachings, and simple "common sense" are also credited with such rights. Natural rights, we believe, are bestowed on us as a result of our humanity. America's founders placed natural rights as the very foundation of the new American society and its legal principles:

"No man has a natural right to commit aggression on the natural rights of another, and this is all from which the laws ought to restrain him." -- Thomas Jefferson

The key principle in the operation of natural rights is that individual rights stop when they encroach upon the rights of others. For instance, the "right" to kill another person. In a free society, one of the roles designated to the government is determining the scope and extent of such delineation between the rights of individuals, and enforcing violations without overreaching.

A nation's laws bestow legal rights. Because our political and legal systems refer to them as rights, we have legal rights. Political and legal institutions can effectively alter, destroy, or enhance these rights because they were granted by establishing legislation. In other words, they became the law of the nation. However, many legal rights are also natural rights, such as the right to life. These are backed up by both legislation and our philosophical understanding of humanity.

Here is a key difference between a socialist society and a Western-style democracy--the United States, in particular. The constitutions of socialist countries believe that citizen's rights provided for in their Constitution are given by the state, the ruling government.

It is the opposite in the United States. The American founders envisioned that our rights are God-given, not arbitrarily handed out or bestowed by any ruling government. It was the philosophy of our founding fathers that the community of people bestows limited rights to the government for the sake of the common good to carry out common goals. The founders were so convinced of this that they did not even enumerate those rights of citizens in the Constitution, implying "all rights" as specific rights. Certain specific rights were then made Constitutional amendments.

By and large, the U.S. Constitution is a procedural document. Built-in checks and balances keep the government in check. No specific group of people is able to dominate others needlessly. Obviously, some Constitutional designs preceded equitable implementation to all groups of the population, such as slavery and the treatment of the native population. However, the Constitution and its foundational principles of American society were the driving force, still implemented by the majority, for reforms favoring disadvantaged minorities, abolishing slavery, and granting voting rights to women and minorities. Eventually, the 1964 Bill of Rights dismantled systematic discrimination. Now, nearly 250 years since its founding, the U.S. legal system and its laws continue to place high value on natural rights.

The road to freedom in America hasn't been without rough patches. Undoubtedly, the remnants, stereotypes, and perceptions of prior historical developments could have led to less-than-fair outcomes for different groups of people. However, judging by the success of millions of immigrants who have come to the U.S. in search of the American dream and applied their desires and abilities to build a better life for their families, America provides natural rights and opportunities for people, unlike any other country in the world.

I am one of those millions of immigrants. I'm grateful for everything this wonderful country has allowed me to achieve since we arrived in this country-me, my wife, our little three-year-old son, and a whopping $110 in my pocket. I received a fine education, which was not easy when my native language was not English. I was offered employment, working for big companies. Eventually, through a grueling schedule of 12-14-hour workdays and many sleepless nights, I built my own legal practice.

America is a one-of-a-kind land of opportunity. The very fact that the majority of U.S. billionaires are self-made entrepreneurs, including some recent immigrants, rather than tycoons who inherited family wealth, proves my point. This nation offers opportunities. Self-made entrepreneurs are the ones who reach out, grab those opportunities, work hard, sacrifice when necessary, and go after their dreams. In most other nations, that is not even possible.

Anyone living in the U.S. who claims they are not given an opportunity is either lazy or entitled. Their energy is spent on placing blame and making excuses. Skin color, heritage, or other factors. "Poor me." This "crybaby" attitude ignores the successes of new immigrants, many of whom were first-generation or descendants of nationalities or races that suffered gravely throughout history. This extends even to recent history in war-torn countries, the deep poverty of Africa, and the decimation of socialist societies.

Here's a little experiment you can do right at home in America. Try to find an unhappy Afghan Uber driver, a Chinese immigrant living on the streets, a Nigerian kid who is not in a 'gifted and talented' program, or a parent from Cameroon who insists their kid be exposed to CRT designed to amplify the already noticeable division between skin color. Try to find an immigrant enjoying the benefits of America who hates the Christian-Judeo foundation of American society. Try to find any of these in America!

These are examples of immigrants who are grateful to be free in America. While they might not explicitly voice it, they came to enjoy the greatest applications of their natural rights. They came to escape their former governments and their broad, empty constitutional declarations.

Now, these are examples of citizens caught in a dismal socialist society. There were four Soviet constitutions in the course of less than 70 years. Those documents specifically granted rights to its citizens as the state gave them. Most of those rights were wishful thinking. Consider the "right to labor." It does not include the right to be fairly compensated for your labor, the right to choose your work, or the right to freely determine what to do with the results of your labor. *That's because all workers are enslaved to and obligated to work for the government.* From the socialist perspective, workers should repay the government for all the "goodness" the government brings, such as labor they did not choose.

The Soviet regime boasted about their "right to "labor" by citing unemployment in capitalist countries. In the mid-1980s, a Soviet journalist was trying to trap Margaret Thatcher about this "inhumane" side of capitalist life. She responded that the unemployed in the UK received unemployment benefits that exceeded the salaries of workers in the Soviet Union several times! The journalist had no other questions.

Another side of the Soviet "right to work" was that it was also an obligation to work. If you did not work, you committed a crime. Such socialist practices continue now in Belarus. If you have no registered employment, the government will fine you and can even convict you for "vagrancy."

This is still more humane than what they did in my time. Back then, the government called it "distribution" as a means of repayment for free education. Recent graduates, including young pregnant women, were forced to take employment in the southern parts of Belarus, known to be highly contaminated with Chernobyl's radiation, dangerous for unborn children. This is another fine example of the "morality" of the socialist state to which you are always deemed indebted, regardless of the price paid. No wonder Belarus had the highest rate of cancer mortality among children. Add that to the long list of reasons people were leaving the country. That was one of the reasons cited by Maria Sharapova's parents for their move to Siberia from Belarus.

Here's an interesting Soviet fact. During the Soviet time, the government determined that playing in a rock band was not worthy of being called "labor." One of the underground rock stars of the popular group "Voskresenie" was convicted of vagrancy. The leader of another band, "Kino," probably the most popular Russian rock band ever, had to shovel coal in the community heating facility. In the early '80s, the Party issued a decree directing local officials to liquidate over 15,000 underground rock bands. The reason? Their mere existence. Ironically, the same rock bands that were banned during the Soviet time are now being banned both in Belarus and Russia for their anti-war stance.

Consider the Soviet "right to health," which really sounds like sarcasm. "Health" comes with a dismal deteriorating medical system in both Russia and Belarus. The highlight of this system is its declining quality. Funding for health care is constantly reduced by the government in favor of law enforcement funding. For what purpose? Solely to protect the rulers. What does it say about the quality of life of the people when their rulers must continually seek more protection?

Many proponents of socialism advocate for "free" socialized medical care. Many in America boast about the so-called benefits of socialized medicine. There is only one reason they do that--they've never experienced it! To put it kindly, they don't know what they're talking about. I have been treated by such a system, and there is nothing to boast about.

Many also boast about the British healthcare system. Before you praise it, consider this--find me a UK citizen with straight teeth. Ask UK citizens where they go for treatment when it matters. They go to the United States! The British healthcare system isn't free, isn't inexpensive, and isn't worthy of boasting. Especially when your health actually matters to you.

Now let me share with you some of the finer points of being treated with "free" healthcare under my "constitutional rights" as a socialist citizen. When I broke my leg playing soccer, the hospital refused to treat me since it was only a few days before my 16th birthday. I was supposed to walk about a mile away--yes, walk with a broken leg--to the children's hospital. We had no car. Taxis in the Soviet Union were virtually nonexistent, and the fare for a ride would equal your daily wage. The only reason I was actually treated in that hospital was because of my dad. Remember, he was a former decathlete and very strong. My dad asked me to step (or rather hop) outside for a second. He then literally threatened a doctor in no uncertain terms. I'm not sure that strategy would have worked for the average citizen.

Nowadays, with Putin sparing no military expense while closing thousands of hospitals, there is a famous video where a 12-year-old boy crawled on his knees to the fourth floor on the stairs to see the doctor because the elevator was not operational at the hospital. This is a site too familiar for people born in the USSR. The narrator notes that the boy does not yet know that this hospital is also out of materials to provide a cast.

The Soviet government considered each of its citizens as both its "subject" and "responsibility." Those are such warm and fuzzy descriptors, aren't they? The government mandated (sound familiar?) that every person traveling outside the country for six months or more had to have their wisdom teeth pulled out before leaving. Their rationale? The Soviet government might be forced to pay in valuable hard currency for treatment abroad if one of its "subjects" or "responsibilities" had impacted infected wisdom teeth.

Since I was chosen by my law school faculty to represent Belarus in the exchange program with the U.S., I had to have my wisdom teeth pulled out before I could leave. This was in addition to about five months of red tape. The dentist, however, only had two Novocain shots (with no resupply in sight). I had four strong, healthy wisdom teeth--and a choice. Forego my dream of studying in the U.S. or submit to having two healthy wisdom teeth pulled out "dry." Yes, that means *no anesthesia whatsoever.* I'm proud to say I made it to the U.S. program. Despite the near-torture cost, it was worth it. But that's another warm fuzzy socialist memory I won't forget.

The "right to free movement," or travel, was nothing more than a joke. Peasants did not get their passports until the mid-1960s and could be arrested if they abandoned their place of domicile--in other words, if they went to a place where their labor was deemed most beneficial for society. So, the socialist "freedom of movement" did not provide people with the freedom to move at all. In fact, it was deemed treason, as in the case of figure skaters Protopopov and Belousova and others, to even travel outside the country.

For most Soviet citizens, that "freedom" did not mean the ability to move or travel *outside* the country. As was the case with the farmers, Soviet citizens could not even travel freely *inside* their own country without the government's permission. The definition of any socialist "freedom" is summed up this way: *"If I, the omnipotent government, allow you, then you can freely do that."*

It comes as no surprise that people living in socialist countries would like very much to escape those countries. Since 1934, the Soviet Union required an exit visa--permission to cross the border of your own country--even if you wanted to enter other socialist countries. An exit visa was almost impossible to get, unless you traveled to a sports competition, or with a ballet or orchestra troupe. And, of course, you traveled under the strict scrutiny of KGB officers accompanying any team.

You may recall the movie "White Nights" about Russian born Mikhail Baryshnikov, one of the most famous classical ballet dancers of modern times, who escaped in 1974 and defected to the United States. That movie was based largely on true events, as well as "movie-like" escapes of the first Soviet NHLers such as Sergei Fedorov and Alexander Mogilny.

One of the more miraculous exercises of "freedom of movement" was a daring escape in 1974 when Stanislav Kurilov jumped overboard from a Soviet cruise liner, which was cruising to "nowhere." You can't make some of these things up! The ship was ironically called Sovetsky Soyuz--the "Soviet Union!" The ship departed from Vladivostok and sailed toward the equator and back without entering any foreign ports. Kurilov miscalculated the ocean streams and winds, so he ended up swimming to the Philippine Islands in the open stormy ocean. The trip was around 100 kilometers instead of the planned 20. Kurilov was equipped with only snorkel gear, fins, and a deep desire to be free.

The socialist "one-social pipeline" system, by design, had no checks and balances that would have guaranteed the implementation of either natural or even legal rights declared in the Constitution. The role of the government is so prevalent in a socialist society that it owns you--virtually owns each and every aspect of your life. Most importantly, it owns the results of your labor. You have no choice in that relationship. On the contrary, you are effectively indebted and subjugated to the government for life.

Granted, in a capitalist society, you have no choice as to whether you pay taxes. We could agree taxes are a type of "taking" by the government, whether you are willing or not. There are two significant differences, however. First, in the reasonably developed contemporary society, taxes do not rise to the level of expropriation--taking your property away from you for public use. The earner is still left with enough. They have the incentive to work, invent, invest, grow, and enjoy their life.

Second, in a free society, the taxes paid by citizens to finance their government are limited. That is because the government follows the rule of law and is ultimately accountable to its people, or it is replaced at the voting booth. However, the current American trends are not promising.

One might naively suggest that there are courts through which one may challenge government overreach. However, under a socialist system or systems that follow it, such as in Belarus and Russia, the courts become intertwined with the executive branch and lose their independence. Courts and judges are deeply ingrained in governmental bureaucracy. It's all driven by the "Party line." As an example, one of my classmates in Belarus was a judge. When he refused to give a harsh sentence to a member of the opposition, within the next few months, he ended up in jail serving six years on drummed-up charges of bribery.

|| *Having the FBI direct Mark Zuckerberg, the founder of Facebook, to censor all stories about the "Hunter laptop," which the FBI referred to as "Russian propaganda," when they knew they were lying and were well aware of exactly what damaging evidence was on that laptop- just weeks before an American presidential election in order to protect the candidate they preferred- bears frighteningly close resemblance to the Soviet-style of law enforcement used to prop up the preferred political side and banish the other. It's the same song, second verse with Twitter, yet another willing and submissive social tool of overbearing law enforcement and the Swamp. Of course, the laptop, per the FBI*

operatives in their typical Soviet-style "open letter to Father Stalin," had all the "earmarks" of Russian disinformation. Unlike the anti-Trump fake dossier, right?

To give you another example of the socialist rationale, my law colleagues in Belarus argued in court that additional taxation on foreign investment is averse to the interests of investors despite the "grandfather clause" that prohibits it. They proffered that the court should follow the rule of law and disallow the increase. After hearing their argument, the "kangaroo court" first ruled that the court was a "state court." Therefore, it should first reflect the interests of the "state," not the law or private interests. Its second ruling stated that, because taxes collected by the government go to the government, those taxes provide benefits to the people, including the investor. Therefore, the increase in taxation is not an act "adverse to the interests of the investor," making the "grandfather clause" inapplicable. Try to make logical plans for your business when faced with that logic in that legal environment.

As you can see, freedom of speech in socialist countries is non-existent, and unfortunately, there are signs the United States is sliding into the same abyss.

But even worse is the status of economic freedoms. I recently enjoyed the Twitter spat between Sean Spicer and AOC regarding the "socialist system." Mr. Spicer commented that AOC used the capitalist system to sell T-shirts to promote socialism. AOC then noted that Mr. Spicer apparently "does not understand" socialism. She went on to offer her "rationale." Because socialism is a "system" and because the "'tax-the-rich' T-shirt is a transaction," which, according to AOC, is neither socialist nor capitalist, it's "just a transaction."

AOC is being just a bit coy. Every society, whichever system it adheres to, operates through transactions among its members. Whether you buy a T-shirt or toilet paper (if you're lucky), there is really no society outside "transactions." To amuse ourselves, let's view AOC's 'transaction' at issue as a hypothetical situation in the Soviet Union. Let's take the 1970s because, if we were to choose Stalin's socialist era, any independent economic activity was essentially treason. The person involved in such activity would be summarily executed within a few days, per Section 58 part 2 of Stalin's Criminal Code. So, let's presume the "transaction" occurred in a more "mellow" version of socialism--Brezhnev's version in the 1970s or '80s.

Let's also imagine a hypothetical person named Alexandra Okasievna Kortezova (AOK) who came up on her own with a unique design of T-shirts. Let's also assume AOK decided to order production of such T-shirts to someone else for 20 rubles. AOK would sell them at around 30 rubles apiece. Then AOK would keep the profits for herself or use them for charitable or political goals in her passionate pursuit and furtherance of the world's socialist revolution.

Now, let's look at how this "non-systemic" transaction would be viewed through socialist lenses.

First, a "transaction" is judged by society on a Marxist moral scale. That means if AOK pays the workers less than the 30 rubles sale price, per Marx and Lenin, she robs the workers or the proletarians, who are otherwise unequivocally entitled to 100% of the fruits of their labor. Business ideas and design, appreciation of assets, management, finance, business risks, investment opportunities, time value of money, entrepreneurship, distribution, and supply chain skills are all largely irrelevant in the Marxist theory. Therefore, in the "socialist system," AOK's little venture is considered morally and socially objectionable and repugnant.

In a capitalist society, a big question is: What will you do with the profits? That is irrelevant in a socialist system because people are not in charge of society's finances and priorities. That is the sole prerogative of the government. Any attempts at doing so are seen as attempts at usurping the power of the "People." In a socialist system, "People" means society as a whole rather than individual citizens. In other words, in the Soviet Union, the T-shirt transaction would be "morally canceled" at every level.

Let's assume that, notwithstanding its capitalistic moral repugnancy, the entrepreneurial and daring AOK proceeds with her T-shirt transaction in the Soviet socialist society. Since there are no rich people under socialism to tax, we'll assume the T-shirts bear the message "Kill the rich!"--a sentiment that is so dear to many socialists around the world.

We've amused ourselves with this little scenario, but the reality is quite serious. Under the Soviet socialist system, if you conduct economic activity along the lines of the T-shirt "transaction" outside the bounds of state employment, you have committed the following crimes per the Criminal Code of the Belorussian SSR:

- Article 66 - "Sabotage." Punishable from 8 to 15 years in prison. The accused conducted activity outside the state employment and "committed actions directed at undermining the state's industry... or trade." Essentially, if you hire someone to do work for you outside the government's services, you are enslaving people and undermining the very basic tenet of the socialist system. As a result, this crime is placed in the grave category of "Particularly Dangerous State Crimes."

- Article 85 - "Violations of hard currency operations." If AOK were to decide to pay or get paid in U.S. dollars rather than rubles, then the charges under Article 85 would apply. Punishable from 5 to 8 years in prison with confiscation of all the person's assets, not just the assets involved in the crime. In fact, in the 1970s, some people trading in hard currency were executed under Article 85.

- Article 87 - "Theft of the Socialist Property." As there is no free "market" for cotton, in order for someone to produce T-shirts, they would have to steal the fabric from the state enterprise or bribe someone to have it allocated to AOK's underground production. AOK is likely to be found guilty as a principal or complicit in a crime, and the charges under Article 87 would apply. Punishable from 1 year to 5 years in prison with subsequent exile, usually to somewhat unpleasant and definitely cold places.

- Section 50 of the Criminal Code - Engaging in "Private Entrepreneurship" because the T-shirt enterprise "transaction" lies outside state planning, production, or hiring. Punishable by up to 5 years in prison with confiscation of the accused's assets or exile of up to 5 years with confiscation.

- Article 151 of the Criminal Code - "Speculation." Buying something at one price and then reselling it at another might be the cornerstone of the capitalist system. "Buy low, sell high" transactions enable competition, logistics, and the search for profit and growth. In essence, it enables wealth creation. However, in the Soviet society, making any profit by resale outside of state channels was considered "speculation"--a highly immoral and utterly illegal feat. Punishable by up to 7 years in prison.

- Article 153 - "Defrauding the Consumer." If the state sells T-shirts at a set price of 29 rubles and you decide to set your price at 30 rubles for whatever reason, whether seeking profits or even a fair compensation of true expenses, this is not just price gouging. In the Soviet society, this is defrauding consumers. Punishable by up to 7 years in prison plus confiscation of assets.

It's a sobering list, for sure. But here's the good news--and "good" is definitely up for debate. If you are weary of computing the potential sentences that AOK would receive, do not worry. Under the Soviet Criminal Code of the Belarusian Soviet Socialist Republic, one cannot be convicted for one "action" for more than 15 years in prison. This is where the true "human nature" of socialism shines! So, whatever crimes AOK would be convicted of would be commuted to a maximum of 15 years. But I guess that really is "good" news--in the latter days of socialist development (late 1970s/early 1980s), economic crimes "against the socialist state" carried the death penalty, much like under Stalin and Lenin.

I'm sure AOK would enjoy starting her life from scratch in exile somewhere in Siberia. And I'm sure she wouldn't mind confiscation of all her worldly assets, however meager. I'm sure she would look at the bright side. At least she won't owe any student debt. Only her life.

You see, this is how "Tax the rich" or "Kill the rich" works in a society that preys on the "rich" and anyone who would dare to strive to become rich, or even a little bit rich--through either efforts or ingenuity. Hence, the common Soviet disparaging expression--"Do you need more than others?" and the derogatory accusation--"Do you think you are smarter than everyone else?"

I just realized there's another sobering item to add to the list. If AOK were lucky enough to live in contemporary Belarus, she'd face another obstacle. Since her T shirt sports an "illegal" combination of white/red/white - the historical Belarusian colors of protest - AOK or the person wearing her T-shirt would get about two years in prison for illicit demonstration and displaying "unapproved" symbols. And it wouldn't matter whether it's the box from an LG-TV or an AOK T-shirt with an anti-capitalist slogan.

Still, this is not as outrageous as the recent arrest and conviction of a young woman in Russia for displaying "I love my father." In the eyes of the police and the judge, this was deemed an anti-war/anti-conscription protest- -a statement derogatory of the Russian army and worthy of a hefty fine.

I know it reads like science fiction, but I assure you *it is real.* To my fellow Americans, I plead with you. A socialist society is filled with empty promises and meaningless declarations--until it comes to the punishments inflicted for crimes against the system. I assure you--they are not empty promises. There are thousands of people in prisons right now who are living proof of this-- though not all were lucky enough to still be living.

Look carefully at the freedoms and choices you take for granted in America. Believe me, you do not want to trade with the unfortunate people who live in socialist societies. Detrimental activities and attitudes promoted by the Left today are short-sighted. They disparage American society and its great history, paint American forefathers with broad strokes of oppression and inherent racism, urge angry people to destroy this beautiful nation under cries of alleged "progressivism," and are willing to submit to the inequities of a socialist society when they have *no idea what that will mean for daily life*.

If you have difficulty relating to the miseries experienced by residents of the former Soviet Union, don't despair. You can enjoy the same miseries today. Book a short "vacation" to current-day Venezuela, North Korea, or Cuba. Never fear, you'll find some of the same socialist miseries and sadness on every corner. Then, see how successful you are at finding or enjoying the freedoms and happiness that are part of everyday life in America.

Paternalism is a term used to justify when a state or an individual interferes with another person against their will, claiming the person would be better off because of the interference, protected from danger, or perceived self-harm. Some paternalism is evident even in a free society. Examples would include Laws imposing limits, such as anti-drug legislation, or requiring passengers to wear seatbelts. Workers are required to contribute to a pension scheme by the government (aka Social Security). Motorcyclists are required to wear helmets. Individuals are prohibited from swimming at a public beach if there are no lifeguards on duty. Requirements and conditions imposed to operate a medical facility, practice law, or sell alcohol. These are all designed to protect the public before it makes an informed choice. They are typically justified from the points of view of public health costs.

However, excessive paternalism is yet another feature of a socialist society. It tends to take upon itself roles that would be more efficiently performed by a private business without the interference of government.

There is another side of paternalism. Self-preservation of the big state. The eyes of "Big Brother" are constantly upon the people to fiercely protect the power and privileges of the leaders.

// *Some might say this is the function of the "Swamp" in Washington-to retain power for the sake of power.*

An example of "socialist-like" paternalistic policies is the confiscation of guns in Australia. Watch how one paternalistic movement led to another. Confiscating guns led to an unbelievable expansion of the state function, followed by increased enforcement against "wrongs." Before long, people who did not follow the vaccination mandates were gathered and sent to "camps." From guns to vaccination choices! Though some predicted the slippery slope, it is sobering how quickly a democratic state could turn into a repressive machine doing away with the basic tenets of a free society.

While I believe in vaccination, similar overreaching certainly occurs within the U.S. government. Perhaps we should take a lesson from Australia before we go from the frying pan into the fire. Consider the paternalistic way in which Covid has been handled. First, the information provided by the CDC to the public, while allegedly relying on science, continues to be inconsistent, contradictory, and ever-changing. Two masks are better than one? Three are better than two--seriously? This inconsistency is a far cry from Dr. Fauci's initial claim in the spring of 2020, namely that masks provide no discernable benefits. That's still not as atrocious of a lie as "this is a pandemic of the unvaccinated."

The same stubborn inconsistency of policies is yet demonstrated by banning Novak Djokovic from competing in the U.S. Open tennis tournament due to the absence of vaccination. This is despite the fact that we now know vaccinated people only present a heightened risk to themselves-- and even that is questionable, at least in young people. Furthermore, there is no discernable difference between the spread of the virus among vaccinated and unvaccinated people.

Using this logic, explain why hundreds of thousands of people who cross our border illegally are allowed to stay regardless of their vaccination status? Yet, one of the top athletes in the world with probably the strongest immune system due to his health and exercise regimen, has the door of "justice" slammed in this face?

Second, the measures that were implemented were perceived by many as arbitrary and capricious. Many businesses and the livelihoods of their owners were crushed by contradictory regulations while creating privileges for others.

Third, politicians from Speaker Nancy Pelosi to Governor Gavin Newsom failed to follow their own mask and isolation mandates after continuous insistence upon obedience by American citizens. A glaring example featured Stacy Abrams sporting a maskless face (well, a face worthy no less than Star Wars!) in a publicity picture with masked elementary school kids.

Perhaps the craziest and lamest excuse would be LA Mayor Eric Garcetti, who claimed that he was holding his breath during his mask less picture with Magic Johnson. Oh, so he did not inhale?? Hmm, *haven't we heard that somewhere before?* Of course, having your picture taken with Magic Johnson is worthy of ignoring your own laws--oh, that's right, those were CDC regulations! Stunts like these are the epitome of the duplicity of the Left.

The American public is savvy. We do not tolerate hypocrisy. We easily recognize when the paternalistic application of the law applies to the general public but not to politicians making all those intrusive restrictions. We also recognize when paternalistic policies contradict science. Vaccine mandates fail to take into account "natural immunity." In other words, the immunity of people who have overcome the disease. Vaccine mandates appear to have no scientific foundation--particularly in light of Dr. Fauci's assertions from a decade ago.

Vaccines are certainly necessary and provide benefits, particularly for those vulnerable members of our population. But to keep beating the same dead horse--when paternalistic policies do not work--appears extremely shortsighted. And logically, the overbearing measure of the mandates does not make sense. This is like a guy wearing a life jacket screaming to the other guy who is not, "If you do not put on a jacket, I will drown!"

Americans are smart. We can think for ourselves. We can be convinced by solid arguments. But we will not be lectured or looked down upon. It appears that many politicians are enjoying the superpowers bestowed on them via the pandemic a bit too much. While the numerous measures they implement seem to go against both science and logic, yet they are apparently worthy of unfounded accolades by the media and Hollywood. Why in the world would you reward Governor Cuomo with praise and awards, including an Emmy, when his directives--namely, the ban on refusing to accept Covid-positive patients in eldercare facilities--brought an onslaught of tragic infections and deaths among the most vulnerable people in our society? That Emmy was later revoked, but for a somewhat 'wrong' reason. Allegations of sexual misconduct are serious and should not be diminished. But that charge pales in comparison to the heartbreaking deaths of thousands of people. Deaths that could have been avoided.

While we're on the subject of frivolous awards, many Americans are still waiting for the revocation of Pulitzer Prizes given essentially for regurgitating a disgusting, though creative, fairy tale about "Russian collusion" and a "golden shower tape." These were made up by unscrupulous politicians, including Ms. Clinton's electoral camp, and media lackeys holding the country hostage for three long years. Clearly these paternalistic actions did not protect us from danger or make us better off than we would have been without their "Russian collusion" interference.

While the "true" Soviet socialist economy was overwhelmingly paternalistic in each and every aspect of economic and social life, another example of the extent of its continued paternalistic socialist policies is exhibited by countries such as Russia. We certainly gripe about some of the bureaucracy in the United States, with good reason. My law firm did a good deal of business with Russia. A few years ago, we learned first-hand that opening a business in Russia requires 39 different permissions and licenses and up to two months of red tape. This nightmare process was still necessary despite the fact that the business at issue had nothing to do with anything that would be considered a regulated field in the U.S. Putting the matter into perspective for you--a new business of that kind in the U.S. would have been operational in a day or two.

To those who are eager to embrace socialism, I warn you: be prepared to be strangled like a mummy in red tape. There were instances when Soviet authorities required a certificate (called "spravka") from visitors for the purpose of proving they were "alive!"

U.S. bureaucracy is slowly moving toward that type of "spravka." The U.S. energy industry, and gas prices in particular, are direct "benefactors" of Biden's red tape wave against business. And the strangling has only just begun. Small businesses are on standby, awaiting the 89,000 new IRS agents capable of using weapons allegedly designed, of course, to go after "rich" people. We believe this almost as much as we believe that printing more money for senseless government handouts will reduce inflation.

Now, the newest wave of reformers claims that the United States is not capable of evolving and improving itself. Instead, they want different kinds of reforms. The "progressive ideology" as championed by the anti-American "Squad" portrays that America is no longer the pinnacle of freedom or beacon of liberty. In whose eyes? Patriots who built this land nearly 250 years ago would strenuously disagree. The "Squad" and their followers, in their depth of wisdom, have concluded that improving the system by making gradual changes to America is no longer feasible. It is interesting because America has been very effective with policies such as slavery, prohibition, women's suffrage, the right to vote, and the desegregation of schools.

This new clique of socialist reformers claims that both the policies and the legacy of this country need to be destroyed. Smashed to the ground. Just as they've done to countless beloved statues and monuments. Their reform philosophy is to "give back" the social wealth to those who have "produced" that wealth. Their list of people deserving this "give back" includes Indigenous peoples, the poor, migrants, women, and even the land itself. This follows the familiar socialist utopian premise that the restoration of social wealth and equity will mean the empowerment of those who have been "dispossessed."

They claim that social wealth can be restored by starting a mass movement. In everyday words, that means another bloody socialist revolution right here in America. In such a movement, they would "reclaim" the resources from the so-called influential class and give them back to the people who have "worked for it." In this mass movement, they attempt to virtue signal so they will not be seen as "greedy." After all, the communists are always after someone's wealth, aren't they? Serious attempts are being made to supplement socialist slogans--so we won't notice that their intentions are really socialist intentions! Instead, they use overbearing goals and catchphrases--"Defund the oil" and "We will all die in twelve years."

These types of tactics and ideological psyche are nothing new. Dmitry Sakharov, a prominent Soviet dissident, physicist, and Nobel peace laureate who had the strength to single-handedly challenge the Soviet regime, observed:

"A gigantic biological energy ripens inside of a fool. He is not constrained by conscience or doubt. The particular danger, even horror, is posed by a 'cultural' or 'educated' fool who relies on authority and knowledge. His ego has no bounds. Morals are unknown to him. He can do anything he wishes, but he is particularly drawn by his passion for destruction, for redoing the world. I think the world will be destroyed by 'cultured idiots.'"

So, do not be that "cultured idiot." Do not bite the bait of the sugarcoated poison of socialist changes.

A prime example of such paternalistic overreach, of the desire for change for the sake of change, is the Left's overbearing fascination with climate change, manipulating it to ruin fossil fuel and other successful industries and, at times, the environment as well. While we all should obviously focus on protecting our Earth, many of the claims of the doomsday crowd are exaggerated, ill-advised, and lacking pragmatism or common sense. In prior generations, hundreds of thousands of people died from environmental causes. As civilization has become more sophisticated with advances in technology and society in general, now these deaths are limited to only a few thousand.

The increasing temperature of the Earth is being pinned solely on human consumption because that fits their paternalistic narrative. Yet, notice the irony. Largely due to government overregulation, firefighters in California were unable to prevent and effectively fight raging fires. Those destructive out-of-control fires in California caused more damage and carbon emissions than all the cars in California combined.

The latest paternalistic policy on the way for lucky residents of California seems to be a prohibition against sales of any new gasoline-powered cars. This brings interference into the lives of citizens to a new high--or actually, a low.

A foolhardy decision like this could cause a ripple effect of devastation to families, businesses, and industries.

The issue of "climate control" is complex. It represents another example of when an understanding of yesterday's history can have a positive effect today. There are credible scientific reports (including the so-called "Milankovitch cycles") that the temperature of the Earth depends on its inconsistent orbital movements and cycles in a 72,000-year period due to the "wobbling" effect of the Earth's axis. Science seems to indicate that human activity is not the prevailing factor in temperature change cycles.

// *The Biden administration champions climate control as one of our greatest threats and clamors for institution of policies that further their agenda. But they make no concrete attempts at real change. During the Trump years, despite him being portrayed as an anti-environmentalist, the carbon footprint of the United States was reduced by almost 20 percent. The world's main polluters China, India, and Russia--show no interest in matching that marker. If anything, they laugh and take advantage of America's own attempts to destroy ourselves. The advance in actual environmental protection during the Trump era is a testament to the fact that true capitalism is not only about money or greed, as it is accused. This reduction proves it's possible to be socially conscious and achieve actual results in the "green" field without destroying the economy and livelihoods of our hard-working citizens.*

The universal neo-Marxist philosophy declared by AOC and followers of her "Green New Deal" along with modern socialists under flags and banners and policies of various "colors," whether in the legal, social, educational, economic, or environmental fields--is nothing more than a repeat of the numerous Red Deals.

They all result in mass murder, famine, the devastation of economic and social life, and the taking of homes and property earned through a lifetime of labor. They all bring human misery and degradation and loss of natural rights and freedoms.

I remember a certain cartoon during the Soviet time. For some strange reason, its pretext was not seen by the rulers as criticism of the regime, but we knew how to read between the lines! The story went as follows:

Two cubs found a large piece of cheese and did not know how to divide it fairly. A cunning fox suggested that she would divide the cheese equally between the cubs. When the fox cut the cheese in half, one of the pieces was larger than the other. The cub with the smaller piece protested my piece is smaller! So, the fox took a bite from the other piece. Now, the other cub was furious as his piece was now smaller. So, the fox took another bite from the first piece. The action continued until both cubs ended up with the same tiny--but equal--pieces. You may even call them "equitable" pieces.

The moral of the cartoon? When communists call for equity, they usually see themselves as that fox who keeps "dividing" until virtually nothing is left. Yet the cunning communist leaders, like the fox, never go hungry.

The sweeping calls for the destruction of the American way of life and system as it exists ignore all the positive things that America and its hard-working people have accomplished. And this includes all people--from the rich and wealthy to those trapped in poverty. For almost 250 years, America's people built cities, and communities and families, as well as schools, churches, and skyscrapers. They developed technology and entrepreneurship and then shared them with the nations of the world. Americans built the largest middle class and raised the social quality of life in a world where few nations even dreamed of such a thing. America's achievements are unmatched in every field of human development--from the invention of drugs to consumer abundance, cultural and artistic freedoms, and rights for all citizens.

People around the world do not vie to immigrate to socialist Venezuela, Russia, or Belarus, for example. The American flag flies in liberation movements around the world, including Hong Kong and Taiwan, as a symbol of freedom. Our flag represents a "Go for it and achieve it!" attitude. So different from the paternalistic "Big Brother" who will take care of you with a paternalistic hand. Do you still say socialism sounds good? Unfortunately, by the time you realize you have no say in any of the decisions of your life, it will be too late to change your mind.

Democratic Nations Fulfilling Nations' Requirements

In democratic nations, unlike those that follow socialist principles, people choose their government, then limit the scope of power of that government and the mob protecting essential freedoms and liberty. They elect people they feel will work for the betterment of the country. Then those people make it to the higher offices. If those people or parties fail, they are replaced in a peaceful transition of power due to established political and social institutions.

// *The failure of the Democratic Party to listen to the voices of parents voicing concerns against the CRT, Left-leaning teachings in school, and other nonsensical policies is an example of a socialist response. Their failure brought a crushing defeat for the party in the 2021 elections in Virginia. (And the GOP wave is likely to increase in 2024.)*

An opposite example would be the defeat of the former president in Belarus. That defeat brought violence, arrests, and expulsion of political opponents by the loser grabbing power with his "blue fingers" (as he once said he wouldn't do)--for the lucky ones. It has been seen that countries with a democratic government are the only ones that can perform well economically. The general public within those nations has a reasonable living standard with liberties protected, including economic liberties. You might ask: How are democratic nations able to do that? What is the key element for fulfilling the requirements of their people?

The Same Law for Everyone

In democratic nations, there are laws for everyone. But recent tendencies of certain politicians in the U.S. to adopt restrictive measures for the public, yet not require themselves to follow those measures, should be earnestly labeled as "dictatorial" or "socialist." Under the rule of law, no one should befavored based on influence, money, class, or political position. If someone belonging to the highly influential class commits a crime, he will be held accountable for it by the same standards as every other citizen. That's one of the main principles of a free society--and that should be guarded zealously.

The attempt of the legacy media and social network oligarchs to cover for Hunter Biden by burying the New York Post story, banning the oldest U.S. newspaper, and suppressing any and all mention of the story in any public discussion will be remembered as one of the most embarrassing rejections of social freedoms--in particular, freedom of the press. The suppression occurred despite numerous sources offering reasons for American citizens to believe crimes were committed and unwarranted political influence was exercised.

Yet the Left covered for its own. The Left exhibited still another trend toward the arrogant behavior usually seen in authoritarian or military-led nations, such as Putin's loathsome covering for his army's recent horrendous atrocities.

While success in any venture, including the operation of social systems, is impossible to guarantee at a 100% rate, the legal system in the United States still appears to work at a high level of veracity. On the one hand, there was a "not guilty" verdict in Kenosha for Rittenhouse in a clear case of self-defense --and that despite the media, Joe Biden, and the government peddling to the contrary by reciting a disgusting, unjustifiable "white supremacy" narrative.

At the same time, while legacy media constantly finds the U.S. guilty of racism, the court also did in the case of three white men guilty of murdering Ahmaud Arbery. Compare that with the fact that there are almost 900 political prisoners in Belarus right now simply for their tenacity to oppose the repressive regime. Compare it also with the disappearing, arrested, and murdered journalists and political activists who dared to criticize Putin and his corrupt ways of governing, i.e., starting a violent war against a peaceful neighbor.

Arbitrary applications of the law seen in the U.S. in recent years are more akin to a banana socialist republic's persecution of political opponents than to due legal process worthy of the vision of American founders. Consider the following examples--the case with General Flynn; the FBI SWAT team's unnecessary display of gratuitous force and weaponry, arresting Roger Stone (a feeble and elderly confidant of President Trump) in apparent intimidation tactics; clear abuses with FISA warrants; and made-up impeachment charges and hoax dossiers, just to name a few.

Amazingly, the Department of Homeland Security, rather than working on solving the spikes of crime--namely, uncontrollable border crossings-- chooses to focus on the "Orwellian Ministry of Truth" by establishing an organization called the Disinformation (Misinformation?) Governance Board. This GB board has no ethical, theoretical, or legal foundation. Ironically, the acronym "GB" (pronounced GeBe, "G" as in "game" and "B" as in 'bear') was one of the slang terms for the Soviet KGB. It was called MGB between 1943 and Stalin's death in 1953. Ministrestvo Gosudarstvenoi Bezopasnosti ... eerily similar to "Misinformation Governance Board."

In today's culture, it's difficult to find or define truth. That is nothing new. Pontius Pilate asked that very question in Jerusalem over 2,000 years ago. What are the legal standards, enforcement mechanisms, and authority for the determination of the "ultimate truth?" Of course, other than the brazen display of ideological bias?

Today, Barak Obama (the same leader who promised Americans, *"If you like your doctor and insurance, you can keep it"* and who "didn't raise taxes once") now wants the government to supervise and define for us what is true and what is not. And the DHS wants to assure us that it is designed to combat national security disinformation propagated, for instance, by Russia.

Are they talking about the same "Russian Hoax" made up and propagated by the Left, which weakened the United States and its credibility? Notably, Nina Jankowicz (current head of that same DGB) referred to Christopher Steel (one of the main actors in the "Russian Hoax") as a source of authority "which provides some great historical context about the evolution of disinfo."

I can't help but wonder--is this the very type of "disinformation" by "disinformants" that we should be concerned with?

It's not even important on which side of "disinformation" Nina Jankowicz and her Ministry of Truth lands. The DGB's very existence is defiant of the foundation of our free American society. Note that neither the leading philosophers, legal scholars, nor American founders ever thought of "misinformation" or its place in the U.S. Constitution. Or maybe they did ... and they called it "freedom of speech?" Wasn't truth supposed to be something that crystalizes in the public discussion? Rather than supervised dogmas and silly songs by Nina Jankowicz, a clearly biased political operative. This same operative also just recently pushed the partisan "truth" narrative that Hunter Biden's story was somehow Russian "misinformation." Clearly, the revelations by Elon Musk relating to the suppression of freedom of speech, manipulation, and despicable censorship resulting from the appalling collusion of the state and American IT oligarchs clearly is just the tip of the iceberg. And we got to see it by virtue of mere accident.

Let's describe this scenario in everyday words--They just put a drunk in charge of our anti-alcoholic campaign. Correct me if I am wrong. The same person who was on the wrong side of the most scandalous "misinformation" scheme becomes the law-enforcement arm of the Left to supervise... misinformation? You can't make this stuff up.

Friends, I've been down this road before. Does America really need more proof? This is an extremely dangerous and prejudicial slippery slope headed straight into a dystopian society--remember, that's a society where there is great suffering and injustice. A society that tries to control people's thoughts. But even more than that ... to control our essential liberty to speak freely.

I am okay, though, (tongue in cheek), if the MGB is established to check and ensure that there are no more statements from government officials that make us cringe and laugh at the same time.

Let me remind you of a few such gems. "The border is not open." "The epidemic is over/is not over." "We don't release immigrants into the U.S." "The economy is growing [while reporting on the GDP contraction of 1.4%]." "The $3B [expenditure bill] will pay for itself."

And, of course, the classic: "I have 'direct evidence' of [Russian] collusion by the Trump campaign." It all reminds me of the movie *The Wizard of Oz* when the "wizard" realizes that Dorothy and her friends can see him and cries out, "*Pay no attention to that man behind the curtain!*"

Right to Question the Government

In democratic nations, the public has chosen the government. Therefore, the people have every right to question and hold their government accountable. For example, if the leaders of a country come up with a law, political act, or process that is not acceptable by the masses, then the people can surely protest against it.

In socialist nations, it's quite different. Attempts at trying to suppress such voices inevitably lead to disconnect and outbursts of social protest which are then immediately quelled by the socialist government. Are we seeing these same activities in America? Social media recently suppressed conservative voices and peaceful legal processes for questioning the legitimacy of our political processes, including our elections. Such actions inevitably led to disconnect and outbursts of social protest here. While the events of January 6th were regrettable, they were also avoidable.

Let's look at the actions that caused such a response. A heavy dose of propaganda aimed at silencing the people's voices, slanting "polls" in favor of the Democratic Party. For example, outright lies were reported repeatedly that both Hillary Clinton and Joe Biden were winning in the polls by double digits. Double digits, no less! Lies are clearly designed to suppress the vote as people feel they will have no influence in a "landslide." Information adverse to the Democratic Party was deliberately eliminated from newscasts to ensure that the public would not know about Hunter Biden's shady dealings and the compromising info on his laptop.

The FBI readily followed the "Party line" and forced Facebook to follow directions in deleting the "Russian disinformation" when they all *knew* both the laptop and its contents were authentic. These types of suppression, fortified by clear collusion of law enforcement with the ruling party's command, are reminiscent of Soviet tactics used in totalitarian states and socialist banana republics. I've seen it all before. I've lived it.

Questioning the government is the fundamental right of citizens in a free society. America is a free society--or at least it used to be. If indeed our government has nothing to hide and if its actions are legitimate and above board, then why go to such lengths to suppress the voices of so many people?

Their theory that such inquiries somehow "jeopardize the democracy" is bogus and laughable.

It's not up to the government to avoid inquiry by conspiring with the social media giants or determining at its discretion if public questioning is justifiable or not. If the Left wants to turn into a communist party, it will indeed become an omnipotent and flawless institution that one may not dare to question. Not even among themselves.

When Khrushchev mildly, yet shockingly for Soviet society, criticized Stalin, after his death for his "excesses" and abuses, someone at the Party Congress yelled from the seats, "Why didn't you criticize Stalin when he was alive?"

Khrushchev yelled back at the sitting crowd, "Who said that?"

After no one dared to respond, Khrushchev quipped, "So you are afraid, right? And so was I."

Unfortunately, U.S. society is also fusing into an atmosphere where people are paralyzed with fear of retribution. After all, their social standing can easily be "canceled" for the slightest infraction. For now, it's a 'light' version of Big Brother watching us. But a little bit of power always desires to morph into more and more power.

What happens if one day we are led, for instance, by the "Squad"-- today's proverbial four "horsewomen" of the apocalypse? If given power by Big Brother, do you really believe the Squad would feel mercy for their "deplorable" political opponents, the ones who are defending America's foundational principles, the ones they have already painted as "Nazis," "semi-fascists," "racists," and the "worst threat to American society?"

Do they really believe the worst threat to our country is our own people expressing their disagreement with the government in a non-violent but energetic fashion? That is exactly what landed Navalny, Tikhanovsky, and thousands of other peaceful protestors in Russia and Belarus in prison. Tikhanovsky is the husband of Svetlana Tikhanovskaya, who picked up the baton after her husband was arrested and clearly won an overwhelming majority of the votes. Or as DHS's Secretary Mayorkas called such people in the U.S.: "The domestic violent extremist, the individual radicalized to violence because of an ideology of hate, false narrative, personal grievance."

Hating the government--particularly its often-senseless actions, be it war in Vietnam or in Ukraine--is the very foundation of a free society and a distinctive and proud American trait. Considering that it's not up to the government to regulate what is a "false narrative," said government may not complain that people have the right and passionate desire for personal grievance against such government's actions. The notion of being able to petition your government for redress of grievances without fear of retribution stems from the Magna Carta, the very foundation of Western civilization.

Now we have the Biden administration, almost as boldly as Putin, daring to insist that people are extremists because they hate their government. Very Stalinist, in my view.

The relationship of the Left throughout the world to violent criminals (as long as they do not cross the ideological party line) is uncanny. The American Left now wants to open prisons. Motivated by a contrived and misplaced "social justice," they have already been partially successful in filling the streets of American cities with violent criminals. The ensuing and totally expected result--huge crime spikes.

In a paradoxical feat, since Putin is incapable of building a modern army of motivated soldiers, he has recruited violent criminals directly from prisons for his cartoonish, bloodthirsty hordes. All this is yet again in pursuit of some nebulous "Russian equity and justice." One who has never experienced socialism might find these anecdotal similarities as pure coincidence. Others--yours truly included--see that the Left everywhere in the world ignore and condone violence if it serves their purpose. We have learned that they always put their "historical" pet projects and ideological "deals" above morality--and, frankly, sanity.

Friends, it is important to recognize and pinpoint authoritarian tendencies in American society. We must not tolerate the creation of an environment of intimidation where people are afraid to speak or question the government for fear of any version of "Roger Stone-style" retaliation.

One of the worst modern examples of oppression in civil society must include commissioning the FBI to go after outspoken parents. For what purpose? To suppress and censor their non-violent speech concerning the moral, psychological, physical, and ethical well-being of their young children. It becomes even more threatening when the government, aided by the muscle of the media in its back pocket, then intimidates hard-working citizens for criticism, political activism, or political affiliation, while at the same time condoning criminals, rioting, and clear violence against "thought enemies."

That is exactly how fascism, one of the types of socialism, crawled its way into power in Germany, the Soviet Union, and today in Russia and Belarus. While America and Western society might still be far from sending its people to Gulags for criticizing or dissenting--the Australian Covid "filtration camps" notwithstanding--it is important that Americans recognize we have indeed taken the first large steps. We have stepped onto that ominous path.

So, what can we do? We must resist that trend right now to the fullest extent possible. Otherwise, we know where that ominous path leads-- the eventual surrender of all fundamental freedoms and eradication of Western civilization.

DMITRI I. DUBOGRAEV

Chapter 5
Political Correctness and Canceled Culture

Freedom of speech is an absolute natural right with very reserved and narrow limitations designed to protect human life, not human feelings. Such limitations include a ban on yelling "Fire!" in a crowded theater--an example of actions that deliberately cause chaos--or directly inciting violence. These exceptions are not designed to ban the content of the speech. Their purpose is to prevent actions that may cause harm to human life. Their intent has nothing to do with human feelings or "false narratives."

In recent years, however, political correctness and its pinnacle, "wokeness," have relentlessly encroached upon the sanctity of our freedom of speech. Obviously, the First Amendment explicitly protects U.S. citizens from the *government* violating freedom of speech. But the natural right clearly extends further than the government. This right should also be defended against *society* encroaching on that same freedom.

No one in their right mind would defend a position that citizens are free to say anything to anybody with no fear of penalty. There are clear and pronounceable legal limitations. Our society has ethics, social interactions, and standards that clearly act as "self-censorship." They prevent us from vocalizing each and every thought we have. As an example, no one would defend the right of the worker to call the boss a "jerk" and not face consequences. Hopefully, that's not the feeling of my employees!

Similarly, levels of societal development and ethics of a nation restrain the speech of its citizens. Clearly, different countries, communities, and religions differ in what citizens "can" and "cannot" say. For a long time, in that sense, the United States has been a society whose citizens enjoyed the greatest scope of freedom of speech. Today, that freedom is being stretched somewhat on both sides, including President Trump's infamous tweets, which many of us viewed as "going too far.

However, "wokeness" and extreme political correctness have indeed gone way too far in the other direction. Excusing themselves under the guise of their desire to prevent hurting someone's feelings, their actions are actually killing real journalistic reporting and even the usual open human interaction. Our value of achievement, our reflection of reality, and even our humor are now tainted by biased and denigrating reporting. Political correctness is having a chilling effect on political activism, instilling fear of any open debate. This is one of the greatest attacks on the fundamental structure of American society and its cornerstone principles.

American society was founded as a meritocracy. In a meritocracy, individuals holding office and wielding power are elected based on their abilities. As "wokeness" invades our culture and crushes the value of debate, officials will be elected based only on the "correctness" of their political views and other irrelevant attributes, such as gender or skin color.

An inherent problem with "wokeness" is its unpredictability. That which was loved yesterday is rejected today. If the light is the best disinfectant, the murky and unpredictable nature of wokeness is a breeding ground for decaying and rotting politics. What was socially correct and revered as a tradition for years is suddenly eliminated. "Wokeness" is killing the authenticity of revered social norms, traditions, and realities we have known and treasured all our lives.

Initially, "political correctness" was essentially a term referring to political language used with the intention of assuring the least amount of offense possible in a political speech. The concept then poured over to any speech or debate, whether given on the university campus or scientific study. However, as the "sensitivities" of spoiled generations grew, "untouchable" subjects have expanded with cosmic speed.

There is irony even in America's politically correct frenzy. In line with the tradition of American socialists, the term "political correctness" was essentially borrowed from Soviet jargon. It made its first appearance in Marxist-Leninist terminology right after the Russian Revolution of 1917. At the time, its definition expounded to a way of describing adherence to the principles and policies of the Party Line. Which party would that be? The Communist Party of the Soviet Union.

Political correctness became a naturally effective political weapon of the communists throughout the world. It led to repressions against anyone who dared to doubt the superiority of Communism or the ruling class. In fact, even a scintilla of doubt was considered a "thought crime"--the most serious crime under Communism.

// *Sound familiar? Today's D[isinformation]G[overnance]B[oard] ... a modern-day KGB or the Orwellian Ministry of Truth?*

We have looked back at the repressions against citizens during the Lenin, Stalin, and Mao times. The result-a staggering tens of millions dead just on suspicion of political "incorrectness." What about today? Let's look at and learn from how dictatorial and other "red" socialist regimes apply political correctness now.

A Belarusian athlete, Kristina Timanovskaya, was set to compete in the women's 200 meters at the 2021 Tokyo Olympics until she dared to make a critical post on Instagram about the incompetency of members of the Belarus Olympic Committee. As a result, she was removed from the team and ordered to return home. What happened to Kristina next? She escaped with the assistance of foreign embassies in Japan. Otherwise, she would have been jailed like many other Belarusian athletes who challenged the Lukashenko regime, particularly his propensity for stealing elections and then defending his crime with violence and torture. That incident, while tragic for the young athlete, was outdone by more outrageous incidents. For example, forcibly diverting an international flight filled with people in a terrorist-like manner in order to arrest one person: Roman Protasevich, a blogger who dared to publicly criticize the Lukashenko regime.

In a similar fashion, a Chinese tennis player named Peng Shuai, who made allegations about sexual harassment by Chinese officials, disappeared from the radar, causing an international uproar. Not surprisingly, a remorseful Shuai appeared later offering "voluntary" retractions of her misguided allegations.

In another glaring demonstration of the danger of veering from political correctness, Alexei Navalny, a Russian opposition leader and the head of the Anti-Corruption Foundation, was jailed on some drummed-up charges after exposing corruption in the Russian government, including the mention of luxurious palaces built for Vladimir Putin.

One may argue that American "political correctness" characteristically used to come into play only when it related to politicians. Today the American public is drowning in "political correctness," trying to disassociate itself from the possibility of offending groups on hot-button items such as race, gender, culture, or sexual orientation. Judging by the mass media reporting, anything can be racist and all roads lead to racism--from math and punctuality to proper speech and city roads. Political correctness has been a bit of a slippery slope for years, though most Americans paid very little attention to it. They simply kept their opinions and feelings about "political correctness" to themselves, fearing they would end up with an unpleasant label just for raising their voice against political correctness. Consequently, political correctness snowballed. Now, there is no end in sight for its expansion.

As an example, the politically correct continue to artificially divide American people against each other because of skin color, largely by abusing the very concept of racism in American society. It seemed to me to be self-defeating when I arrived here years ago, and frankly, it seems worse now. When I came to the United States years ago to study, in one of my first private conversations with a classmate, I noted that it was inappropriate, in my opinion, to have a "black law student association" to the same extent it would be offensive to have a "white law student association"--which of course, they did not have a white one. As you might expect, it was suggested to me that I keep my view to myself as it was not "politically correct." I was advised that the organization was not promoting racism. I dared to disagree because, if not promoting, it was still contributing to the division of society by skin color.

You either divide people by skin color or you don't. There is no "in between," no "soft" or "good" racism. Hence, I countered, if the U.S. were to eliminate racism, the color of someone's skin would have the same meaning and social effect as the color of their hair or eyes. I also mentioned that disgusting and discriminatory racism by instituting other artificial and trivial. How has all that worked out for racism in America over the past 20 years?

Well, clearly, my views about racism did not align well with "progressivists."

// *Now America has "progressed" to instituting an anti-Constitutional fascist mandate by New York authorities to consider race when distributing life-saving Covid treatments and to consider skin color and gender as the primary "qualification" for government appointments. Sound familiar? The opposite of a meritocracy.*

This is how the fundamental principles of our American society erode. Rather than minimizing differences, we escalate and exacerbate them. We turn "classes" of people against each other. We ruin compassion, equality, and fair competition. Ultimately, we ruin America.

Electing or nominating someone to public office because of their gender or skin color is immature and, frankly, foolish. If you were choosing a pilot for your airplane, would you give the color of someone's skin any weight? Governing a democratic society is still a tough assignment, requiring skill as much as flying an airplane. So, why does the Left continue to give so much credence to irrelevant "woke" traits rather than human achievements? It's no wonder our safety, economy, and social progress are in a tailspin.

Many of those "signs" in American society have been exploited by unscrupulous politicians and media figures for years, creating "problems" where there were none. But by the 1990s, the Civil Rights movement clearly won. Affirmative Action and other programs made huge strides in providing opportunities and erasing factual inequalities. Systematic racism was eliminated.

On January 20, 2009, the U.S. inaugurated Barack Obama as the country's first black president. America was predominantly white then ... and is still white now. Yet, this went against any and all claims of America's racial "tribalism" or "white supremacy." If Barack Obama's election was not evidence of the end of racism by and large, then what is?

America's inner cities and black communities have persistent and apparent problems--high crime rates, high mortality of young people, and deep poverty. It's a vicious cycle that perpetuates the desperation of the ghetto lifestyle. Young people are sucked back into the same petri dish of problems despite attempts to escape-- while politicians continue to fail them.

Sadly, politicians spend much time justifying their own existence and very little time focusing on "root causes" and solutions to problems that plague black communities. For example, the staggering lack of the presence of a father. Over the past 60 years, fatherlessness in black communities has risen at least 500%. Gang activities fill the gaping hole left by missing fathers and mentors. Misguided priorities by people in charge, particularly politicians.

Instead of virtue signaling and empty political rhetoric, politicians must return to prioritizing and improving education and schools, providing job training for today's work economy, developing a lifelong desire for learning, and providing a path for achievement and success in both school and work settings.

But most importantly, through education and family pressure, there has to be a social turn. It's clear the "victimization" outlook only breeds discontent. We need a refocus from negative to positive. Rather than rewarding or punishing based on skin color, we need an optimistic "You can do this!" environment focusing on merit and achievement. Everyone wants to succeed until you ostracize the values of education and effort as racist and oppressive. Every child of every race must have dreams and goals to work toward, and the help of their society and community leaders to achieve those goals.

Numerous examples of achievement and success have emanated from the inner cities. People like Condoleezza Rice, Colin Powell, Tim Scott, and Charles V. Payne would be excellent role models to inspire inner-city teenagers, proving that success is indeed possible. Instead, "martyr" criminals --people who happened to become victims of police misconduct and abuse- -simply fill black teenagers with more discontent.

If our schools, entertainment industry, and society as a whole would highlight and celebrate the many people from "inherently disadvantaged" beginnings whose stories turned "from rags to riches," maybe our inner-city communities could capitalize on these stories and make a real difference in the lives of children.

That same focus applies to the numerous immigrants who arrived in the U.S. truly disadvantaged from multiple points of view-- language, vastly different cultural practices, and true financial poverty. They weren't looking for handouts from politicians. They worked hard, built communities, inspired each other, and seized success. That's the true path to the American dream. Put aside whining, begging, and blaming. Ignore leaders who entice you to depend on the government. Instead, take advantage of what this country offers everyone--freedom and opportunities.

Racial division, stoked by political correctness, still existed and widened when the PC/wokeness culture provided both the tools and fertile ground. That division first surfaced decades ago. In 1994, in the firestorm that defined the O.J. Simpson trial, black Americans and Leftist media took a position that could be summed up this way: "Since we used to be oppressed by racists and the cop is a racist, then *actual guilt does not matter.*"

This attitude would mark a change in thinking. Thus, the non-guilty verdict was seen by white Americans as clearly erroneous at a minimum and appalling otherwise. A large part of the American public perceived the verdict as letting O.J. get away with murder. But the law is the law, and the jury of peers has spoken.

On the other side of the spectrum, black America cheered the verdict as "we got one free," with a questionable point in the "win" column.

The same attitude was demonstrated in modern times when the PC mass media took the side of Jussie Smollett in an obviously orchestrated hoax. Despite all the "fake news" signals, the media aligned deeply with the narrative of the Left. The claim that America is racist and oppressive was "proven" by hordes of "deplorable" MAGA people roaming around Chicago at 2 o'clock in the morning with nooses and bleach, frantically looking for an obscure gay black actor to beat him so badly that he would not even drop his sandwich? Every single outlet of the Leftist media took the story and ran it without fact- checking. Why? Because it perfectly matched their made-up narrative reality. And, of course, it had no "earmarks" of Russian disinformation.

The sheer absence of brain function by the so-called journalists at CNN, MSNBC, and the like was only overshadowed by Smollett himself. He actually performed a "dry run" of the hoax in front of the same street cameras and paid the fake attackers with his personal check. Now obviously, any instruction manual for fake racist hoaxes would note that such behavior is a "no-no." Actually, the State of Illinois Criminal Code came to the same conclusion.

If racism is still alive and rearing its ugly head in America today, it is alive in all colors and should not be divided into "acceptable" racism on the one hand and "white supremacy worse than Hitler" on the other hand. As a matter of fact, no race can claim it is free of idiots and assholes. Thus, if we insist on dividing ourselves, we should first divide people into two groups--smart and stupid. Once we settle that, then the group of stupid can be further divided into stupid white people, stupid black people, stupid brown people, stupid purple people, etc. The word "smart," as a predominant trait of a group of smart human beings, would have no more bearing on the amount of pigment that gives one's skin color than the color of one's hair, eyes, or pants.

Racism should be condemned equally on any grade, any level of melanin in the skin, any color of the rainbow. Racism is dangerous on multiple levels. Most importantly, because while people of any nation are busy dividing themselves into groups and hating each other, they weaken their nation and set themselves up for takeover--*from within or from without.*

The media is relentless in its search for the next "shocker," always playing the blame game, continuously stoking the feeble sparks of racism. They do this by creating an artificial divide, i.e., reporting on the "whiteness" of explosive stories like Sandman or Rittenhouse or the racism of math or good manners. Yet they fail to report on the race and utterly racist propensities of the perpetrator of the Waukesha terrorist act. The simple truth is there are rotten apples of every skin color. Rotten apples in and of themselves do not make the whole race racist.

Despite the false Washington Post reporting, it was not an "*SUV* [that] slammed into Wis. parade and killed [6]," including innocent children. It was *a specific person.* It was *an American.* A jerk and racist. A murderer and terrorist. His color did not matter. He was evil. But if you report the color of the skin in other racist instances, you must report this one, too. Call a spade a spade, even if it does not fall into your narrative and made-up agenda. I know its wishful thinking on my part, but journalists should apply the same standards and logic to *factual* reporting. Otherwise, our media effectively becomes complicit in the search for useful idiots. And there are many to be found!

In the Western world, the theory is that people are influenced to different degrees by external sources. Politically correct language exerts a lot of influence on the unsuspecting masses. Political parties have taken that theory to heart. As an example, political parties increased the usage of sexist language in the expectation that it would promote sexism and sexist opinions in the audiences, which they could then use to their advantage.

The use of racially-charged language is particularly disturbing in such a context. The more politicians accuse with racially-charged language, the greater its effect on instigating violent content. In actuality, at the very heart of their concept is this question: Who decides what is acceptable and what is not in American society?

Once we settle that, we can determine which joke is below the belt and which is not, which label-in-jest is allowed and which is not.

Politicians have agreed on a new truth-self-restraint and a person's ethics no longer matter. Big Brother now establishes the rules and the norms that citizens must follow. At times, in lieu of the law. Being "politically correct" has been regularly used to silence any dialogue of disagreement. Being "politically correct" has been used to limit freedom of speech, with its snowballing effect permeating new horizons every day. Being "politically correct" has also been an effective censorship tool to drag down any opposition to the Left's agenda.

Today, America is experiencing the threat of "social suppression." It's nothing new. Socialist nations have been using it for years. Social suppression involves using language that forces a speaker to speak in statements and speeches without the benefits of freedom of speech. It inhibits citizens from speaking the truth for fear of "insulting" or "violating" the feelings of others. Citizens are forced to comply with a rigid, tightly-held use of self-censorship. The rules and scope of this censorship are ever-growing, while permissible boundaries are ever-shrinking.

And what is the result of all this? Thanks to the bloated media, politicians win votes. Ordinary people willing to "toe the line" advance their careers by reading off a carded script. That script eventually turns into a "Party Line."

I never dreamed that America could one day have its own "Party Line" of politically correct censorship. Friends that is the stuff of socialist nations-- not the beautiful United States of America. Political correctness supercharges the trend in modern-day political games for the purpose of ostracizing any individual from professional, social, and media circles when they veer off the Leftist course. Even "speech sins" committed in the past, even in childhood, can be used against you.

Cancel culture, or "call-out culture," has grown to be a dominant and poisonous phenomenon. A media weapon in the hand of the Left. It is used by the media to gun down virtually any person in any situation if they disagree with the Left. Cancel Culture uses smear tactics to accuse concerned citizens of being racist and bigots "worse than Watergate/9-11/the Civil War."

The media is developing an almost godlike power to silence those who disagree. A glaring example is ex-U.S. President Donald Trump, who was permanently banned from the popular social media platform Twitter on Friday, January 8, 2021. It should cause great concern and agitation to Americans to realize that while their ex-president was banned, enemies of the U.S. like Putin and

ISIS were not banned. But Trump was not alone. Numerous conservative groups and many discussion forums that did not fall squarely in line with the "dominant view" have suffered the same banning, whether their sin was criticism of the Biden administration or frustration with the flip-flopping positions of the CDC.

The expression "cancel culture" holds a unique meaning in today's society. The person being "canceled" is subjected to ostracism from society and considered officially 'canceled' in their social, political, or even professional life. It's quite arrogant to think that a society can "cancel" one of its own as if they never existed simply because they disagreed. Those unfortunate public figures, now private citizens, suffer severe negative implications. Sadly, there is no "statute of limitations" for the far-reaching implications of "cancel culture." Even prior youthful sins and "incorrectness" from kindergarten to high school can come back to haunt you! Until you submit to repentance--or at least reverse your misguided opinions.

Interestingly, "cancel culture" never seems to seize those on the Left. Have you noticed that? A free pass is given to Leftist politicians. This free pass allowed Barack Obama to change his mind and his once-staunch position regarding marriage being a union between a man and a woman. And allowed the former Governor of Virginia, Ralph Northam, to dress up as a member of the KKK or sport a blackface (he can't "remember" which) with no consequences. Perhaps because neither the puffed-up media nor the pompous governor himself could decide which behavior was more offensive. Hence, the odious Northam--another Left politician-- escaped cancelation!

Of course, the media forgave Governor Cuomo of New York for his incompetence in handling Covid, which resulted in thousands of deaths. He even won an Emmy in the process-- and it wasn't for best role as "Dr. Death!" That proves the depravity of today's culture. Interestingly, being disrespectful and harassing women turned out to be over the line, even for Cuomo! I guess the Left has a few scruples.

"Call-out culture," a sister form of "cancel culture," has become a method where an individual, even celebrities and hosts, are boycotted or shunned for speeches or statements they made if they contained comments on controversial or questionable topics. Sadly, the called-out person has no chance to receive forgiveness or outgrow their stupidities and youthful errors. We have seen a substantial rise in these called-out punishments being carried out recently against respected public and political figures.

In the same way, the Soviet Union canceled scientists, activists, and even members of families. There was actually a term coined –"member of the family of the enemy of the state." Using the same logic, after the civil war, the Soviet Union gathered the cream of the crop of the Russian intelligentsia and simply "canceled" all of them–well, those who had not been previously executed–by putting them on a ship and expelling them from the country.

Luckily for the West, those same people became part of the engine of the social, cultural, and scientific progress of the West. They included the inventor of the helicopter, Sikorsky.

Similarly, today, Belarus and Russian officials jail or expel anyone who is not in line with acceptable political correctness or official views about the war. In fact, the words "war" and "peace" are both banned in Russia today. As I'm thinking about it, I guess Leo Tolstoy's novel will have to be retitled in Russia to simply say "*** and ***."

Opposition leaders in Belarus are subdued by prison sentences ranging between 12 to 20 years simply for running the elections or, in the case of attorneys such as Maxim Znak, even for representing the interests of the opposition leaders. Those who "like" or post unpopular opinions on social media are a little more "lucky." Their sentences range between 2 to 5 years. Similar criminal cases are pursued against protestors and journalists in Russia, including Alexander Nevzorov and Ilya Yashin, who were sentenced to 8½ years in jail for denouncing Russia's war crimes in Ukraine.

// *The persecution of conservatives in America, including Facebook's snitching to the FBI regarding the activities of groups on the right, follows the same Soviet logic and embarrassing pattern-- without the prison sentencing. They use state resources to fight anything they consider to be political dissent.*

Another example of modern-day ostracism in the form of "cancel culture" has been inflicted on Alexei Navalny. Due to Navalny's support for freedom of speech and his openly-targeted statements regarding Russia's corruption and Putin's inept presidency, he has faced not only cancellation but also persecution, arrests, and even a homicidal attack with a toxic nerve agent. Amazingly, Navalny survived the attack and was able to trace his assassins, even duping one of them, Konstantin Kudryavtsev, into confessing the crime over the phone. The assassin admitted to Navalny that the Novichok (poisonous agent) had been placed in a pair of Mr. Navalny's underpants. Since then, blue underpants have become a symbol of the shameful and vindictive nature of Putin and his regime.

Unfortunately, proponents of socialism in the United States see nothing wrong with cancel culture. There is very little doubt that, if they are given sufficient power, the cancellations will not stop at just social media or careers. We can expect that certain politicians and members of law-enforcement institutions, such as Congress and the FBI, will continue their power grab by knighting themselves as god-like puppet masters. They will use their high moral ground power to cancel any politicians they do not like. They will also fix the results of any elections they do not like by securing "insurance policies" --such as pushing the "Russian hoax" button and other clandestine tactics they used to displace and undermine duly-elected President Trump.

Abusing FISA warrants, weaponizing the FBI against the sitting President of the United States, and openly threatening him with the powers given to those law-enforcement agencies--any of those actions are worthy of the most prolific banana republics. However, it is sobering that such actions took fertile ground here in the United States and were executed with impunity.

Here is just a small list --

Bruce Ohr held a prominent office with the Attorney General while his wife was involved in the infamous fake "Russian dossier."

Senator Schumer said the intelligence community was very angry at President Trump and mentioned they had "six ways from Sunday" to get back at him.

Peter Strzok took upon himself the task of correcting the elections in case they went the "wrong way." Such actions came with the blessing and likely active participation of other FBI operatives such as James Clapper, former FBI Director James Comey, ex-Deputy Attorney General Sally Yates, former National Security Advisor Susan Rice, and former Deputy FBI Director Andrew McCabe--all either openly leaking classified information, undermining the President's decisions, sabotaging, and even threatening the sitting President.

Anyone familiar with the ins and outs of the operation of the Soviet system immediately finds scary parallels. The U.S. social system, unfortunately, is slow to react to such repulsive displays of abuse of public trust and law enforcement authority. House Intelligence Committee Chairman Adam Schiff was key to fueling the feeding frenzy over the fabricated dossier. He reiterated repeatedly that he had "proof" the dossier was real and President Trump was compromised. Remember, Schiff was not a layman but Chairman of the *Intelligence Committee.*

Chairman of the Joint Chiefs of Staff, Gen. Mark Milley, when he was not busy pushing the racist Critical Race Theory as the key element of U.S. military readiness, was even willing to go around the Commander-in-Chief and call his Chinese counterpart--essentially an enemy--in his secret and treasonous reassurances of Beijing regarding U.S. foreign policies and war tactics. Interestingly, Critical Race Theory doesn't seem to be on the minds of the brave Ukrainians fighting for their lives. Nor is CRT lacking in Russia's abysmal military operations or dreadful weapon production, notwithstanding the use of Soviet-era outdated armaments designed to wipe out entire cities.

This slew of virtual creeping military coups is akin to Russia being overtaken by the KGB (now known as FSB) and then running the country outside the electoral process or the rule of law. The "cancel culture," as the weapon of the socialistic Swamp, does not cancel itself unless the people of the United States first face it, call it what it is, and eventually cancel it. That brings the media back to reporting rather than fueling propaganda lies. That returns the government machine into the legal framework. While certain "cancellations" have had successful defenses in the courts as infringement and violation of free speech, and while the Special Counsel Durham investigation bore some fruit with indictments (and, surely, more to come), that is not enough. Society as a whole must realize that this is cancer on the republic, and if we do not, in Trump's words, "fight it like hell," it will kill us.

However, far more peculiar was Donald Trump's January Twitter ban, which came only days after the Wednesday, January 6th violent invasion of the U.S. State Capitol. Trump was viewed as providing encouragement for the participants, despite his clear statement in his speech to "walk peacefully and patriotically to the Capitol."

In light of that statement allegedly being a violation of the "Community Guidelines" set forth by the company, there is still, however, no banning of terrorist organizations. They remain present on the very same platform. We assume the beheading of the captain of the women's volleyball team in Afghanistan is not something that Twitter, other social media, or women's rights groups are concerned with because that would be "Islamophobia." Nor is there a banning of a plethora of accounts using "hate speech,"--whatever that is--a clear incitement of violence against conservatives, or violent imaging against Trump and the then-presidential team.

Ayatollah Khomeini's existence on Twitter is just fine by the fact-checkers and other liberal media. Apparently, nothing to be concerned about. All Khomeini does is call for--and provide a careful elaborate justification for-- total destruction of the only democratic state in the Middle East and long-term U.S. ally--namely Israel. However, if you are Republican and provide contradictory statements about the vaccine like Marjorie Greene, you are banned for life. That did not happen to Dr. Fauci because his statements are all so "consistent."

If you are a Democrat, like then-candidate Biden, you can lie that you have a federal plan to shut down a virus and state a "person"--making a clear reference to President Trump-- "anyone who's responsible for that many deaths should not remain as President of the United States of America." This is despite the development of the Covid vaccines during President Trump's unprecedented "Warp Speed" plan.

Yet, President Joe Biden--being president during the period culminating in more Covid deaths than during Trump's era--now admits that he has no federal plan that the states should take care of the Covid strategy.

In addition to dropping the ball on that front, there is more. Multiplied by uncontrollable and unvaccinated, non-tested illegal immigrants, Biden's administration completely botched testing plans and production. As of the beginning of 2022, Biden was no longer even trying to show any semblance of consistency or scientific basis in Covid protocols, CDC incantations, or required safety measures.

Biden continues to get a complete pass by the liberal media, which is baffled and dumbstruck by his low popularity ratings. None of his misstatements or outright lies, however, were banned or questioned by social media. Why would that be? Any inaccuracies, puffing, or stumbles by Trump received a scorching fire from the media.

We are still waiting for any media reaction to Biden's boast: "I will shut down the virus. I will not shut down the economy!" Why should we expect anything different? If the baffled media believes Biden's catastrophic pullout from Afghanistan, the unnecessary deaths of 13 marines, and abandonment of billions of dollars in American military equipment to an enemy was a success, of course, he receives a complete pass.

So, there is a clear trend in the cancel culture, and it goes only one way. Again, as declared by the French Revolution, for the Left, "There are no enemies to the left." The ever-increasing frequency in the usage of cancel culture on strong opposition members in a political party is one of the fundamental reasons behind unfair elections (as strongly believed by many), whether it be rigged by the monster media, irregularities of ballots, or faulty voting systems that can be manipulated to deliver the scores required.

It has become popular for the Left to be walking on eggshells when it comes to criticizing violence by any Leftist movement. Similarly, the Soviet Union supported and financed numerous "leftist" African dictators so long as they decried "imperialism" and declared their adherence to the "socialist course." These ominous "socialist" characters included the President of the Central African Republic, Bokassa, who declared himself an Emperor and spent the country's entire GDP on his Napoleon-like coronation, while being credibly accused of cannibalism and mass murders.

*/ / * *In the eyes of the Leftist media, even if a child rapist got shot by Rittenhouse in a clear case of self-defense, such rapist may still rise to the level of sanctity and martyrdom just by virtue of his participation in the "righteous" BLM riots.*

At the same time the contemporary liberals, and their extreme Leftist wing in particular, easily trample upon the free speech of those who disagree with them. They ignore our Constitutional and liberty-based foundation and surreptitiously defile and morph it to suit the requirements of the Leftist party line. The mass media and Leftist partisans make sure to skew the reality so that what you see is never real. The sheer volume of repetitive material spoken by most of the leading members of the Left is staggering.

"Repeat a big lie often enough, and it becomes the truth" is a quote often attributed to the Nazi propaganda boss, Joseph Goebbels. More importantly, however, he is known to perfect the propaganda by mixing lies with the truth, by inserting small but critical pieces of propagandistic falsehoods into veracious reporting to gain ideological indoctrination.

The contemporary propagandists follow pageant-like scripted statements. They keep clear of the ever-expanding "acceptable-speech code" designed to avoid any "violation" or even a perception of violation. They're like puppets being "puppeteered" by the rise of politically corrected speech. It is yet to be seen whether journalists and other public figures are truly ruled by the fear of being canceled in the public's eye–particularly by the loudest but not necessarily the most honest or smartest voices--or by the steroid-like feel of power over unsuspecting politically-incorrect souls. That is where the desperation of both the Swamp and oligarchy begins to leak out and bleed across their assurances and public pledges. Desperation to cling to power, to be accepted, to win another term, and to continue in that power role, drives them. They are eager to use overbearing words to define their objectives, play fast and loose with truth and objective reporting, and cover up for "tribal" preferences.

These leaders and false figures of authority promote an idealistic and utopian state. Such talk marks their assignment as a laughable string of linked unrealistic promises and picturesque expectations. Most of those promises will, in all probability, never touch the light of reality. That's the Soviet, or "sovok" way too. I've seen it all before.

The task for society is to identify the falsehoods and make appropriate corrections--accomplished through legal challenges and elections.

Pinpointing lies becomes more and more tricky, particularly in light of the heavy Left lean of information and infatuation with utopian self-mutilating socialist ideas. The histories of socialist countries and their miseries are being obfuscated, confused, and muddled by modern-day socialistic ideologues and apologists. They accomplish this by promising "new" revolutionary ideas for political gain--sprayed with a "new" color. Much like with racism, again, the "color" is secondary to the underlying principles, ideology, and causation. These tactics are certainly supplanted and heavily employed by such outlets as CNN, MSNBC, NBC, and the like, although their results are intermittent.

On the one hand, the mass media was relatively successful in convincing at least half of America that active, rowdy, raucous Trump was "Hitler-like." That Trump was essentially responsible for the Covid pandemic and its devastating economic ramifications. That feeble-minded Biden, propped up by the Left, would somehow bring equilibrium and reconciliation to our society. Remember, we were promised an "adult in the room." We have the person who shakes hands with air and cannot string a sentence without a teleprompter. Of course, having a Vice President who declares that we have a "strong and enduring" alliance with the Republic of

North Korea (!??) brings us no comfort as to either the sanity or competence of our leadership. Obviously, slip-ups are easily forgivable if superseded by a list of achievements. While that list remains largely blank, we will take the liberty of laughing at each untimely cackling, for instance, when discussing war refugees with foreign leaders, or non-sensical speeches with circular "passage of time" passages aimed at grade-level pupils. If anything, that level of incompetence and derogation from her duties is a great disservice to the very cause of nominating minorities and women to the high offices.

At the same time, while a 70-80% drop in viewership of CNN by awakening America is encouraging, it's far short of a full payback for all their lies, cover-ups, and sheer propaganda--from the Russian hoax to the perverse, never-ending "systematic racist America" angle. Reporting on those falling ratings, however, was done with typical Leftist media bias and misreporting. For example, Leftist media conflated the ratings of Fox News-- which were up--with the ratings of CNN and the like, then concluded the "average" trust and ratings of news outlets was down by a certain percentage. This is like reporting on a one-sided match where the final score was 6 to 0, summarizing that the average number of goals allowed by each team was 3, leaving the remainder of the "details" outside the brackets.

Those same tactics are even more perfected by such ominous regimes and personalities as Putin or Lukashenko. Prior to the occupation of Crimea and the Ukrainian War of 2022, Russia and Putin's illicit yet feeble attempts at influencing U.S. elections--and anything else related to Russia, other than Ovechkin chasing Gretzky's record--were out of both the public view and interest of Americans. In fact, it had deliberately been that way for decades since the end of the Cold War.

For all practical purposes, the Cold War with Russia is over for Americans. But that is not the case for the inept rulers of

Russia. And therein hides the danger. Putin, in his pretense for war, was able to convince a large portion of the Russian population of the very "real" Western threat. He imprisoned any meaningful dissent, took over traditional media, and banned or severely limited Russia-based internet news outlets by indiscriminately labeling them "foreign-influenced" or "disinformation." "Foreign" influence, of course, is a deliberate inference to the Western threat--namely, America.

With his most recent moves, the regime's kangaroo courts banned "Memorial," an organization formed by Dmitri Sakharov, a Nobel Peace Prize laureate. "Memorial" was dedicated solely to tracking and reporting atrocities and victims of Stalin's communist regime and didn't even focus on Putin. However, Putin's methods and affinity are apparently way too similar to former ruthless rulers not to draw a clear parallel, if not the desired legacy.

This expression may reflect the psyche of Russian society and policies:

"Our democratic so-called writers and opposition pour dirt on our country, working off the money paid by the West. Such opposition exists on the American money, and they are nothing more than lapdogs of their overseas masters; it's not a secret that so-called "opposition" is an enemy of our people and financed by the plutocratic West and lives of its handouts."

Ironically, the statement above--while ringing true with what is going on in North Korea, Belarus, and Russia today--was actually uttered by Goebbels, the head Nazi propagandist. Many Americans may find this type of view of America having an allegedly aggressive stance toward Russia surprising, if not befuddling. But it's definitely in line with the mindset of both Goebbels and Putin. To demonstrate, here is the actual statement made by Putin that enabled him to apply his heavy-handed cancel politics and war waging in full swing:

"The problem is not that I am a bad economist or a bad president, but that we are surrendered by enemies. And because enemies--and the main enemy, NATO--around us, we do not have time for economic happiness, growth, or salary increases. We have to survive. We are under siege. And in the fortress that is under siege, you do not elect leaders. It's wartime. There is no time for an election or meetings. We have to be careful."

So, in order for the cancel culture to be even mildly successful, you have to entirely ignore facts, sanity, and reason. You have to employ fear mongering to the full extent. You make up the most ridiculous enemies as "American threat" (in the case of Putin), or "white supremacy," or "flatulent cows" (in the case of Green New Deal proponents), or "sparrows" (in the case of Chairman Mao). On their face, the most ridiculous hysterical claims appear to be existential. So, you are thus ordered by the propaganda to march in lockstep while ignoring your government's corruption and shortcomings. If you do not, you become, in fact, the "enemy of the state/the enemy of the people."

By the same token, arrogance multiplied by ignorance (not knowing what a $3 billion tax credit is?) caused Rep. Ocasio-Cortez (D-NY) to cancel the "enemy-of-the-people" Amazon, preventing it from investing billions of dollars and creating tens of thousands of jobs in New York. Virginia, by the way, said "thank you very much" and welcomed the jobs and economic boost it received.

Not to be outdone and following her tribe's smoke signals, Senator Warren with her questionable appetite for truth and lacking a discernable record of any contribution to society other than her priceless contribution to Native American cuisine and false "diversity" of the Ivy League faculty, went after Elon Musk for not paying his "fair share." Elon Musk–who made the largest tax payment in the history of the United States, who is responsible for creating hundreds of thousands of high-paying tax-bearing jobs, who is advancing U.S. technology, space exploration, and economy. They attack him for simply proclaiming the need for Twitter to be a bastion of true freedom of speech. But remember, for socialists the definition of freedom of speech means freedom to say anything freely *for as long as they agree with it.*

In a "tax the rich" mentality, what's the next "natural step" in going after the rich? Just taxing (to the order of three commas) will never provide enough to finance utopia thrift-spend projects such as Build Back Better, a precursor to the catastrophic Green New Deal. This "great" deal is so appalling, it must be supplemented and supported by lies and elimination of any open debate.

Logic bears asking: Can you actually and reasonably tax someone more than $11 billion--which is more than the entire state budget of numerous countries--without 'expropriation' crossing your mind? Those of us who lived under socialist rule know painfully well the meaning of 'expropriation'- -taking property from its rightful owner for the use/benefit of the future public "good." *Taking your hard-earned property from you.* And just to clarify-- those who part with the fruits of their labor or ingenuity are never part of the "good" or the "future."

If Russia or Venezuela are not enough of an example for our ultra-Left, they should study Sweden, quoted by modern U.S. socialists as an example of where American "imperialism" should turn. But *which* Sweden? The Sweden that existed between 1970-1990, or the Sweden before and after that period? It makes a significant difference. Sweden and other Nordic countries tried "socialism" for two decades. They also followed a form of utopian socialism, both politically and socially. Utopian socialism was formulated by Marx and Engels around the mid-19th century and later adapted by R. Owen and Fourier. The concept grew from early communist and socialist ideas.

Sweden, for example, raised taxes up to 90%, doubled the size of its government, and significantly increased welfare programs. As a result, the country virtually squandered all the wealth it had accumulated over a century of capitalist development.

What saved countries such as Sweden? I offer three answers, which made one true evolutionary step. In a nutshell: Enough with revolutions! Instead, frank, open dogma-free discussions. Actual honest, at times self-deprecating, analysis of their dismal "socialist" policies. Self-correction, which made the society turn an about-face from socialism and return to lowering taxes, encouraging private enterprise, rewarding work, cutting welfare, and focusing on care for the truly needy.

Therefore, before Left-leaning politicians turn "irreparably inequitable." America into "socialist" Sweden they may want to brush up on history, geography, and actual economic and political analysis. Unless, of course, they are keener on turning the U.S. into the Soviet Union, North Korea, or Venezuela, like Lenin and Trotsky. Easy to rule. Hard to live in. Unless you are the one in power.

Green New Deal

The proactive weapon of political correctness today involves putting forth loud-sounding policies and virtue projecting, but it is extremely impractical and usually counterproductive. Opposing or criticizing such loud policies makes you a "fascist"--and not just the semi-type. The full-on type. One of those policies is the "Green New Deal."

The term "Green New Deal" (GND) is a blanket term being used to describe the various set of policies put firmly in place to make for systemic change, promoted under the flag of immediate existential threat to humanity in the range of 10-12 years. Its goal is to thwart the existing economy and make a switch to "green" and renewable energy. The idea isn't new. We watched the United Nations (UN) push for global policies under the same name in 2008. Those same ideas have been added to the platforms of many green party candidates in the past, including the likes of Barack Obama, Ralph Nader, Bernie Sanders, Jill Stein, and H. Hawkins. There is certainly a clear need for practical policies and incentives focusing on the environment- -but you don't burn the barn to get rid of the rats.

In the current situation, the set of policies under the Green New Deal name has broad implications. First, it is estimated to cost the country over $80 trillion. To put it in perspective, this is four full years of Gross Domestic Product (GDP) of the U.S. or the country's over 100 annual military budgets. It will also bring the virtual death of numerous industries, livelihoods, and businesses that have been an integral part of policy debates across the country. Pushing along the lines of typical virtue-signaling socialistic "goals" and "plans," substantial credit for this utopian, unproven, and unrealistic program goes to Rep. Ocasio-Cortez (D-NY). As the youngest woman ever elected to Congress, AOC has been courted as one of the Democrats' favorite potential candidates for the presidential election set for 2024, along with Andy Cuomo, Michael Avenatti (if the legal troubles for both magically disappear), and other brilliant thought and "spiritual" Leftist leaders, supported by the "Cuomo-sexual" media.

To boost her chances of success, AOC will probably need to improve her basic knowledge of economics. It appears that many of her statements lack a basic economic foundation, let alone any logical basis. Statements such as, *"We need to invent technology that's never even been invented yet"* should be cause for great concern about her leadership.

The GND, a broad and vague 14-page nonbinding resolution presented to Congress, has become a lightning rod for economists who deride the plan as frantic government overreach lacking reasonable details, pragmatism, and financial realism. Strikes also come from a more humorous side. Ms. Cortez, in promoting her green views, produced the infamous 'flatulent cows' documents, which thankfully never became part of the bill and have since been taken down. They were, however, part of the fact sheet provided to the media outlets by Ms. Cortez. It's likely they will be remembered for their absurdity.

The text explained the role played by cows in rising global temperatures due to the production of methane gas, a byproduct of digestion in most cows released into the air in the form of flatulence, primarily. While agriculture clearly contributes to pollution, including animal waste and its byproducts, technology, and environmental regulations have made huge positive strides in dramatically reducing pollution--particularly in the U.S. and EU. These are in response to increasing demands for mass production of healthier foods to remediate world hunger.

That's why AOC's "cow" documents were, in essence, a self-inflicting wound that made people take environmental initiatives less seriously. The deprecating nature of the GND became inevitable when "cow" issues became a target of Trump's labeling and criticism. While at times sophomoric and unnecessarily disparaging, it was yet effective and catchy. In one such rant, President Trump joked--not without some truth--that the Green New Deal calls for banning cows. His words, which were then comically plastered across the media platform, were, "Cows are out ... They don't want cattle; they don't want cows." Fortunately, despite Trump's somewhat humorous predictions, Biden did not fully heed the progressives and did not support the "banning of cows" or the Green New Deal itself.

There is a real peril in policies such as GND, as with any "Red" deal that reeks of the impracticality of socialism with various beams of social justice. They become a "First-world" problem for people who are either too obsessed with virtue-signaling or can't be bothered to figure out the details of their plan or its real consequences for society as a whole and its poorest and most vulnerable members in particular.

While Biden did not push the GND through, he clearly took a large part of it and voiced it on the electoral trail--or in his basement in those days. He claimed he would make strides against the oil and gas industry and made a bold promise to ban oil and gas licensing on federally-owned land. That promise, supported by various policies, is now viewed by many as one of the main reasons for high oil prices and inflation. After the elections, Biden clearly started making good on his promise with such policies. One example is the Keystone pipeline closure. Another example is the removal of the blockade against Putin's Nord Stream 2, which is one of the main sources of support for Putin's Soviet revisionist policies and his brutal Ukrainian war.

The cited fear of climate change influenced Biden to take such massive measures as shutting down all oil and gas lease sales from the country's vast lands in his first few days in office. Biden had not implemented even 1% of the GND (aka, per yours truly, the "Red New Deal"), and yet gas prices almost doubled. Obviously, this massive measure was a monkey wrench thrown into a working plan for American energy independence.

In addition to killing around 300,000 blue-collar American jobs, as predicted by the University of Wyoming, the measures gave rise to gas prices which clearly acted as a much heavier burden. It was, in effect, a tax on members of the middle and lower class in our society. No wonder it has been reported that an average American family's expenses for necessities rose on average by almost $4,000 in 2021 and even higher in 2022. Declaring "social" equities as your moral telos is one thing. Taking practical steps to achieve them beyond futile rhetoric is something different.

Defunding Law and Enforcement

The rallying cry during the protesting and rioting against "systemic racism" was actually against a number of isolated instances well addressed through the punishment of the culprits. During the protesting and rioting surrounding the BLM cause, the "call-to-arms" was focused on black lives lost due to isolated cases of "abuse of police." Curiously, those protests were actually silent about the hundreds of lives lost due to warfare-like shootings in Democratic-run cities, or the miseries of those dying due to fentanyl overdose caused by open border policies. However, there were more than a few select activists who initialized and propagated the campaign to convert the catchphrase of those protests--"Defund the Police"--into a reality across U.S. cities.

The slogan was picked up by unscrupulous "woke" politicians looking to score easy political points. This scenario was *strikingly similar* to disbanding the police in Soviet Russia and Nazi Germany when socialists came to power.

The unfortunate death of Breonna Taylor, shot by Louisville police officers in 2020 during a botched raid on her apartment, aggravated the situation further. Despite charges being brought against the police, that tragedy was a pretext that triggered more uprisings, destruction of cities, and violent riots.

Those unprecedented events caused conditions to be put into play one upon another, culminating in measures finally taken to *actually* defund law enforcement agencies across the country.

Did defunding the police *actually* cause any reduction in crime and/or deaths of people of any color? Of course not. In fact, there are numerous indicators that such policies caused further hardship, particularly to vulnerable minorities. This is yet another example of such "New Red Deals"--an emotional virtue-signaling feat bringing the opposite result.

A year later, the cities that yielded to such nonsensical policies reverted their stance and sought additional funding for police to fight the spike in crime, particularly in urban areas. Unfortunately, the society's peace and prosperity--its very life and human existence--depend on its policing power. That feature of society has been a necessity for thousands of years. Unless and until the "root causes" are eliminated, along with the crimes they caused, you will not be calling a social worker when someone robs your house. It is highly unlikely that criminals will abstain from committing crimes after being warned by a member of the local PTA.

The crime problem was obviously exacerbated even further with the influx of Soros-elected prosecutors hell-bent on changing the societal architecture. Their new methods included intentionally failing to prosecute crimes and, instead, adopting "revolving door" policies featuring easy release of violent criminals at pre-trial and post-trial reforms. These superimposed policies that encourage crime, i.e., "smash and grab" robberies rampant in our cities, are not yet likely to affect elite gated communities or politicians who seek to remove protection from average citizens while enjoying an abundance of personal security for themselves and their families. Some "defund the police" politicians have been chased by their own karma when they've experienced carjacking at gunpoint.

However, the reduction of police is a growing burden to a much greater degree on our poor and a curse on disadvantaged members of our society.

Another disturbing feature of socialist "wokeness" is that it does not know when to stop in its pursuit of "equity" or "non-offending" rhetoric. Therefore, it is unable to correct its course or put itself in harmony with reason, causation, or science (which they "like" so much). In their skewed perspective, wording and feelings are much more important than being "factually correct."

As an example, let's look at a current issue. Women have fought for their rights since New Zealand became the first country to give women the right to vote. The Achilles' heel, if you will, of the women's equality movement has been for women athletes to receive equal pay, scholarships, and recognition for their athletic achievements.

Title IX, a federal civil rights law in the United States of America, was passed as part of the Education Amendments of 1972. While not explicitly mentioning "sports," it became a foundation for furthering equality and the development of women's sports. Since then, there has been clear progress in sports equality. Grand Slam tournaments now pay women and men equally. Many women's sports occupy higher slots in viewership. However, the reality is such that WNBA will likely not be able to compete successfully with the NBA. Neither will men successfully compete with women in Victoria's Secret Angels shows. The latter example is not so much about women being sexual objects but something much different and more dignified than the Left wants us to believe. Throughout thousands of years of human history, the arts and literature have always signified not only the beauty of "women" but the beauty of mankind. The Left has turned that longstanding, well-documented cultural thread of society into an embarrassing and degrading social phenomenon.

Biological science is such that men's bodies have greater strength, higher testosterone, and greater capacities of the heart, lungs, etc. As a natural result, women are not able, Title IX notwithstanding, to compete on equal footing with men in most sports. In pole vault competition, as an example, men clear over six meters, while women barely clear five. This is supported by relative results in other sports as well. In my view, this is a fairly representative sample of a comparative ratio of pure physical/biological abilities of the sexes. Competition, hard work, perseverance, and talent are important in physical sports, but nature's pure propensities are a critical advantage.

So, when the "woke" crowd, echoed loudly by the liberal media and politicians, sees nothing wrong with biological transgender men competing against biological women and obliterating them on the track and field or swim lane-this is more than wrong. It's insane. It's fundamentally unfair to women and their parents, who invest their time and money to prepare female athletes for competition. However, pure natural biology does not get a "like" from the Left.

Imagine a 250-pound male boxer deciding he identifies as a 100-pound man or even a 100-pound woman. With today's threat of being called out for fat-shaming or body-shaming, should we now allow that 250-pound man to compete against a 100-pound man? Or woman? Does it ever cross any "wokester" mind that winning by 38 seconds in swimming is fundamentally unfair to actual biological young women competing fairly? Or that this grand "win" did not happen in an "equal" setting?

Winning at all costs is everything if you prescribe to an East German-like obsession with sports. However, this might be the case in America if Americans were to follow the path of Putin. I am still puzzled as to why Putin didn't come up with the idea of replacing all women in Russia's Olympic sports with men identifying as women. But, of course, there's always the next Olympics for such nonsense.

However, I am sure if Putin did call, there would be plenty of athletes willing to cross gender lines. *But never the Party line.* As I reflect on this, I realize that a simple call would be so much easier than Putin going through the trouble of employing the powers and ingenuity of the FSB (former KGB) to replace urine samples through intricate bathroom wall holes and empty vial tubes. Nothing is too much trouble to avoid the World Anti-Doping Agency (WADA) disqualifications.

If you recognize the validity of science, which says that men and women have over 2000 distinctions, and if you have any attachment to reality, then you recognize that winning a swim meet by 38 seconds is neither fair nor sane. In a world of increasing discrimination (i.e., fat-shaming of heavier athletes?), this must indeed be seen as a form of discrimination against biological girls who put their heart and soul into doing the best that the physics of nature allows them to do.

The "woke" approach is indeed the opposite of Jesse Owens, a black U.S. track and field athlete who won four gold medals at the 1936 Berlin Olympics. Here is yet another example of a point I made early in this book- namely, the value of knowing history.

In 1936, Jesse Owens was an affront to Hitler and his followers, just as he would obviously be in opposition to the U.S. "woke" movement today. Jesse dismantled the Nazi claims of a "superior race." His victories and gold medals redefined the principles of fair play and respect that athletes deserve when competing on an even playing field.

// *I do not recall reading that any U.S. politicians instructed Jesse Owens or other American athletes not to irritate Hitler's despotic regime in 1936. However, a similar instruction was given to U.S. Olympic athletes by Speaker of the House Nancy Pelosi prior to the Beijing 2022 Winter Olympics, warning not to anger the Chinese Communist Party due to the social stance of any U.S. athlete. Many U.S. athletes and Hollywood elite are quick to heed those instructions regarding the power of Chinese money. They would not dare to "irritate" their lucrative Chinese sponsors with appeals for freedom and liberty, or even their own "woke" values.*

DMITRI I. DUBOGRAEV

Conclusion
How to Spot and Say "No" to Socialism

The degrading and devastating nature of socialism in economic, social, and ethical aspects of civilized life as implemented by various countries around the world is obvious and unquestionable. It might explain why Putin, when occupying Ukrainian cities in his brutal and unjustifiable war, resurrected the statues of Lenin which had been removed by the Ukrainians vying for a free society. The ugly realities of socialism are easy to spot.

But could there be a "softer" nature of socialism? Can you borrow the "slogans" and desired results of socialism without all the destruction, misery, usurping of power, snowballing lies, repressions, and economic devastation?

Many countries have tried. None have succeeded in that pursuit. To this day, the historical answer remains an unequivocal "NO."

Except that today, there seems to be a "maybe" in American thinking. Maybe if we kowtow to China's success, like Google or the NBA? Maybe if we consider China's economic might and payouts now as more important and valuable than the repressions, lack of freedoms, and concentration camps for dissenters/religious believers that will surely come later?

America, listen carefully. Learn from history. Apply critical thinking. Follow causation. Stick to the principles, but be flexible and ready to have your views evolved. We must understand and ingrain this in our society-- *Taking the "soft" approach was exactly the means by which Russia achieved socialism.* That exact mindset--"Let's do it again because Stalin was the problem, rather than the Party or socialism."

Russians couldn't have been more wrong.

But the goal itself was also well beyond the realm of being ethical or humane. The desirability of achieving socialism is a dubious reward to say the least, despite the masses of citizens who are taken in by empty slogans.

// *Defund the Police is a sobering current example. Remember that the conflict between socialism and capitalism is not only in the "outcome" or the fruits of the labor, i.e., redistribution of the "positive," such as property. Capitalism favors you keeping your stuff. Socialism insists that "you did not build it" (remember Obama's remarks) and that society needs your stuff for the common good more than you do.*

There is a larger conflict between the two systems relating to the "negative" or responsibility for your actions. Capitalism, and the freedoms it provides essentially says that you are responsible for your plight and liable for your actions, including crimes. Socialism, however, constantly excuses itself with high-brow goals, willing to give a pass to the so-called "oppressed" when they commit crimes, blaming society as a whole as the "root cause" for anything that an individual did or committed. The socialist approach can be summed up in a few philosophical words uttered by John Belushi in the movie "The Blues Brothers-- "We are on a mission from God..." and "it's not my fault." Just to remind you--that was a comedy.

All in all, the Left is willing to excuse crime and allow criminals to roam and rule the streets because it's "not their fault." To the Left, it's the fault of a few--literally, a few-- unscrupulous policemen.

There is a saying, "What doesn't kill you makes you stronger." That doesn't apply to socialism. Socialism will either kill you or make your life miserable. Weaker, but never stronger. There is one exemption--if you are among the few in power, the few spewing out utopian concepts to obtain and keep that power. For the rest, the hard-working citizens, the masses, one thing is for sure--*socialism deprives you of your liberties.* No matter what color those socialistic policies and goals are painted with--red, green, brown, or any other color.

Nikolai Berdyaev, a famous Russian writer, summed it up with eloquence:

"Freedom is the right to be unequal. Equality (if it is perceived to be broader than formal legal equality) and freedom are incompatible. By their nature, people are not equal. You can reach equality only by force, but the equalizing will always be performed to the 'lowest level.'

"You can equalize the poor with the rich only by taking the wealth from the rich. You can equalize the weak with the strong only by depriving the strong of their strength. You can equalize stupid with smart only by turning intelligence from being a benefit to a flaw. The society of universal equality is a society of poor, weak, and stupid based on coercion."

So, in essence, fighting for socialism is nothing more than a path to power. Turning various parts of society against each other for the sole true purpose of being more politically active. Benefitting from the strong, bright, and wealthy at their own expense.

At the same time, there is clearly some fluidity of wealth, knowledge, and power within the social horizontal and vertical lifts. There is some forcible "taking" or "sharing" that inevitably occurs, the libertarian ideology notwithstanding. Despite the "socialist" vocabulary permeating our lives in various contexts, it's likely that "socialism," even on paper, can no longer exist in its purest Leninist/Marxist form.

On the other hand, judging by the strong middle class in most industrial countries, capitalism has acquired a "human" face. It is no longer the brutal uninhabitable force enslaving the workers (proletarians) that, as Lenin said, "Has nothing to lose but their chains." As a result of this evolution, many welfare programs, government actions, programs, and interference are, at times, in jest, called "socialism."

So, it bears asking the question: When is there indeed "too much socialism" in the capitalist society that the society either gets seriously ill and severely hampers its development or is so significantly damaged that its social, ethical, or economic recovery is no longer feasible? When is America doomed to the standard socialist plight of misery?

Each person has their own scale of when "too much is too much." When the adverse changes reach an unacceptable level, it's the predominant perception that the well-being of society, as a whole, turns the society one way or another. Some objective/subjective evaluation should help us determine the breaking point. That determination is vital because after the breaking point, the country essentially progresses onto a slippery slope and descends into the socialist inferno.

How do we acquire such an objective/subjective evaluation? By the study of history and a little bit of geography. Contemporary societies should be evaluated by approaching modern practical "socialist" phenomena and historical facts. I'm not talking about "pure" Marxist dogmas voiced in the 19th and beginning of the 20th centuries--although they are raising their ugly bloody head again in the 21st century under "different" colors and pre-texts.

This means that the social underpinnings should be held to mirror the *actual* social events and *actual* consequences suffered by socialist societies. This does not mean accepting virtue-signaling "declarations" by modern politicians or even the proclamations of the "wishful thinking" Marxist theoreticians.

This approach should provide proof of evidence for our future actions and plans as an American society. In addition, it would also be instrumental for our younger generations. We all must evaluate the existing socialistic "sores" infecting America's spirit and degrading its continuous endeavor for a "more perfect Union." How did we get these "sores" and when did we get them?

We should modify our perceptions of socialism as it conceivably reappears in modern society. It is a different world. We should not focus on the Marxist's hopelessly outdated "ownership of means of production." (NASDAQ stocks already exceed Lenin's outdated expectations for public ownership.) We should not focus on the "dictatorship of the proletarians" (i.e., workers) nor "red terror." Items such as the required number of Gulags for the "rehabilitation" of noncompliant citizens are not the focus of our American society, even in light of socialist analysis. And Twitter bans do not count as Gulags, although calling one-half of voters semi-fascists is not encouraging.

Using the four-dimensional R.E.D.S. scale, Americans can make an informed judgment based on their own personal perception of the following:

R – Ruling by oppression

E – Enterprise (private) deterioration D – Denying the rule of law

S – Speech restrictions

The application of this 1-10 evaluation should not be made on the perception as to whether an event is "widely spread." Rather, consider the event for "how deep" it goes against the norms of a free society even while being condoned or accepted by that society or the government *without proper legal redress.*

Simply put, there need not be 100 Gulags. One political prisoner scores a 10 on the socialist scale. When your score is often 20 or more, you should then be concerned that socialist propensities are now dominating *your life.*

Be warned that once we consistently reach the score of 30, I am not sure if reversal from socialism will even be possible in American life. We are not trying to diagnose how to spread the cancer of socialism yet.

This scale analyzes how benign or potentially terminal a particular "spot" or "sore" on society's skin will be if left untreated. Absolutely no "socialist" value should be assigned based on the natural color of anyone's skin. Note that we also did not assign any "R.E.D.S." socialistic value to feelings or "puffing." Unless they rise to the level of political or legal actions, they are largely irrelevant and should be confined to one's private life.

As we examine events against this scale, the system's occasional lapses or flaws, particularly when they are rectified by legal action, should not be counted toward the upper side of the scale. They could be the "sick spots." However, regardless of the degree of their threat, they are surgically removed through legal recourse. No matter how heinous or socialistic the crime is, if the society provides legal relief, the act does not move the needle of socialism to the left. However, if the punishment or lack thereof encourages that act to be repeated or sets incentives for the spread of the problem, that should move the needle left.

Let's look at each category on the four-dimensional R.E.D.S. scale.

R – Ruling by oppression

The general consequence of a socialist society is that it moves further and further from voluntary exchange and transactional interactions between people into forced behavior and coercion. At times, the impermissible encroachment could be carried out through a law that goes way beyond what is necessary for the fundamental goals and functions of the government.

As an example, in the case of Nazi Germany, the majority of the nation decided through a legal process that Jews were no longer desirable members of the society. While that was the "law" of the land, it was a law of oppression violating the natural rights of people. A law that went way beyond.

Everyone is free to set their value scale. Here are two examples and my view on them. Stalin sending people to "kolkhoz" (collective farms) by expropriating (taking) their private property and killing those who voiced a protest would get a 10. The actions of Derek Chauvin in the George Floyd case would get a 10 because a police officer acted on his own volition while vested with authority. But if the justice system works and the perpetrator is convicted, no "socialist" or "dictatorial" points should be awarded (violent riots notwithstanding).

Unfortunately, American society is not yet at the stage where crime is 100% preventable, even in cases of clear abuse of power. Nonetheless, the free society governed by the rule of law applies the law in an even and nondiscriminatory manner without giving a pass to classes or rulers.

Let's compare this with Russia. A leak of electronic surveillance showed the prison warden torturing and raping the inmates with mops, which appeared to be fully sanctioned by the prison authorities and those in power above. Obviously, the leak produced no criminal prosecution--other than against the person who leaked the tapes.

Let's look at Belarus. What happened after the peaceful demonstration against the fraudulent elections? In the best tradition of Stalin's NKVD, hundreds of people were snatched from the streets by plainclothes officers, at times under the disguise of medical emergency vehicles. Those people were then beaten and tortured. Several people, including Roman Bondarenko and Vitold Ashurak, were beaten to death.

Belarus and Russia get a solid "socialist" 10 for the manner in which they handle civil disobedience and human rights, on the one hand, while on the other hand, condoning those who abuse power as long as they are loyal to the regime.

Now, let's look at America. Failure to account for Ashli Babbitt's death after the January 6th events with virtually no investigation, keeping protestors without bail, denying a speedy trial, handing out excessive sentences, and harassing people who participated in the peaceful part of the protests get a solid "socialist" 8. This takes into consideration the fact that the January 6th rioters were indeed acting illegally, and no one was tortured.

Forgive me for resorting to socialist tactics of "whataboutism" to make a point about the unequal application of the law. What about the rioters who burned and looted American cities for months, causing billions in damage and killing dozens of people? Where was the tough justice there? Where was the public and media condemnation of those who incited and encouraged those riots? Was it less of a crime because the precious lives of politicians were not in peril? After all, those victims were "regular" people, business owners, and policemen.

Or was it because the current Vice President and other politicians were encouraging such behavior, bailing out rioters but *not bailing out* peaceful protestors? The media might say that Kamala Harris encouraged peaceful protests rather than violent rioters. However, when cities are burning, when police are being shot, when ongoing looting is taking place on national TV, and the Vice President vows, "They're not gonna stop," people take words at face value. Particularly when you do not specify what you meant.

Here's another similar mistimed and misplaced (or at least insensitive) quote by Ms. Harris. You do not boast that America is "moving" as a result of your wonderful policies when your administration and the Secretary of Transportation were amiss while people were stranded for tens of hours on a frozen Virginia highway. When no help ever emerged from the docile office of Ralph Northam, then-Democratic Governor of Virginia. When Northam, in fine democratic tradition, blamed the travelers for their troubles! All the while the government abrogated its duties when it was entrusted with protecting the safety of its citizens on public highways.

Similarly, Putin blames all the heinous atrocities committed by his army against Ukraine on the Ukrainian people's resistance to Russian occupation. He again echoes the Nazi sentiment, claiming that there would have been fewer war losses if the Ukrainians simply gave in, stopped protecting their land from an evil invasion, and stopped killing the "mostly peaceful" murderous Russian army invaders.

Mr. Northam, Ms. Harris, and Ms. Lightfoot each get a solid "socialist" 8 for sheer hypocrisy and socialist dereliction of duties to the public. These bureaucrats turned the dial of oppression on citizens by ignoring their primary public service duties.

Here's a particularly innate feature of the socialists--Blame the victims. Kamala Harris commented on "smash and grab" crimes in the cities, while abdicating her responsibility for the safety of those citizens by shifting the burden onto the tax-paying shop owners. It was *their* duty to protect *themselves*! Her socialist message to American citizens was clear--You are on your own even if I, the government, caused your trouble.

Sending Sergei Tikhanovsky to prison for 20 years in Belarus just for daring to participate in elections. Sending the entire bagpipe band to prison for two years for playing at a peaceful protest--truly peaceful, not "mostly" peaceful. Both earn a socialist 10. Most recently, a Belarusian singer who covered a Ukrainian song titled "Give Me a Hug" was convicted for "disparaging the Belarusian and Russian statehood."

Planning a KGB-like coup by the United States FBI, spying on a political campaign through FISA abuse, and getting away "scot-free" also gets a 10. Americans are still awaiting legal redress to remove that mark.

Setting a country's tax rate at 90% gets a 9. Stalin would get a 10 for taking all the property on a whim. Similarly, Putin looted Russian banks, large enterprises, and independent media one by one. Setting a tax rate at 30% gets a 5. Contrast that against countries having a 5-10% tax rate, which scores a 1 on the R.E.D.S. scale.

In any event, an imposition of the will of the authority onto a person against their will and outside the scope to where such actions encroach on another's rights clearly has a "socialistic" value and should be treated as such. A glaring example would be attempts at canceling the U.S. energy system through the Green New Deal against the will of the people and to their tremendous and immediate detriment. Of course, the authority would counter that it is "thinking about the people's future."

This red herring tune that socialist warriors of all kinds sing throughout their inevitable fiascos would be graded high on the "R" scale.

E – Enterprise (private) deterioration

A key aspect of a free capitalist society is private "enterprise," a unit of private commercial and personal family life activity. Against the dominant will, overpowering it by society imposing its arbitrary rules and taking the fruits of such enterprise is socialism.

A five-year plan and a complete ban on private enterprise in the Soviet Union gets a 10 on the R.E.D.S. scale. Particularly in light of the fact that the tiny gardens people were allowed to cultivate for their own families produced over 50% of the vegetables in the Soviet Union while accounting for less than 1% of the available agricultural land.

Forcing Tinkoff to sell his share in the most successful bank in Russia, named as his namesake, at 1/30th of market price just because he opposed Russian aggression against Ukraine amounts to nationalization. This clearly gets a solid "fascist/socialist 10." The so-called "common interest" overpowered private property, individual liberty, and even mere decency.

Forcing Michael "My Pillow" Lindell in the U.S. out of ads, banks, and social media for his support of President Trump and conservative causes gets a 7. The only saving grace is that, unlike in Russia, there are some remaining free markets and free media outlets still providing Lindell with a platform.

Biden closing down the Keystone pipeline and overregulating the oil industry while forcing an artificial boost in economically unjustifiable solar energy scores an 8. That's a high "socialist" grade due to the devastating economic effect of his actions, coupled with nonpractical Soviet-like rhetoric. The next time you pump gas, you may tend to give an even "higher" grade.

Interference by government or society in someone's religious beliefs, forcing them to employ their imagination and artistic abilities to produce a cake for gay marriage--which happens to be against such a person's religious beliefs--gets an equally high 8. Forcing the public to employ hundreds of pronouns is equally detached from basic biology, intruding on rational people's daily lives and gets around an 8--lowered simply by sheer irrelevance of the issue outside of fantasy land.

However, for our sake, the Supreme Court recognizes such society's coercion as being abusive. Obama's reference to private businesses, "You did not build that"--an expression with which every private business owner took offense, including yours truly--gets a 6. Obama clearly had this principle in reverse. As Margaret Thatcher noted, there is no government money. There is people's money. And it's not the "government" that built the roads, communications, etc. that enable private businesses--an implied message of President Obama's statement--but it is the businesses that employ people and pay taxes that "built"--including building this great country.

For private business owners who lose sleep, work 24/7, and pour their hearts and souls into their enterprise, such disparaging connotations from the Left rise to a similar level as degrading the sacrifices and efforts of the police. While it was "just" an expression of a "feeling" by President Obama, it clearly translated into his suppressive policies against private businesses supplemented by the government's subsidized jobs, resulting in the slowest post-recession recovery in U.S. history.

Obamacare gets a clear 9. The one point less than 10 is given just for the fact that it gave some people health insurance as a safety net. Otherwise, Obamacare made private health insurance prohibitively expensive and almost killed it. Its oppressive features are lengthy. Restricting competition, banning across-state-lines insurance transactions, depriving patients of their doctors and insurance--despite Obama's repeated assurances to the contrary--increasing insurance premiums three to five-fold, and consuming a large portion of the federal budget along with the family budgets of working people, just to name a few. Did the writers of Obamacare really believe that persons who were unable or unwilling to pay $300-400 premiums for health insurance could actually afford to pay $3,000-5,000 deductibles?

Placing all the oil companies under his oligarch's direct control while criticizing Yeltsin-era privatization gets an easy 10 for Putin.

Venezuela's nationalization of the oil fields, turning one of the fastest developing countries with the best investment climate into one of the poorest countries, also gets a 10. Its citizens literally lost tens of pounds on average because of starvation and malnutrition. While we recognize that obesity is a problem in the United States, there are probably more humane ways to fight it than socialism-caused starvation.

New York Mayor Bill de Blasio's expression, "...*there's plenty of money in the world. There's plenty of money in this city. It's just in the wrong hands,*" would get a 9. One point less than 10 is given in reliance on operational U.S. courts from the ideological standpoint, but a 0 from the point of view of practicality and IQ scale.

California's bans on independent contracting in the trucking industry get a solid honorable 7 for demonstrating to Americans how "good-sounding" socialist "economic" measures can be, yet so disruptive in supply management, i.e., the infamous socialist "shortages," just on a smaller scale.

Americans regard the family as a "private enterprise," the foundational cell of society. We also regard parents as having the primary responsibility for raising their children as good citizens. With that approach in mind, the government's educational system should be viewed as the provider of educational services, with children and their parents as the primary "customers." There is no education just for the sake of education. The government should not be in the business of raising obedient government servants or brainless devotees of "greater purposes,"--which is how education is primed in the socialist/fascist society.

This trend of going deep into the society through educational outlets is portrayed in today's Russia. Their education system hides its atrocities and glorifies its ruthless war through school "agendas," "verified information," and forcing kids to march in goose-steps in Z formation, the modern-style Russian swastika.

Obviously, the carefully crafted public-private partnership between American parents and the state eventually benefits society as a whole--as able, smart, law-abiding children eventually become contributing parties of our society. That might explain why the "socialistic" approach of using children as guinea pigs of the state's indoctrination and social experimentation ensured a crushing defeat for the Democrats in the 2021 Virginia gubernatorial elections.

The roots of the eventual defeat by Democrats in Virginia were planted when former Gov. Terry McAuliffe confidently announced that he did not think "parents should be telling schools what they should teach" children. As a result, an otherwise "blue" Virginia-- largely due to its Northern Virginia liberal population who are kin to the "Swamp" of big government--showed that even centrist parents, let alone Republicans, disagreed with that approach. McAuliffe's comment secured his crushing defeat by the Republican candidate Glenn Youngkin and his team, despite Republican former President Trump being soundly defeated in Virginia in 2020.

While the government has a massive role in providing education for children, caring parents--and only caring parents--can ascertain if the educators are doing an excellent job in providing education in a safe environment for those children. President Biden followed suit by labeling parents "terrorists" and unleashing the power of the FBI to go after those parents. For what purpose? Essentially because those parents dared--in a loud voice! --to question the inappropriate agenda of bureaucrats.

The outraged parents righteously opposed the growing list of liberal interventions- the teaching of the *racist* "critical race theory," providing "woke" literature of pornographic nature, indoctrinating elementary school pupils with sexually-explicit materials or topics, covering up sexual assaults and rapes committed by transgender students, and arresting parents who dared to call administration out for such actions at school board meetings. All these calamities get a solid socialist 9. The one point less than 10 is given as a discount for the ability of angry parents to fight on all fronts--including the voting booth--against Biden, teachers' unions and their reactionary "boards," and the FBI.

Many politicians declare their intention to "fight crime" and then reduce armed robberies or theft under $250 into parking-ticket-type misdemeanors. This path of hypocrisy and delusion was seen as the means to "protect" society, making it "safer" and "equitable," according to newly-elected Manhattan District Attorney Alvin Bragg. Take note: Bragg is another Soros-sponsored prosecutor. Along with other Leftist prosecutors, such as George Gascon in California who refuses to prosecute crimes, Bragg also believes the casualties of crimes are neither the victims of those crimes nor the failing safety of society. According to the standard Communist view, criminals are not responsible for their deeds because those deeds are simply the derivative product of society and its oppression.

In their twisted logic, Leftists believe the individuals whom society has defined as "criminals" since ancient times are now actually the "true victims." Yes, you read that correctly. The individuals who commit the crimes are now the "true victims" in the eyes of the Left. Consequently, in those same eyes, decriminalization of crimes and lifting punishment for perpetrators of crimes is in the best interest of society.

These clearly insane, counterproductive, and extremely damaging policies have already caused a spike in crime in Democrat-ruled cities across the U.S. This suicidal trend is nothing more than twisted-mind logical acrobatics-- victims become criminals; criminals become victims. What is the ultimate purpose behind this lunacy? Pursuit of their ill-conceived and nebulous concept of "equity" by way of some sort of moral, historical reparations for the "disadvantaged?" As a result of their brazen impunity, *prosecutors now encourage people to steal rather than earn.* Rampant crime in our cities is clear proof of their failed, twisted approach. Unless, of course, this was their purpose in the first place.

I would agree with those ridiculous policies on one condition. The D.A. should publish his home address and declare that "victims" can rob his house!--and as long as the value of each robbery is below $250, you will not be prosecuted! Then we'll see how long the lunacy lasts.

Society still suffers now from the O.J. Simpson communist-manifesto effect. The logic was this--As long as you are part of a class that used to be oppressed, whether it was 50 or 100 years ago or more, as a proletarian or formerly-oppressed class, you now have the right to rob, loot, and even kill with impunity. For what purpose? To swing the pendulum back to the other side. Shouldn't society stop that swing rather than replace one alleged historical injustice with this present one?

D - Denying the rule of law

This criterion should cover not only the denial of fair treatment by the law but also an arbitrary and selective application of the law, particularly *"the law is for thee and not for me."*

In its classical application, "rule of law" means not only strict enforcement of the law as written but also the democratic and equitable process of the creation of such laws. Such process must be bound to three basic principles-- first, it should be adopted by a majority of the people to which the law applies; second, the law should not overstep the natural bounds of its reach (i.e., applying only to the extent required without treading on natural liberties); and third, it should apply consistently and non-discriminatorily.

As an example, suppose the people decide that stealing is a crime. In that case, stealing *is* a crime. The duty of the prosecutor is to prosecute that crime. It is not the duty of the prosecutor to apply insolent social activism and "wokeness" and unilaterally decide what a crime *should be* based on the moral or political scale of said prosecutor. Today, that is the case with individuals like Ms. Foxx, Mr. Bragg, Mr. Krasner, or Mr. Gascon, among other "Soros"-elected state attorneys general. The term "Soros"-elected officials means they were elected by using Soros' vast financial support. The motivation of George Soros appears to be hell-bent on destroying the tenets and foundation of capitalist societies, if not civilization as a whole. While Soros' ideology and billions fail our grasp, his "Soros-elected" prosecutors get a solid "socialistic" 10.

You need not be a scholar of socialist studies to see that Mr. Bragg zealously implements the quintessence of Stalin's prosecutorial practices-- "Find me the man, I will find you the crime"--in trying to "bring Trump to justice." While Mr. Bragg routinely downgrades felonies to misdemeanors in New York causing a spike in crimes, he is eager to be a puppet of the Swamp in doing an unprecedented "political hit job" to skew the next presidential elections. We were all apprehensive of potential "Russian interference," but it pales in comparison to our domestic ultra-socialists' use of our own legal system to actually break up the very foundations, principles, and traditions of our society. Such an ill-conceived endeavor of the Left to abuse the law for political purposes will live in infamy as the most embarrassing misuse of political power in American history. We can only hope it will be countered with the proper response from the courts--and, ultimately and decisively, from the American public.

When citizens elect a legislature that votes for the law to decide what constitutes a crime, if socialist activists then usurp the role of "law god" upon themselves, they deny citizens the application of criminal law and the rule of law which those citizens elected. Namely, a law that defines victims as victims and perpetrators of a crime as illegal, and not vice versa.

When Putin made it a crime to reveal the property values of corrupt politicians, he defined those corrupt state officials as "victims." However, journalists who reveal such looting and corruption or report on war atrocities are deemed perpetrators spreading "disinformation" about the corrupt state and the army. Sound familiar? In Russia, the criminal is now the victim and the victim is now the criminal.

Furthermore, as Putin largely failed to replenish his army through draft after heavy losses in Ukraine, he now authorized picking conscripts from jails in exchange for their freedom. In other words, those who raped and murdered people are offered freedom in exchange for the opportunity to commit more rapes and murders without consequences. Doesn't this run slightly contrary to the "high morale" of the "Russian world" propagated by Putin?

Why would citizens of the United States want to follow the same dangerous path? My fear is that when it finally dawns on Americans that socialism is a scourge, it will be too late.

No wonder Russia and Belarus, since the August 2020 fraudulent elections and the Ukrainian war, eliminated all independent news outlets and exerted substantial efforts to block foreign-based media. This is the very nature of upside-down justice worthy of intrinsic socialist regimes. Alexei Navalny was thrown in jail for corruption reports about Putin. The Belarusian athletes who organized the Belarusian Sports Solidarity Foundation and signed a petition *against* violence were themselves labeled and prosecuted as criminals. These types of fascist suppression and twisted misapplications of law get the highest 10.

Well, the hypocrisy of U.S. politicians might not be as severe as sending people to jail. But hypocrisy can cause suffering and deterioration of trust in a system built on law and liberty. When you force other people to abide by mandates and then you ignore those mandates and parade yourself to a fancy restaurant or barbershop (the likes of Pelosi and Newsom), while it may be on a smaller scale of causing human suffering and hypocrisy, you still get a 7.

When Kamala Harris brags about bailing out violent rioters and "mostly peaceful arsonists," and then the courts delay pre-trial for several hundred January 6th trespassers for over a year, such behavior appears to be a clear inconsistent application of the law. Judging by their walking alongside policemen, those trespassers clearly presented no real danger of violence then and no danger now. That gets an 8.

You say, well, the January 6th rioters did break the law. Similarly, sending hundreds of people to jail for marijuana use and then laughing when asked if she smoked marijuana, as Kamala Harris did, is the epitome of hypocrisy rotting the system from within. This outrageous display of hypocrisy gets a solid socialist 10--this is *exactly* how communist bosses operated and lived their lives. We witnessed this firsthand. It shocks me to see the impunity offered to the "Party bosses" and "neo-proletarians" in the US.

When the FBI tipped off CNN, then employed SWAT teams and made an intimidation spectacle of Roger Stone's arrest to exert pressure on Trump and his inside circles, that was a KGB-worthy tactic. That gets a 9. Some reduction is given for not beating up or torturing the accused, as is routinely done in Russia and Belarus.

When the schools and Biden administration directed that same FBI against the vocal parent at Loudon County, Virginia while ignoring and covering up the reports of rape--for Biden, that is a solid 10. Denial of the rule of law and an abomination against the parents and the victims of rape.

This is the very pinnacle of socialist thinking and legal theory-- that the application of the written law must serve the "greater" good of the society, not the natural law. The socialist "rule of law" heavily relies on the "letter" of law typically adopted by puppet legislatures designed to protect the rulers. Of course, they cannot be wrong. After all, they have a "larger" goal to think about. They cannot be bothered with details or "insinuations" of corruption. Under the socialist application of the law, the court would rather give slack in prosecuting or rendering sentences to violent criminals as compared to moral criminals since they're the ones who dare to shake up or doubt the unfairness of the "system."

True to that principle, Russian or Belarusian citizens who dare to "like" or repost "statehood degrading" posts or question fraudulent elections will get more extensive prison sentences than violent police officers or other criminals. Granted, such officers are loyal to the "system" and probably voted the "correct way," torturing people under investigation, even if they get arrested. It is noteworthy that none of such policemen were detained in Belarus or Russia or in the instances of war crimes committed in Ukraine. Of note, the person who leaked the videos of tortures in Russia was declared an enemy of the state and had to flee the country. The torturers did not. This gets a solid "Stalinist" 10.

Here's an example of how new anecdotes on that topic reflect the realm where the "neo-Soviet" system operates:

A policeman is beating a man with a baton.

The man screams, *"Don't beat me, I voted for Lukashenko!"*

The policeman replies, *"Don't lie to me! Nobody voted for him!"*

It's no wonder that "hurting feelings" of the arbitrary, inconsistent, and inept-be it Putin, Lukashenko, Nazarbayev, Biden, Harris, or Fauci-is typically made into a "crime" by the system. So, it is in Russia and Belarus. So, it is on CNN and Facebook. Russia went so far as revitalizing a concept of "other thinkers" ("inakomyslyaschie"), which was popular in the Stalinist Soviet Union and Hitler's application of his "Mein Kampf." Russia even proposed a bill that would strip those people of Russian citizenship.

// *In a similar fashion, those who do not vote for the Democrat spend-thrift and system-altering agenda are painted by Joe Biden as "domestic enemies." Biden equates them with Bull Connor, George Wallace, and Jefferson Davis, insinuating racist and reactionary undertones for anyone who dares to vote "the wrong way." In his proverbial "deplorable moment," Biden went so far as calling the "MAGA crowd"--i.e., virtually half of American society--"the most extreme political organization in American history" and "semi-fascists."*

Obviously, the objective and practical achievements of the MAGA agenda notwithstanding, denigrating political opponents to a level that considers them "worse than" KKK, Nazi, ISIS, Antifa, or BLM is not an implementation of Biden's electoral promise of reconciliation and civility of the American society. At the same time, Antifa's "brown shirt" violence and BLM leadership's corruption receive a pass.

It's tough to put a "grade" on Biden's rhetoric that has yet to materialize in any concrete actions. But such an angry, mumbling mess brings back some unpleasant childhood memories of Nikita Khrushchev's threatening speeches. Furthermore, by proclaiming half of our country as "semi-fascists," Biden appears to give an unfettered tool to his followers--Use whatever force and means you deem necessary to get rid of any outcast outside of the normal election process.

S - Speech restrictions

Freedom of speech is probably the easiest and most vulnerable tenet of a free society to be violated, as well as the hardest to be returned and recultivated. The reason for such a dichotomy is that freedom of speech is not trampled upon and gutted by the law. Instead, it suffers from an overwhelming internal human fear. Such fear is the fodder that encourages government power trips, poisons journalism, corrupts academic debate, chills critical thinking, and permeates the human soul. It's not like Big Brother needs yet another justification for its insatiable desire to tread on the line of submitting those who disagree with its power.

Government excesses are a given fact. That is why the founders designed our system of limited government, even adding the sacred First Amendment to limit and fight such excesses. When the media, including private social media and academia, become the lapdogs of the Leftist party line, particularly when such party line merges with the tenets and principles of socialism, they cross the line from regretful to scary.

Objectivity in American journalism will never outweigh the need for sensationalism. But objectivity cannot dangle around zero in the single-digit percentage range when reporting on President Trump's clear and unequivocal achievements in our burgeoning economy and foreign policy (i.e., keeping enemies at bay, Israel-Arab diplomacy, absence of new wars, strengthening NATO, and transparency, at least from the point of view of what the president was thinking and doing, which could have been a bit too much at times).

It is fine to go after people in power aggressively and excessively, though peacefully, particularly when someone like President Trump welcomes it. However, where are that same journalistic aggression, excessive questioning, and inquisitiveness in evaluating Joe Biden, his family dealings, or other democrats? The country was traumatized by the fraudulent dossier--a product of the collusion of Democratic operatives and the FBI--and nonexistent pee tape for four years. That collusion caused the country to doubt the legitimacy of the 2016 elections.

Why is it that credible reports of corruption, one way or another, concentrated in the information found in "Hunter's laptop" get zero inquisitive interest from investigative journalists? *No follow-up questions.* None at all. After Hunter Biden's response, "It could be my laptop, it could be a Russian setup." *Seriously?*

What about a question along this line, "How about the verified communications, wire transfers, and documents found on that laptop? Are those true, and what do they mean?" There was no follow-up on the obviously corrupt payments from Yelena Baturina, wife of Luzhkov, Moscow's corrupt mayor, whose sole goal in life was to be richer than the British Queen. Nothing about Kazakh, Ukraine, and Chinese entities tied to corrupt and communist structures?

And who is the "Big Guy" in those communications for whom a certain percentage of the projects was "reserved?" Isn't that Joe Biden? The social media and mass media suppression of those kinds of discussions and stories about alleged corruption, with live witnesses, verifiable evidence, and accounts prior to the 2020 presidential election, deserves a solid "socialist" 10. In the socialist society, the obedient press gives the rulers a pass for their corruption while pursuing the accusers of "Party-line" corruption.

Encroachment on freedom of speech starts slowly with small things. It's much like the frog that jumps out if thrown into boiling water but slowly boils to death when the temperature is increased gradually. Society tends to let the small things go. Soon enough, however, you can't tell a black, gay, or transgender joke. You can't criticize a woman or a minority in their government position for fear of being ostracized, labeled as a "racist," and ultimately rejected or canceled by society. Aren't we all still equal? If they can't take a proverbial political and satirical punch and we are all forced to walk on eggshells around such an artificially designated class of people, doesn't that make them weak and denigrates their true achievements? One good thing remains in humor-with the "woke" crowd it's still okay to tell a Russian, Polish, or white hillbilly joke. And we are OK with that!

And today, when you are in a fight, the consequences of insulting someone during a fistfight--*and you do insult with bad words*--are now more aggravating for the person than the fistfight itself!

Twitter and Facebook closed down numerous conservative groups, including a few Russian-speaking republicans, for "misinformation," an ominous recently-coined "woke" term amiss from the U.S. Constitution or even prior concepts of free speech. A debate, an opinion, hate speech, wrong information – these concepts are the whole point of freedom of speech. *If you allow only the "correct" speech, then it is Soviet socialist "freedom of speech."* And that has nothing to do with our founders' original concept.

Drawing a parallel to Bulgakov's "Master and Margarita," it's like saying this is a "socialist" fresh fish or giving a degree of freshness of the fish--rather than just "fresh fish." If you need to qualify or grade the concept of "fresh," it is not fresh. If you need to qualify the "freedom of speech," it isn't freedom either.

It is embarrassing and humiliating for our society how American pen and keystroke lackeys--formerly known as journalists or social media monopoly warriors--have willingly knighted themselves with the less-than-noble role of government censorship. They are cloaked with the Rule 230 exception, or "community rules," under the false pretenses of "the public good."

So much is at stake in our society depending on our freedom of speech-- and yes, even journalists and IT gurus have political affiliations. Still, they are, first and foremost, the social watchdogs keeping the government--not an opposing opinion--at bay. If they "let it slide" and compromise their integrity once because of their personal preference, political affiliation, or money, they become moral-writing prostitutes. Yes, you can make mistakes and be forgiven, but you cannot intentionally be a "mostly correct and objective" reporter.

Do you know the difference between a bucket of honey with a spoonful of manure and a bucket of manure with a spoonful of honey? The answer is that there is no difference. Both are buckets of manure.

Former President Trump was censored and his accounts were closed for his alleged role on January 6th, despite his calls for "walking patriotically and peacefully." However, no such ominous measures were hammered upon any Democrats who openly encouraged "mostly peaceful" riots (which they were not) and openly called for violence against Trump or conservatives.

Ironically, social platforms are content with keeping RT channels and accounts (sponsored by the Russian government)-- which openly call in prime time for the burning and drowning of Ukrainian children for the simple fact that they want to be Ukrainian, not Russian.

However, isn't it ironic that questioning the 2020 election's legitimacy through legitimate discussions, free debate, and peaceful exchange of opinions got an immediate ban on all social media? Yet, when Joe Biden and other Democratic operatives frivolously challenged the 2016 elections as fraudulent and then pre-emptively questioned the 2022 elections, that is all just fine by these "f... checkers." Along the lines of Putin and Lukashenko banning all independent and opposition media, the American social media and mainstream media get a solid "10" in their relentless (and, in large part, very successful) attempts to quash freedom of speech in use by the conservative side.

Under a thinly-veiled socialistic pretext of "equity," racism, and oppression, there is a very real, full-frontal, unconstrained attack on freedom of speech in most areas of public life. The following are the most visible examples:

- Humor: mainstream humor is no longer funny, nor is it relevant (*and that's the only way to be funny*).

- Science and biology, in particular: As it relates to the male and female natural designation.

- Sports, specifically women's sports; Note that we see no need to add "naturally born women" because it is redundant.

- Education: Achievements in real education and STEM are deemed racist, while indoctrination with socialist and openly racist theories and irrelevant studies is just fine. Recent attempts by Virginia schools to hide the achievements of top students, thus depriving them of chances for better colleges and scholarships--all in the name of "equity"--is utterly evil.

- Police: Trashing and denigrating police while glorifying insolence and criminal behavior as "victimization" by society rather than personal responsibility.

- Race: Highlighting the perpetrator's race when it suits the narrative of "white oppression" while referring to an SUV or a gun as being a "perpetrator" when it does not.

- Media reporting: Covering up for the Left (whether Epstein, Cuomo brothers, Weinstein, Avenatti, Swalwell, or Pelosi) yet digging in deep when it concerns Trump or other conservatives.

- Elected officials: Questioning the quality and performance of elected and appointed officials as the self-suppressed "freedom of speech," while the partisan approach prevents legacy media and social media from reporting on government failures–from supply management and transportation issues to uncontrollable inflation and the severe border crisis. (Yes, it is a crisis!).

- Economic policies: Denigrating people's legitimate concerns about the Left's failed economic policies by making insane comparisons, i.e., if you want to fight inflation, then you are Hitler because Hitler also successfully fought inflation. By the same logic, do you know what else makes you "Hitler?" Beer! Since Hitler liked beer, if you also liked beer, you must be Hitler.

- Criminals: The wholesale glorification of criminals, i.e., BLM's racist, communist, pro-criminal stance; the vilification of victims of crime and police officers, even those killed in the line of duty.

- Crime: Silence on the spikes in crime due to progressive socialist policies.

- Transportation: While Peter Buttigieg's caring for a child is commendable, as is childcare by any male or female parent, somebody–hopefully somebody competent–has to take care of the transportation issues in the meantime. Would you give Uber a pass for your missed ride if you learned your Uber driver used parental childcare leave as an excuse for failure to show up? Why does the media give a free pass to the government and transportation secretary when there are critical crisis-like issues with supply management and transportation in particular? Is that less important than an Uber ride?

You may want to evaluate these aspects and others on the "S" scale based on your own moral compass and perception of truth and prejudice.

I would like to go over two specific examples. The first example is the self-censorship by Hollywood and professional sports leagues regarding their catering to the needs of the Chinese Communist Party. In the United States, Hollywood and big sports are super-proactive in their social positions and activism. You can kneel against the American flag or burn it because Americans enjoy unfettered legal freedom of speech and social activism despite, at times, being misplaced or disrespectful to our veterans or our country as a whole. But freedom is freedom whether we like it or not- including an athlete's greed and hypocrisy. It's our choice to cast our vote with our dollar or our ratings.

However, what disposes of the legitimacy of their proactive endeavor is its utter hypocrisy and lack of consistency in their annoying moralization of society. While acts such as defunding the police and other extreme social proposals are done under the flag of fighting against discrimination and alleged police violence, these activists completely close their eyes and embarrassingly kowtow to the interests of the Chinese government. In other words, they "talk" when it's allowed, with little consequence to their paycheck other than ratings. At the same time, they prefer big bucks rather than big social ideas when it concerns the Chinese market and the ability of these activists to voice their position about atrocities by the Chinese government, including the concentration camps for Uyghurs.

Unless you subscribe to Joe Biden's position, of course, that this is all about "cultural differences." If that's your stance, then just stick to dribbling the ball. At least have the guts to be consistent. And no, you will never be "better than Michael Jordan" from a historical perspective because the "greatest of all time" could never be stained with kowtowing to the Chinese Communist Party. For the same reason, due to her affinity with Hitler and the Nazi Party, no one will likely dare to call Leni Riefenstahl the greatest woman filmmaker ever.

One of Putin's cronies, Kadyrov, through threats of violence, forces Russian people, including politicians, judges, and even military troops, to apologize if he considers someone's accusations or statements to be hurtful. John Cena, saving his wallet but not his dignity, took a page from the book of Putin and Kadyrov's clan. He profusely and sheepishly apologized to the Communist Party of China for stating in passing that Taiwan is a country. Spinelessly playing to the tune of the actual Communist Party and its brutal policies unavoidably gets a red bull's-eye 10 on the "socialist/fascist" scale for elitist athletes, Hollywood, and the press that covers up for them.

Obviously, the current pandemic and Russian aggression add a new dimension to re-evaluating our freedoms and government incursion into our private lives. Freedoms are freedoms because they concern the fundamental aspects of our lives. Not because the government has a "higher" interest than people's lives, interests, and freedoms. So naturally, the Covid pandemic became a barometer of the measurement of government intrusion on our freedom of speech, among other freedoms.

First, the liberal media, Joe Biden, and Kamala Harris attacked the "Trump vaccine." Yes, of course, we all have an image of Trump mixing fluids in glass vials while burning the midnight oil in the Oval Office. Then, as it got more hypocritical, they acted surprised that people did not want to get vaccinated or that people didn't take seriously the advice of Biden's administration regarding vaccines, especially when that advice was highly inconsistent. By the way, no posts from either Biden or Harris were ever banned by a media outlet as "misinformation" despite being filled with lies, hate messages against police and border patrol agents, contradictions about vaccines, outright lies in family business affairs, or insults against journalists. Not to mention stocking hate about those "MAGA Republicans."

I want to go on the record that I am fully vaccinated, having lost my mother to Covid due to the lack of *real vaccinations* in Belarus. Rather than an anti-vaccine stance, I personally stand for vaccination, particularly for the vulnerable, although recent studies cast doubt as to the need or efficacy of vaccinating younger people. Still, I believe that vaccines mitigate the dire consequences of the infection. So, let's imagine that vaccination is the bridge by which humanity can get from the insane Covid place where we are now to a safe Covid-free society ... soon.

While the media was busy making up stories about Joe Rogan taking horse medicine (which was not true), one matter of legitimate public concern was completely missed. Namely, the consistently inconsistent information fed to the public by the CDC and Dr. Fauci through the media. At the time of this writing, in 2023, they are still guiding us over that bridge with misinformation. The media's infatuation with Fauci and his "science" brought about the most anti-scientific public approach to a real medical event. Not to mention a full media ban on credible news stories about a lab being a potential source of the virus rather than an exotic food market. But then, that might implicate U.S. officials as well. Questions that could have verified conclusions and challenged inconsistencies were constantly rejected. The CDC's claims about the "bridge" we all "have to cross" were anything but consistent.

However, whenever anyone–including high authorities on the subject, such as Dr. Robert Malone–dared to question any of the policies, efficacies, or medical conclusions, they were immediately censored and banned from various media outlets. Americans aren't children. We don't like to be spoken down to. We are willing for you to convince us, but we don't appreciate having your position shoved down our throats.

So, if the "bridge" is secure for those who cross it, why is it dangerous for the ones told to cross the "bridge" to discuss its safety features or "blind spots"–just in case there are issues? It's not like the government is ever wrong, *right?*

We were told on numerous occasions that if you get a vaccine, you will not get infected, nor will you transmit the infection. We were told that it is a pandemic of unvaccinated. Neither of these was true. The latter was the most dangerous lie of all because we were led to believe we could let our guard down among the vaccinated. That was definitely not true. I am sure this contributed to the spreading of the illness. But don't you dare to raise that discussion! These misleading positions were voiced again and again by the Biden administration, including Joe Biden himself, as well as Leftist loudmouths like Rachel Maddow.

We now know that was a total lie. So let's gauge the discussion process and this type of "misinformation" from the "can't-yell-'fire'-in-a-crowded-theater" perspective for the sole purpose of evaluating the potential need for restriction of that speech.

In the view of the liberal media, Zuckerberg and Dorsey who sanctioned the "thought police," if you question the safety of the "bridge" or the fact that it might not take you where you want to go, you are the "enemy of the people." You are to be banned, canceled, and censored. At the same time, Biden and company unequivocally stated to the public that the "bridge" makes you immune from the disease. The "bridge" makes you safe among your loved ones. Both ended up being totally false and utter lies. Weren't such statements akin to silencing a guy yelling "Fire!" when there is possibly an actual fire in the theater? When you tell people they are absolutely safe, even while they are exposing themselves and their surroundings to the disease, isn't that the same? Of course, President Biden, and Rachel Maddow and the many others confidently reporting Biden's false message day after day were never banned or censored for speaking utter lies. Or, at the very least, "misinformation." And this, despite the clear and present danger of their statements to an unsuspecting and vulnerable public.

When people question the "science" they are being asked to base their health and potentially their very lives upon, and the sweet assurances of a treasure chest at the end of that proverbial rainbow, doesn't that always serve and continue to serve the public good?

One can't infringe on freedom of speech just because the subject matter is important or crucial. All subject matter is important. That's not the way freedom of speech works, especially in America. Freedom of speech offers freedom about important and unimportant subjects alike. That's the whole point--unless you sell your soul to the red communist ideology. Otherwise, free people don't just concede their freedom to speak.

Epilogue

I'd like to end my book by telling you a story. Some people say it is a true story. Others say it is a made-up anecdote, a parable. Either way, it rings true as to the troubles and perceptions of people living under socialism.

Beer was one of the few pleasures in the dreary socialist society of the Soviet Union. It was often sold from transportable large kegs on wheels, each with a capacity of about 250 gallons. This beer was not cheap. Sanitary conditions were less than exemplary, i.e., reused mugs and minimal rinsing. Still, such kegs would gather large lines of people. At one such sale, when the man next in line stepped up to buy his portion, he loudly declared that he had purchased the entire keg so everyone in line could drink beer for free! The crowd cheered!

After a few minutes, however, people started behaving badly-- cutting in line, allowing friends or family to cut in line, arguing as to their place in line, selling their place in line for "free" beer, and over-pouring their share of beer into large containers. Fairly soon, a fight ensued, and the entire crowd was involved in a nasty brawl. The police were called. When the police asked the people the reason for the disturbance, everyone pointed at the man who had purchased the contents of the keg and offered free beer to the crowd.

So, the police questioned the man as to why he created the disturbance. The man responded: "I am terminally ill with cancer. I won't live to see communism, where people live like brothers and fully enjoy many free things. So, I decided to buy the keg and give it to everyone for free to replicate how communism would work. I wanted to witness it before I died. *Now I have seen exactly what communism looks like.*"

I hope my little story and observations cause you to think. It is imperative that each of us realize--America is at a crossroads. Which way will we go?

Where is America right now with our "affection" for socialism? How soon until America is "infected" by socialism? Are we at the point of no return? These are heart-wrenching questions. I do not believe so. Not yet.

However, judging by our recent regression from freedoms we've enjoyed for over 200 years into a society with clear tendencies toward oppression, "Big Brother," and censorship, America's bright future is no longer certain. We can no longer promise our children a "better" life than their parents. If we do not reverse our course, if we as a people do not go to battle in the social and political arenas, I believe America as we know it will fall into the socialist abyss. And it will happen quickly.

Some people ask me: "But is there a way to get the 'good' parts of socialism without getting its 'bad' parts?" Judging by my firsthand experience living under socialism as a boy and by history itself, including the most current events in Russia and Belarus, my only clear answer is: "No!" Socialism is a social, economic, and moral decay. The more it is developed, the more rotten it is.

In actuality, socialism's perceived 'good' side is really its worst side. Socialism touts equity. But that's deceiving because socialism's 'equity' levels everyone into misery as the lowest common denominator. It reverses Darwinian selection. Socialism selection is choosing the weakest and worst in character but most loyal to the government or party line.

Leaders in tyrannical socialist states are not chosen based on honor, merit, honesty, or integrity. Socialism chooses leaders based on irrelevant factors such as loyalty to the ruling tyrant or party line, sexual orientation, skin color, or level of virtue projection. Absolutely no consideration is given to merit or one's ability and competence to serve.

As an example, would you even hire "pothole mayor" Pete Buttigieg to mow your lawn, let alone be in charge of our country's transportation? Based on his abysmal performance and arrogance, one wonders if he is there just because he "checks the box," representing a certain allegedly "oppressed" group.

Why is that in any way a serious, if not sole, consideration for the job? Is this an example of our government now building as Putin and Lukashenko built so "successfully"--by choosing people loyal to the party without any regard for their competence?

Once socialism shifts into a higher gear, the goal and result become a destitute society. This is achieved by granting an overwhelming amount of power to an inflated government. Eventually, the inflated government suppresses all forms of individualism and ingenuity. Inevitable cutbacks in personal freedoms, liberties, private property, entrepreneurship, prosperity, and wealth continue--until individualism and prosperity die.

Finally, the long-sought-after 'equity' rules the day. Except in socialist equity, citizens share equally in poverty and misery.

I am pleading, especially with the "woke" who view socialism through rose-colored glasses and hold affection for equity. You do not know what you are bringing onto yourself. You don't realize that you are suppressing not only your fellow citizens with whom you disagree, whom you frivolously call Nazi and other names. No! You are also inviting your government to crush *your freedoms, your rights, and your dreams*. You must realize that before it's too late.

Even if, in your view, you think I have exaggerated some of the points, at least consider reasonable and factual arguments. Observe what is happening in America and ask yourself if you like the direction your nation is going. Look at the tragic consequences of destructive social policies, for example, "defund the police." Look into our schools where police must guard our vulnerable children, where our children are failing to meet even reduced educational standards in reading and math--while the progressives continue to focus on wokeness, gender, and irrelevant and useless studies.

Our education system suffers from misdirection. Children are being exposed to materials that would cause adults in the workplace to be arrested. Investigate. Make decisions for yourself. Analyze facts. Consider joining the discussion. Push the pause button temporarily on feelings. Ask hard questions and hear the opinions of others. Note that Voltaire's "I disapprove of what you say, but I will defend to the death your right to say it" is the cornerstone and quintessence of free society, and America's social landscape in particular. No one is asking you to die for my opinion. I just need you to hear it, or at least I need to have the right to express it without fear of prosecution (I am OK with your dislikes). At the end of the day, we are all Americans. Our children are our future.

When you fall--and we all fall--get back up and try again. Quit the toxic blame game. Everything isn't always someone else's fault.

Step away from the victim mentality that is poisoning our culture. You are not a victim. Stop feeling like and acting like a victim. Be an achiever. Be a difference maker. "Merit" is not a dirty word. The Left's crusade to destroy traditions, freedoms, holidays, and unique aspects of everyday life that Americans have held dear for generations will ultimately destroy you too.

Respect entrepreneurship. It's exhilarating to build your own business. Owning property is a satisfying accomplishment. The American Dream is real. Many Americans are living proof. Read their stories.

Don't blindly follow the crowd. The mob rarely knows where it's going or even why. Think for yourself. That's one of the most important freedoms you will ever experience. Don't allow it to be taken from you.

When we pursue frivolous, even dubious, virtues and ignore the fundamental principles and values of a free society, we end up with nothing. No dignity. No freedom. No values. No virtue. No hope. No future. No country.

The alarm bell is sounding for those who are committed to "woke" ideas. Stop attacking our freedoms. *Those freedoms are yours, too!*

Come to your senses and recognize the benefits you enjoy by living in the greatest free nation on earth. *Millions of Americans know what tyranny is because we once lived in a nation that was not free.* We recognize this threat of socialism because we've been there.

And there is only one kind of socialism--the miserable one. Just ask any American of Russian, Belarusian, Cuban, Vietnamese, Chinese, or Venezuelan descent. American families defended this nation in the past, and they are willing to defend her liberty again. Liberty is worth fighting for.

You might have noticed I've equated the American Left--the "woke," Antifa, extreme politicians, etc.--with communist leaders or left movements elsewhere. Maybe you're insulted. Perhaps you feel that I've embellished the point. However, even though our nation still operates under a democratic system, these similarities are very sobering. I want to show you three expressions by today's politicians. I want you to notice how similar American politicians and communist counterparts like Putin are in their arrogance, disregard for human life, and abrogation of their duties.

- *"What difference does it make?"* --Secretary of State Hillary Clinton exclaimed when questioned about the circumstances and reasons for the Benghazi disaster when our U.S. ambassador (the first openly gay ambassador) was dragged onto the streets, tortured, and murdered.

- *"It sank."* --Putin's terse reply when asked what happened to the Russian submarine and why its sailors weren't rescued when there was a chance to do so with the assistance of technologically advanced marine countries.

• *"But it was last month!"* --Biden quipped, as if it did not matter when asked about a botched withdrawal from Afghanistan and how he felt about people clinging to the sides of airplanes trying to escape the Taliban and falling to their deaths. Or perhaps he hoped with the passage of time, the horror of the story would subside, and no one would care anymore?

While I am critical of the Left, the Republicans are not without guilt either. The responsibility to protect our nation from socialism falls on both parties. These examples of varying degrees show where Republicans have fallen short or exhibited shortsightedness.

• Ted Cruz chose to place Mother Russia--an image of the statue called "*Rodina [Mother Russia] is Calling*" --on the cover of his most recent book "Justice Corrupted." A statue commissioned by Stalin and erected in the city of Stalingrad. This isn't likely an act of "Russian collusion" because his book points out the failings of our Justice Department. But it is sloppiness to place this statue (which was probably meant to signify Lady Justice, even the broken one) with such deep-rooted Stalinist history on his cover. This is similar to a clumsy mishap by Secretary Clinton's staff when they mistranslated the "reset" button into "overload" while meeting her Russian counterpart.

• Despite most favorable circumstances, Republicans failed to secure a majority in the Senate. If they had worked together instead of giving the impression of incompetence, they would have secured a "Red Wave" in the 2022 elections instead of a disappointing "Red Splash." This is similar to the inability of the Russian opposition to unite, allowing Putin to dissipate any and all meaningful competition for the past 25 years.

• The most disheartening recent failure of the conservative movement is the failure of some Republicans, politicians, and spokespersons, such as Tucker Carlson, to understand the importance of all-out support for Ukraine in its righteous fight against the Russian invasion. Ukraine is the second largest European country after Russia. Be warned. Putin doesn't want only Ukraine. *Putin wants the world.* This is similar to America under the Monroe Doctrine in the 1820s, which decreed that Americans should take care of America first and be "isolated" from world politics. No interference in the politics of other countries. However, it is clear to me and many others that Putin's insatiable desire to rule the world is no longer a "European" problem. It is now the world's problem. We cannot afford to turn a blind eye. Our freedom and our lives are at stake in the long run.

Look carefully at today's socialist leaders. They are true modern-day heirs of Stalin's ideology. Attempts to appease them or come to an agreement with them are totally futile. Many politicians--Bush and especially Obama with his foolish quip in the Presidential debate, *"The cold war is over!"* --have failed to recognize this. The Soviet Union's inherent danger is not dead. It has been resurrected by oil dollars and is very much alive--alive, but not well. Putin and others are former card-carrying members of the Communist Party.

My fellow citizens, Vladimir Putin today is an example of what America can expect of our leaders if our country embraces socialism.

The Red New Deal could lead us to the brink of the events of 1940, if not "1984," all over again. First Hitler. Now Putin. Another megalomaniac attacks Western civilization. For now, the battle line is protected solely by the bravery and dedication to freedom of the Ukrainian people. They consider it their sacred fight, possibly 400 years in the making, to finally make their Cossack land truly free and independent. Today, Ukraine is the shield against that red-brown plague. Ukraine is modern-day proof of the horrors of the socialist agenda.

All in all, the goal of the Left, the "Swamp," is to challenge your freedoms and liberties and paint them bloody Red. The Red New Deal. No matter what phrases they coin to disguise their intentions or make them sound worthy or virtuous--it's "for the public good" or "to achieve "equity"--it is the rotting remnants of Communism, a new public tyranny. Through the pen of Thomas Jefferson, we know, *"If tyranny becomes law, rebellion becomes duty."*

It's time to be a rebel. A rebel for freedom.

Our current American battles of the extremes of left vs. right, democrat vs. republican, liberal vs. conservative, socialism vs. capitalism, and so on, are equally dangerous unless the opponents of such encounters continue to adhere to America's fundamental principles of freedom, rule of law, and personal liberty. Otherwise, the political extremes will lead us into the same terrors and desolation that I lived and experienced as a young boy. Socialism is a curse. It is a red-brown plague. Neither the United States nor any nation should want this for our children, motherlands, human race, or future.

I have one last example to share with you. I deliberately saved this for the end of my book. As you read it, you will understand why. When we begin talking 'crap,' we know we have reached the bottom of the barrel. Perhaps this would be comical if socialism were not so dangerous. But it is dangerous and sneakily deceptive. I hope this will open your eyes and wake you up to the nastiness of socialism.

Socialism trends inevitably to what is called "Kakistocrasy"-- a social order where the government is run by the worst, least qualified, or most unscrupulous citizens. That is typically how socialist countries are run. Ironically, the first four letters of that scientific phenomenon in Russian mean "excrement." Ironically, it describes Putin's regime perfectly. *Why, you ask?* It is the duty of one of Putin's bodyguards to haul around a suitcase. Putin relieves himself in that suitcase. *Why, you ask?* So that Putin's 'valuable' body specimens cannot become accessible to foreign spies or the opposition. Putin takes paranoia to a whole new level. This may be the epitome of the disgusting nature of socialism.

So, whether you take a Greek etymology of the word "Kakistocrasy" or its Russian phonetics, we could say Putin and Lukashenko have essentially built --excuse my language--a

"Shitocracy" in Russia and Belarus. Now, they are trying to spread their socialist waste around the world.

I hope this story and everything I have shared in this book will be a nudge, a reminder of what America once was and should be again. And a graphic warning of what socialism, if we allow it, definitely will be.

From the bottom of my heart, save our beautiful United States of America! Fight for her so all our children and our grandchildren can still grow up in *"the land of the free and the home of the brave."*

The next time a politician makes an attempt to take your liberties while telling you of the wonders of 'equity' and socialism, remember Joe Biden's comment- "This is not about freedom or personal choice."

Make no mistake, friend, it is. *It's about your freedom.*

www.ingramcontent.com/pod-product-compliance
Lightning Source LLC
Chambersburg PA
CBHW062045290426
44109CB00027B/2737